The Hollywood Posse

The Hollywood Posse

The Story of a Gallant Band of Horsemen
Who Made Movie History

Diana Serra Cary

HOUGHTON MIFFLIN COMPANY BOSTON
1975

Chapter 14, "We'll Judge by the
Riding . . ." appeared in slightly different
form in *The Reader's Digest* under the
title "His Greatest Ride." Copyright © 1966
by the Reader's Digest Association, Inc.

Library of Congress Cataloging in Publication Data

Cary, Diana Serra, 1918–
The Hollywood posse.
1. Western films — History and criticism.
2. Cowboys — Biography. I. Title.
PN1995.9.W4C35   791.43'0909'32   75-17531
ISBN 0-395-20437-2

Printed in the United States of America

w 10 9 8 7 6 5 4 3 2 1

To my mother and father and the
Gower Gulch men

Preface

My lifelong association with the Hollywood Posse began in very early childhood, when I was barely twenty months old. When these men were starting their long careers, I was launching my own, as the child star, Baby Peggy. Century Studio, where I made one hundred and fifty two-reel comedies in the eighteen months after April of 1920, stood on the corner of Sunset Boulevard and Gower Street. This landmark the cowboys later made famous as "Gower Gulch."

My father and the other old-time cowmen treated in this book were my constant companions and co-workers, on the set, on location, over meals or riding together on weekends. Father taught me to ride before I was three, and it was my good fortune to have these other men as mentors. Even as I was learning to talk, I was absorbing their mannerisms, their values and the salty flavor of their lingo, much as other children learn their first prayers at Mother's knee.

Like others of his kind, Father possessed an excellent memory. He avoided braggadocio and exaggeration when recounting his experiences, not merely out of self-respect, but also because he would never have heard the end of it from his peers. No one in his band would dare to deliberately distort the facts, when others of their group had been eyewitness to many of the events. These men treated me on an equal footing, more as an adult than a child, and unconsciously I adopted their attitude of respect for oral traditions.

Becoming a "quick study" was one of the first techniques I acquired in life, for it was indispensable if I was to cope with the demands of my job. A shoestring company like Century, with a limited budget, demanded, and got, one-take performances from its actors or one's career was over before it began. This entailed memorizing long, and often complex, patterns of action and dialogue, even though the films I made were silent. Constant practice resulted in a very retentive memory, and because making movies often developed into life and death situations, those eventful early years have never lost their sharpness in my mind. I vividly recall my first visit to the Waterhole, and stabling my horse at the old Sunset Barn. After I moved over to Universal Studios when I was three, I remember greeting the cowboys in the hiring tanks, enduring the studio tours and their raucous guides, and visiting the Western street between scenes of my own productions.

Because my career in movies had been thrust upon me as an accident of fate, I did not choose to continue acting as an adult. Instead, I became a writer and, considering my early association with cattlemen, it is not surprising that the study and writing of Spanish and Amercan frontier history became my special field of interest.

As the years went by, I expected some leading Western historian would come forward and interview these remarkable men, chronicling their contribution to motion-picture history. But in the late 1940's I began to realize that time for this was running out, as, one by one, the old timers began to "ford the Jordan." Determined not to let them be totally forgotten I took up the task myself, recording my own childhood memories, and persuading my father to talk about and write down his own recollections. I went square dancing with Bob Burns, and arranged dinners at my home for Father, Jack Padjan, Neal Hart and others. As artfully as possible, I maneuvered the conversation into channels touching upon the old days, triggering the flow of priceless and brilliantly recounted anecdotes.

These I carefully wrote down and filed away for future use soon after they were told.

It seemed necessary for me to mention the foregoing factors involved in the writing of this book, or risk having the reader assume I had interpolated dialogue and fictionalized those events that I could not possibly have witnessed. In describing such action, I have based my narrative either on oral traditions as told and retold on the set, on the trail and around ranch campfires over a period of many years, or on written memoirs. My special thanks go to my father and mother for keeping the past alive with their colorful brand of storytelling. Herman Hack kindly took the time to write several long letters about his early days at John's Café and the founding of the Chuck Wagon Trailers, an organization of which he was president for many years. I am especially grateful to screenwriter and long-time friend, Leo McMahon. His letters generously and graphically bring to life incidents and anecdotes garnered from his own thirty years as a riding actor. I am also indebted to Mr. Eddie Brandt of Saturday Matinee Shop for his valuable assistance in obtaining some rare and highly graphic stills as illustrations.

I make no claim to having written a definitive history of Western films and those who made them. I do believe, however, that what follows is the first insider's account of the cowboys' Hollywood, as I knew it in childhood and as the old rawhides themselves remembered it. Their contribution to the motion picture industry was indeed significant. If history is to be served it must be stated that this unique band of men — never more than two hundred in number — made the Western movie possible. Westerns were not made by producers, directors or even the splashy cowboy stars, for it was the riding extras, doubles and stunt men who took the greatest risks and provided the real action. Without their courage there would have been no heart-stopping horse and saddle falls, no flaming wagons plunging over cliffs, no lightning-fast getaways and long, drawn-out pursuits, which kept children and grownups on the edge of their seats for half a century.

This book is my personal tribute to the men with whom I was privileged to "ride the river" for many years. It is a book that any one of them might have written far better than I, if circumstances had been otherwise. As it is, I have tried to speak for them and tell the personal story of who they were, where they came from, what brought them here, and how they managed to survive as Hollywood's perennial posse for almost fifty years — long after the real West they knew and loved was gone.

Diana Serra Cary
Encinitas, California
1975

Contents

Illustrations

(*following page 126*)

Ranger Jack Montgomery and his twenty-one year old wife, Marian, descending Arizona's Grand Canyon on the all but impassable Mormon Trail. *Author's Collection*

A scene from an early G.M. "Broncho Billy" Anderson two-reel Western. *Hoblitzelle Theatre Arts Library, Austin, Texas*

Jack Montgomery helps cowboy hero Tom Mix in this still from a silent Western made at "Mixville" in 1920. *Author's Collection*

Jack Montgomery in 1925 when he was doubling actor Ronald Colman in *The Winning of Barbara Worth. Author's Collection*

Child star "Baby Peggy" in 1921, as she appeared in the two-reel comedy *Peg of the Mounties* on the midget Mexican horse, Tim. *Author's Collection*

Three-year old "Baby Peggy" with cowboy extra Jack Dawn in one of several two-reel Western satires. *Author's Collection*

Fred Burns, silent cowboy star turned riding extra. *Ernest Corneau Collection*

Art Acord, short, stocky, fearless and a hard man to kill. *Ernest Corneau Collection*

Neal Hart when he was starring in the "Blue Streak" serials at Universal. *Ernest Corneau Collection*

Al Jennings, sole survivor of the once deadly Jennings Gang, in his favorite portrait, which he gave to the author in 1932. *Author's Collection*

Leo McMahon, playing a Western lead in the late 1930's. *Author's Collection*

Director Cecil B. De Mille in a rare publicity still for the silent version of *The Ten Commandments* filmed in 1923. *Saturday Matinee*

in their feud with De Mille. *Academy of Motion Picture Arts and Sciences Library*

The famous charge sequence in the Warner Brothers 1935 spectacular, *The Charge of the Light Brigade,* starring Errol Flynn. *Academy of Motion Picture Arts and Sciences Library*

Their ranks broken by withering enemy fire, the "gallant six hundred" regroup for a second charge. *Academy of Motion Picture Arts and Sciences Library*

A memorable scene from the MGM release *Gone With the Wind,* © 1939 Selznick International Pictures, Inc. Copyright renewed 1968 by Metro-Goldwyn-Mayer Inc.

Two Gower Gulch men are seen trying to keep their panic-stricken teams from stampeding in the melee of re-creating the flight from burning Atlanta. From the MGM release *Gone With the Wind,* © 1939 Selznick International Pictures Inc. Copyright renewed 1967 by Metro-Goldwyn-Mayer Inc.

Slim Whittaker threatens Buddy Roosevelt in a typical grade-B Western. *Ernest Corneau Collection*

A between-scenes publicity shot of one of the stars of the 1940 MGM action film *Northwest Passage,* together with unknowns who were handling the dangerous stunts and falls. *Author's Collection*

A successful dude rancher in 1944, Jack Montgomery sits astride his powerful strawberry roan trail horse atop a Colorado peak in the heart of the Rocky Mountain National Park. *Author's Collection*

John Wayne leads a band of horsemen into a ruined ranch in a scene from *Dark Command,* filmed in 1941. *Academy of Motion Picture Arts and Sciences Library*

A scene from Warner Brothers' Western, *A Distant Trumpet,* directed by Raoul Walsh and filmed in the early sixties, in which many veteran cowboys were gathered together for the very last time. *Saturday Matinee*

The sheriff's posse is hard on the trail of an exgun-fighter in this scene from Columbia's *Twin Sombreros. Saturday Matinee*

The Hollywood Posse

1

"Where the Hell's Hollywood?"

AMONG old-time cowmen Los Angeles had long been rated a town "with the hair still on it," as the saying went. Ever since the first mountain men ventured overland in the 1830's, its fame as a horse trader's paradise had spread throughout the West. Great herds of wiry mustangs and mules gathered on California's saffron ranges were fetching top prices during the turbulent decades of Gold Rush and settlement.

California *vaqueros, rancheros* and merchants had little cause to greet these *gringo* traders with warm *abrazos*, especially after 1846 when Uncle Sam stripped them of millions of acres and decreed them foreigners in their native land. Still, Angelenos and cowmen had much in common, on a man to man basis, and in many cases formed enduring friendships. Both lived in the saddle, both were aficionados of fine horseflesh, good horsemanship and beautiful women.

But since male Californios were also wizards at the art of sequestering velvet-eyed sweethearts and sisters, their overprotectiveness created a demand for Yankee-run saloons, poker parlors and sporting houses. The vacuum was not long in being filled by the usual company, and soon Los Angeles became a city to remind a man of palmier days back in Abilene and Denver, when he was still a "button" and reaching out for life with both hands. Abilene may have been more carbolic and Denver gaudier, but most agreed that L.A. managed to be as bawdy as both.

After 1880, however, the old girl began to shed her spangles. Years of drought decimated the extensive horse and cattle herds, and brought native ranchers to the brink of bankruptcy. Hard-nosed Yankee land speculators moved West en masse, to launch a systematic dispossession of the helpless California aristocracy, until gold-ripe citrus groves and booming townsites cluttered the once lordly land grants dating back to the Spanish kings. The land boom was followed by the heartaches of war, and peace brought the horrors of the Black Flu epidemic, which in 1918 carried off thousands of Angelenos, native and newcomer alike. Hard on the heels of these catastrophes, prohibitionists dealt the lowest blow of all, hanging padlocks on all the rawhides' favorite whiskey mills. By 1920 this once wide-open city of half a million people had been reduced to little more than the glint of remembered wickedness in an old man's eye.

Now when a cowpuncher delivered a trainload of beef to the L.A. stockyards for some distant foreman in Colorado or Wyoming, he first saw to it that his steers were tallied, paid for and safely in the buyer's pen; then, instead of heading instinctively for some long-familiar rendezvous, he sought out a livery barn whose owner knew where other hairpins like himself were likely to be found.

"No real saloons in this town anymore," would come the disheartening reply. "Only place I know of where you can step up to a real honest-to-God brass rail with cowshit on it is a little one-time saloon over in Hollywood."

"Hollywood?" the newcomer would ask. "Where the hell's Hollywood?"

It was a logical question, coming as it did from a band of men to whom moving pictures and the town where most of them were being made had yet to become synonymous. Cowboys were scarcely movie fans. In those larger cities where nickelodeons mushroomed after 1905, there were always more cowboys on the screen than in the audience. On the rare occasions when they got off the range to blow their wages in a

town imposing enough to boast such "electric" theaters, cowboys had in mind doing something saltier than straddling a
hard folding chair in a darkened store front. Except for the
possible laughs, most wouldn't even pay a nickel to watch some
dude actor from back East — who couldn't ride, rope or spit
like the real McCoy — caricature their virtues and vices on the
screen.

"Hollywood's a little whistle stop just west of here about
twelve miles," the barnman would oblige, and, provided he was
the type to run off at the mouth, he might lace his directions
with several jiggers of unsolicited local gossip.

"Yeah, old man Wilcox come out from Kansas and bought up
a hundred and twenty acres over there during the land stampede in the nineties. He whittled a townsite out of them and
he's got more prohibitionists and retired millionaires than a
Texas steer has ticks. Not much else there except a post office
and some tourist-type hotels, until the last four or five years
when New York show people started movin' west huntin' sunshine to shoot their flickers by. Anyhow, be that as it may,
what you're lookin' for is a plain gray frame building just off
Hollywood Boulevard on Cahuenga Avenue. From the looks of
the outside you wouldn't think they'd serve anything stronger
than Chinese soup, but don't let that fool you. Take my word
for it, you can buy into a poker game in the back room most
any time of day or night, and providin' a regular of the place
vouches for you, bootleg whiskey's so easy to come by you'll
think you're sittin' on a still. You can ride your saddlehorse
over, or stable him here and take the trolley. Only costs a
nickel."

"Much obliged for all the information, but what's the name
of this outlaw saloon I'm lookin' for?"

"Oh, I plumb forgot: name fits it to a tee. It's called the
Waterhole."

✳

Cowmen from every Western state, from Texas, Canada and even the northern states of Mexico, made their way to the Waterhole. They came by different routes, and ostensibly for various reasons, but gradually it came to serve the same function for them as the general delivery window in a small town post office. Here a man could learn the whereabouts of — or better still, run into — old friends he'd lost track of during the Cuban campaigns, the Mexican border troubles or on the battlefields of France. Here he might also learn where wild horse herds still ran free and where two good mustangers with lots of twine and time on their hands could parley six weeks of summer into a tidy sum. There was still good money in catching broomtails, taking the kinks out of the better green broncs and then selling them as gentle saddle stock. They brought seventy-five to a hundred dollars a head. There, too, he might get wind of a new rodeo where an all-around hand could pick up some easy prize money. At worst he might win a silver belt buckle he could hock in a local pawnshop.

True, their common thirst for outlawed alcohol attracted them, but it served more as an excuse than a motive. Before all else, what the cowboys hoped to find at the Waterhole was the desperately needed companionship of their own kind. They longed to hear from the lips of men they could trust that things were not really as bad with the crumbling cattle kingdom as they seemed.

"We've all been through bad times before," a veteran of the northern range could be counted on to say. "My paw before me come through the ruinous Sioux raids along the Rosebud, way back before the Custer Massacree."

Others drew courage in sharing memories of how they had survived the Johnson County War, which had dragged many cowmen's prestige to its all-time low. And certainly a man would be half dead who couldn't recall the silver lining to the blizzard of '87.

"Hell, it buried, froze or starved to death all but a handful of our cows and steers. We was wintering in the open just outside

Miles City, never dreamin' such a storm could hit. Charlie Russell was right when he did his postcard picture of that lone, ganted longhorn, *The Last of the Five Thousand.* Looked like the last of us, too, but that there blizzard drove the foreign syndicates clean off the range, and we survived to see our herds sleek and fat once more." Surely, they told each other in the roseate atmosphere of their clandestine saloon, men who could pull through such disasters and keep their hide could pull off one more miracle. Or could they?

On that bright spring morning in 1871 when Texas drovers and northern cattlemen first mixed their shadows on the high plains, riding point and drag on the nation's earliest great cattle drive, a new American hero was born. Generations of nonconforming youths would renounce city, town and farm to pursue the precarious but liberating existence of their idol, the cowboy. Unlike adventurous youths who had gone West before them, they were not motivated by hopes of finding their fortune in furs, ore, freighting or real estate. Rather, they cheerfully forfeited what comforts and security they possessed in exchange for a paltry thirty dollars a month, and "found," food and shelter, such as they were, and an eighteen-hour day. Nor was there any chance for promotion beyond a certain point, no increase in wages for performance or seniority. Honor and pride were the only bright promises this man-killing profession held out to them, but they sufficed to outshine all material rewards.

The cowboy's survival gear and the tools of his trade he packed either on his back or his saddle. His only map was in his head, his first-aid kit whatever brains God gave him, and his only disability insurance what he termed "a cast-iron tail and guts to match." Merely to stay alive in country where even longhorns winter-killed, he had to become a carbolic rider, a passable veterinarian, an artist with lariat and branding iron and a better-than-average shot with both Colt and Remington.

After the tragedy of '87, when ranchers began winter-feeding stock and fencing in some pastureland to keep their herds from drifting south, the cowboy had to master new pedestrian skills in addition to those he had perfected in the saddle. He irrigated, cut and stacked tons of native hay, raised barns to hold it, dug wells, forked manure, cut poles, mended fence and broke out beaver dams to keep the ditches free. After playing midwife to a downed cow in a Christmas blizzard, six months later he would round up, earmark, brand and cut the same calf he had delivered in the snow. Finally, he might be asked to ramrod a trainload of stinking, frightened white-faces on the thousand-mile boxcar trek to the feed pens of Minnesota or a Chicago slaughterhouse. He was bone-seasoned to working in climates where a hundred and ten in July is termed "tolerable," and twenty below in March welcomed as a warm spell.

Perhaps because his manhood was judged by how well he stood up under this grueling regimen, the cowboy almost never turned to an easier or better-paying trade. The only other goal that tempted him was the dream common to them all that someday an unexpected windfall might make it possible for him to buy a little spread, run his own cows, marry and raise kids of his own. Certainly it never crossed his mind that this vast and powerful empire in which he served as a free-lance knight could ever be brought down by anything short of Armageddon. And yet, in less time than it takes for a green colt to become a used-up cutting horse, the twentieth century overtook the cowboy. He woke up one morning to find the open range transformed into an enormous patchwork quilt, each green and gold snippet of velvet grazing land neatly feather-stitched on all four sides by the ubiquitous and despised barbed wire. Homesteaders infested every mountain meadow with grass, timber and a creek running through. Every acre or section that could be bullied into raising spuds or bearing wheat was fenced, irrigated and otherwise "improved." Ranchers and cowboys from north and south alike buried their ancient rivalries and looked on in helpless rage as the empire they had pioneered together kept shrinking like a green cowhide under a relentless August sun.

All the skills he possessed, the cowboy had learned on the range. Where else could he put his accomplishments to use? Dispossessed and disillusioned, the old hands moved on, as ranch after ranch went under or was broken up for farms. For older men, rendered obsolete by change, only the hope of a miracle remained, the hope that just beyond the next rise a Home Ranch would appear where they might find a haven, so when it came their time to winter-kill they could die among their own.

Younger punchers trailed rodeos working as trick riders, or took part in the ever-stiffening competition for bronc-riding and bulldogging prize money. Not a few hired on with one or another of the still-solvent Wild West Shows — whose tents were likewise tattered — hungry for the hazardous work they savvied and which in turn salvaged their self-respect and pride.

Regardless of the trail he rode to get there, Hollywood's false-fronted, Western-style Waterhole symbolized each man's Last Chance Saloon on a downhill trail of hurt and disappointment, the place where things simply had to get better or he would be set afoot forever. To a cowboy, being grounded was the meanest hand destiny could deal.

One man holding just such worthless cards was Jack Montgomery, when, on an otherwise uneventful February afternoon in 1920, he happened upon the Waterhole. He had spent twenty-six of his twenty-nine years in the saddle and sixteen punching cows. Now, displaced and desperate, his future seemed to have curled up like a dead sycamore leaf cast on the wind. When he arrived he was on foot, without a horse or even a saddle to his name. But there he was shown an entirely new, wide-open frontier, one that he would never have recognized as such, although it lay spread out all around him.

✳

If Buffalo Bill's Wild West Show had not played Omaha in 1897, Jack Montgomery might never have come to Hollywood or found the Waterhole. Chances are he would have finished school and gone on to become a merchant, banker or broker, as his father, uncles and brother had done. But after much preliminary pleading, Jack's mother agreed to celebrate his sixth birthday by taking him to see his hero of the hour. Saucer-eyed with excitement, the boy watched the dizzy, death-defying rides as cowboys and Indians pursued each other in and out of the arena. When the lights in this magic tent show were snuffed out, Jack asked to be taken to meet Bill Cody himself. Off they went to a smaller tent where they found the flamboyant showman surrounded by a crowd of adoring young fans. Jack was dazzled by Cody, who seemed to be a benevolent buckskin-clad Santa, with his flowing silver hair and white goatee.

When Jack's turn came, Cody sat him astride his own iron-muscled thigh. "And you, little tad, what do you want to be when you grow up?"

"A cowboy — just like you!" was the boy's instant reply. And until the day he died, sixty-five years later, Father never changed his mind.

From infancy Jack had ridden and climbed all over the family's carriage horses, and as soon as he could talk, he begged for a pony of his own. When Jack was three his Grandfather Montgomery paid the family a rare visit from his home in Port Hope, Canada. John Thomas was pleased that the boy had been named for him, and especially delighted to see he evidenced such a remarkable love of horses. A superb horseman himself, the elder Montgomery had spent the first twenty-five years of his life on Oldtrim, his country estate in Tipperary, Ireland. Inheriting Oldtrim from his father, who had served as a major in the Second Dragoons, Queen's Boys, young John had improved upon the stable of fine horses the major bequeathed to him. John Thomas rode to hounds, drove a smart rig and was referred to by all the neighbors in the county as "a splendid whip."

Unfortunately less expert in business and legal matters than he was in the saddle, he had unwittingly allowed Oldtrim to be taken from him by a stepmother's extravagant claims. In 1861 he and his wife and infant son (who became Jack's father) took passage to Canada. There they intended to buy another country estate, but the Canadian climate proved a far cry from Tipperary, and he went into the lumber and shipping business instead. Still, he missed the life of a country gentleman, and his birthday gift to little Jack of a sleek, black pony was his way of passing on all that he could of the vanished traditions of Oldtrim.

When he was old enough to attend school, Jack rode his pony there and back every day. Soon after he had learned to read with ease he discovered dime novel Westerns that embroidered the already magnified exploits of such superheroes as Wild Bill Hickok and Buffalo Bill. The hero of one popular series was named Bob Hampton and he became Jack's particular favorite. When the first Western ever made, *The Great Train Robbery,* came to a nearby nickelodeon in 1903, Jack went to see it. Like thousands of other novice filmgoers of the era he was fascinated by the seeming realism of movies — why, when the outlaw turned his gun point-blank on the audience and fired, everybody ducked! For a time, G. M. Anderson, who played the hero, "Broncho Billy," in this twenty-minute masterpiece seemed to fulfill Jack's ideal of everything a cowboy ought to be. But Jack was really projecting himself onto the screen, which served as a kind of magic carpet on which to flee the unhappiness and restrictions of an authoritarian home and roam at will through a siren West that beckoned just beyond the silty waters of the Platte.

The boy's addiction to daydreams, dime novels and Broncho Billy increased in exact proportion to the problems that now began multiplying at home. After months of bitter quarrels and accusations, his childhood world was blown apart by his mother's announcement that she was divorcing his father and

marrying another man! In a respectable middle-class Episco-
pal family in turn-of-the-century Omaha, his mother's act was
tantamount to walking naked through the local emporium. To
compound the trauma wrought by this scandal, Jack and his
stepfather took an instant dislike to each other, providing the
seedbed for a new harvest of discord.

The family moved soon after to Chicago, where the new
stepfather held an important post in a local bank. Here at least
Jack could escape the glares and gossip of long-time neighbors,
but conditions at home remained abrasive. The day after his
stepfather caught him reading a Bob Hampton serial in the
woodshed and caned him severely, Jack resolved not to spend
another night under this usurper's roof. With his mother and
sisters all downtown shopping, a wild solution to his troubles
suddenly loomed clearly before him. He remembered a grand
total of thirty dollars in gold pieces which his Grandfather
Montgomery had given him on special occasions over the past
few years, and which he had kept, untouched, in a bank in his
bedroom. He raced up the stairs two at a time, broke open the
ceramic pig and translated its contents, by simple arithmetic,
into the means of his escape. He stuffed the cache into the
pocket of his knee-length breeches, and packed a straw valise
with the bare essentials needed to survive his immediate
future. Slipping out of the house unnoticed, he made his way
to the railroad station.

"I want a one-way, chair car ticket to Calgary, Canada," he
told the gray-haired man at the ticket window.

"Calgary?" The man peered out from under his green felt
visor and searched the boy's eyes. "Alberta Province is a pretty
far place," he opined while he checked the records for the
exact fare. "You're kinda young to be travelin' that far alone,
ain'tcha, son?"

"Oh, I have relatives in Canada," Jack lied, knowing he was
heading for the opposite end of the continent from where his
grandfather's people could be found.

"That'll be twenty-five dollars."

Jack already had it counted out and ready on the counter.

"Yes, I know," he grinned, grabbing the ticket and running for the train.

As the chair car rolled westward, hunger pangs reminded him of how little money he had between himself and starvation. But this problem was fortuitously solved by a lady seated across the aisle, whose family had provided her with a basket of food for her trip.

"Wouldn't you care to share some of my lunch?" she asked her fellow-passenger. "I declare I won't be able to eat it all before it spoils."

After a polite but unconvincing refusal, Jack was persuaded and wolfed down several pieces of cold fried chicken.

"Going far?" the lady asked.

"Calgary, ma'am," the boy answered, savoring the word as much as the food, for it conjured up visions of the Calgary Stampede Rodeo and the great open spaces where he planned to seek his future.

"What's your name?"

Jack glanced at her and as steadily as though he had been saying it all his life, he replied, "Bob Hampton!"

The dime novel Hampton was anywhere between eighteen and twenty-five, but in the spring of 1904, the other Bob Hampton setting out for Canada was barely thirteen years old. Jack Travers Montgomery, formerly of Omaha and Chicago, sank from sight and would remain a missing person for the next eleven years.

The first cow outfit that would take on the sensitive, spindly legged kid with the enormous brown eyes and the fierce determination to become a cowhand was George Lane's Bar-U spread in Calgary. Lane ran forty to fifty thousand head of cattle and employed a sizable crew of men.

"I've been riding since I was two years old," Jack told George Lane proudly.

"Well, I've no doubt that's true, son," the cowman allowed sympathetically. "Trouble is I got all the hands I can use. But the cook needs help rustlin' up firewood for the chuck wagon, and that's right in the thick of things on a spread as big as this."

The way Lane put it to him, Jack would be doing the cattlemen a personal favor, and that took some of the sting out of his menial chores. Of course, Jack knew he didn't have to spend the rest of his life picking up cowchips for fuel and banging the triangle while he announced chowtime by bellowing, "Come and get it or we'll throw it out!"

One day there was a wrangler's job open and a horse to go with it, and Lane figured both were about Jack's size. After that he was put to topping off green colts in the *remuda,* the remount horses that traveled with the round-up and were held in a rope corral.

Cowpunching led Jack from Canada down through Montana, Wyoming, Texas and Arizona. In Tucson he planned to join up with the Arizona Rangers. While awaiting their decision he stepped into a saloon to kill some time, and fell into a pleasant drinking competition with two Mexican *vaqueros* at the bar. The last he remembered of Tucson was saying goodbye to his drinking partners, an hour and uncounted tumblers of mescal later. He came to, three days after, sitting on a rail fence above several pens full of milling cattle. From the drift of conversation around him, he learned that he had signed a contract with the Chowchilla company to take a trainload of cattle to Athelone, California, and had hired three men to help him, all without remembering a single incident of the intervening three days.

Originally an old Spanish land grant, the Chowchilla Ranch was owned by Isaac Bird, a banker from Merced. One of the last of the big spreads left in California, it boasted a hundred thousand acres along the San Joaquin River and ran about 18,000 head of cows.

Jack arrived at the Chowchilla with his load of cattle in November of 1909. He was still nursing some disappointment at having lost out on the chance to become one of the first Arizona Rangers, but his lost weekend in Tuscon was almost forgotten when he reached the ranch and discovered Stanley Hannah was working there. Stanley was a close cowboy friend he had met and ridden with for two years on the George Lane spread in Canada.

"You got here just in time for the fun," Stanley told him as they sat outside on the corral fence smoking their after-supper cigarettes.

"I figured it that way," Jack smiled. "Fall round-up's over, cattle all shipped off. What the hell do you chili-dippers do out here in California with no winter-feeding, no blizzards and no blue northers to ride around in?"

"Well, we got a winter crop here like no other ranch you ever seen. It grows plumb wild, don't cost a cent to raise and fetches a handsome profit."

"Yeah, what's that?" Jack asked in mild curiosity.

"Wild hogs. They call 'em tule rooters in these parts. They're mean, slippery descendants of some stray razorbacks that got loose from the Forty-niners back in Gold Rush days. Last fall the Old Man shipped three full freight car loads of 'em to Eastern markets, and got as much per pound as a domestic hog. It's found money, and each year we clean out enough sows and boars to keep them from overrunning the place and still leave enough breeding stock for next year."

"What did you call 'em?" Jack queried, his interest kindled.

"Tule rooters," a Californio *vaquero* put in. "That's because they live on the tules or reeds that grow all through the river bottoms here in the San Joaquin Valley. Sows weigh up to two hundred pounds, and the boars have tusks that grow almost two feet long. They're big, ferocious and fast, and a cow pony really has to move to catch one in the first hundred yards."

The following morning the Chowchilla declared open season

on tule rooters, and any questions that went unanswered would
be supplied by the vicious hogs themselves as the round-up
progressed. The foreman sent his crew out in teams of two,
one to rope, the other to tie. Jack was teamed up with Stanley,
for as his old friend explained, "At least one of us has to have
had some experience with these slick sons-o-bitches. The minute you spook one out of the rushes, he's on the prod and will
charge the first thing he sees, man or horse. They're plumb
fearless, and God help you if one catches you afoot and unarmed. That's why the ramrod insists no man go huntin' hogs
without his equalizer on him." Stanley patted the .45 in the
holster at his side for emphasis.

Jack soon learned that Stanley was not exaggerating the
risks. It took nerve and teamwork to rope and tie a tule rooter,
bearing down with a knee behind the animal's ear while managing to keep clear of the cruel, curved tusks. Once their job
was done, the cowboys rode on after further game, leaving the
animals behind to be picked up by a foot crew that followed
with a high-sided wagon. These men, hired especially for hog
season because the cowboys would not work on foot, also
moved in a team. Their job was to pick up the tied hogs and
throw them onto the wagons until they had a full load. The
wagons were then driven into holding pens with loading
chutes, which were located at intervals beside the railroad spur
serving the Chowchilla. The ranch processed cattle in these
pens during the rest of the year, and the chutes greatly facili-
tated the loading operation of steers. But the hogs were not
nearly as tractable as cattle, and cowboys dreaded the last,
loading stage of the round-up. And predictably, it was then
that the worst accident of the season occurred.

Jack and Stanley, still working as a team, had lost a sow to
Jack's hog-shy cowhorse because he had never worked with
tule rooters before and refused to hold his end of the rope.
When they finally got the sow tied and back on the wagon
once more, Stanley drew the sleeve of his shirt across his

sweaty brow, and accidentally brushed past the trap door of the tailgate. The vengeful sow saw her chance and bit him through the thumb. Stanley grimaced in pain, swore under his breath and then automatically removed his neckerchief to wrap up the wound. Just then the watchful foreman saw him.

"What happened, Stan?"

"Oh, nothin'. Just lost a thumbnail to that snaky sow."

The foreman stiffened. "You get on a fast horse and get to the doc in Merced . . . right now!"

"But it's only a thumbnail . . ." Stanley protested.

"I'd rather be struck by a rattler than a rotten-mouthed tule rooter. Here, take my buckskin. He's fresh and he's fast as hell. Get someone to ride in with you."

Jack stepped forward. "I'll go."

The twenty-eight miles to Merced was as flat as a feedlot, and they pushed their ponies hard, but the infection seemed to spread faster than they could ride.

"Goddam hand's already swellin' up like a poisoned pup," Stan observed drily, and Jack noticed that his friend's face was ashen with pain. An hour later, their horses lathered and flinging froth from their bits, the two cowboys jogged onto the main street of Merced. They tied up at the drugstore where the doctor had his office. He took one look at Stanley's arm — it had now turned black and was swollen to three times its normal size, splitting the sleeve of his shirt — and remarked almost casually, "Looks like you just shook hands with a tule rooter."

As the doctor scissored the shirt, Stanley asked, "Am I goin' to lose my arm?"

"If you boys had been one more hour gettin' to town, I'd say yes. As it is, you can thank God you had a fast horse under you." He glanced out the window to the hitching rack. "What do you want for that little buckskin of yours?"

"He's not mine. Belongs to the foreman at Chowchilla."

"If I was you I'd buy him, for luck."

When they got back to the ranch that is exactly what Stanley did.

For two years it looked to both Jack and Stanley as though the Chowchilla would become a real Home Ranch for them, but then, in the spring of 1911, Isaac Bird suddenly sold out to a British syndicate. The announcement was made by the old man in front of the main ranch office. The cowboys were stunned at the news and Jack, Stanley and thirteen others of the regular crew refused to work for the new owners, and quit in a body.

"I'll never work for those damned foreigners," Jack fumed as he and Stanley packed their gear for the move. Although his own forebears had gone skirling into battle behind Scottish kings, and his great-grandfather had been proud to fight Victoria's many wars, Jack felt himself as much a stranger to England as he now was to Omaha and Chicago. His allegiance was to the cattleman's domain. That was his country, where his only loyalties lay.

The disgruntled Chowchilla loyalists drew their time and hit the grubline heading north, figuring they could live on ranch handouts until they ran into some foreman who needed seasoned men. A few days later, as they topped a rise above a secluded brush-bottomed canyon, Jack instinctively pulled his pony up short, for he sensed, more than he saw, riders darting down the opposite slope. A second later they emerged and scattered along the sandy bottom, two of their number apparently falling lifeless from the saddle, although they were moving at little more than a slow lope.

Jack signaled Stanley and the others. For several minutes they sat their horses, watching in mystified silence, trying to make out if the horsemen below were trying to flush out bushed-up cattle or surround an unseen band of mustangs.

"I can't figure out what in the hell they're doin' down there," Jack mused aloud.

"Looks to me like they can't stay aboard a horse for sour owl manure," Stanley ventured, shifting his cud of chewing tobacco to the other cheek. "I just seen two men fall out of their saddles like they was picked off with a thirty-thirty, but I didn't hear no report."

"Looks to me as if they're fallin' off on purpose."

Jack lifted the sweat band of his Stetson to allow some cool air under the crown, and then pulled the brim down hard against the slanting sun. As he did so, his eye caught the glint of something metallic that at first suggested the polished brass-work on a rifle stock. Then his memory identified the image.

"Well, I'll be goddammed if that isn't a camera on stilts! Like the ones itinerant photographers used to haul around to your house and talk your mother into takin' your picture standin' against the pump or the back stoop!"

Just then a stocky, middle-aged man emerged from the general direction of the half-concealed camera, and called up to the riders on the ridge above.

"Hello there! Why don't you come down and join us? I'd like to talk to you."

Jack looked at the other men in his group. "Hell, why not? Let's go down and look around." The drifters kicked their ponies lightly and let the trail-seasoned animals pick their zigzag way down the slope to the floor of the canyon. During the descent Jack was trying to place where he had seen the man before — he looked familiar and, at the same time, ridiculous. He was dressed like a Wild West Show cowboy, with such extravagant extras as brass-studded wrist guards, fringed gauntlets, and a bandanna worn full in front like a lady's big bertha collar, instead of tied tight around the neck to keep dust out and sweat from running all the way down into your boots. Why should such a comically dressed stranger seem familiar to him?

As they emerged from the underbrush of the slope, surprising things began to appear on all sides: an open touring car with a platform built on top of it, a camera on a tripod, and bright silver boards reflecting sunlight back into shaded corners of the canyon. The mysterious riders the cowboys had been watching from above were neither dead nor wounded, but busy climbing back into their saddles.

The man who seemed familiar to Jack strode forward to welcome the newcomers.

"I'm Broncho Billy Anderson," he said by way of introducing himself, "and this is my movie company. We're making a two-reel Western here."

"Broncho Billy!" Jack exclaimed. Suddenly he was a boy again, back in the musty nickelodeon in Omaha, watching the hero of *The Great Train Robbery* dash after the outlaws, his movements made clumsy by oversized goathair chaps and huge roweled spurs. So that was where he had seen the stranger before! It was hard for this seasoned cowboy to believe that once he had thought Broncho Billy's version of a cowboy's working clothes as true to life as a mortgaged homestead.

"Well, by God, I never thought I'd live to meet you in person, especially way up here in Niles Canyon country."

"I thought you picture people were shooting your flickers way back in New York and Chicago on top of flat-iron buildings," Stanley put in.

"No, not anymore," Anderson said easily. "At least not me. I've been out here in California for nearly a year now, sort of scouting out the climate and scenery for pictures. Long enough, anyway, for me to shoot about a hundred of these one-reelers. You boys workin' for some cattle ranch around here?"

"No, sir, not at the moment," Jack answered, continuing to act as spokesman for the group. "We just quit the Chowchilla down by Merced. They sold out to a British syndicate." He gave solemn importance to the last sentence, but the implications of the treachery in that sale and the cowboys' nobility in refusing to be a party to it were lost on Anderson. Instead, he noted their dress, and how they sat their horses — all with a newly practiced eye. Broncho Billy may have started out as a janitor back at the Edison studios in New Jersey, but along the way he had learned the value of good horsemen, if only to substitute for him in those scenes in which he was supposed to ride.

"Well, if you're lookin' for work, I've got some for you."

The cowboys squinted their eyes under the shadows of their Stetsons and sized up the company riders suspiciously.

"Doin' what?" Jack asked, his curiosity tinged with humor.

"Oh, saddle falls, chases, stunts — you know the kind of things 'Broncho Billy' films are made of. I've got a posse sequence to shoot tomorrow and don't have but enough men and horses for the outlaw gang." He pointed to the other cowboys. "You Chowchilla boys would do just fine for the posse."

Jack's blue roan, Cowboy, impatiently tongued the cricket in his bit, making the racket for which the roller was named.

"We're lookin' for steady work," Jack explained, an edge of pride in his voice and bearing which spoke for all the men behind him.

Anderson nodded. "Sure, I understand. It's true, I'd only need you for a few days, but I'd make it worth your while. Good riders are gettin' hard to find up here, and so I pay two dollars a day — your horse thrown in, and we feed you both. How's that sound to you?"

The grubline riders were staggered by Anderson's munificent offer. A dollar a day was the most they had ever earned for managing to stay aboard the slickest bronc any ramrod could cut them. If one could get paid twice as much for bailing off a bronc as staying on, well, they could learn to do that, too. It took only an exchange of glances for the riders to communicate their decision to Jack.

"Okay," he said. "It's a deal."

As soon as the sun rose the next morning, both posse and

outlaw gang had already breakfasted and were in their saddles. The camera car (as the converted touring car was called) was loaded with crew and cameras, and Anderson climbed into the front seat beside the driver. With the cowboys following on horseback, the company drove out to a different location just a little beyond the mouth of the canyon to a hard-pan plain, tufted with clumps of sage and grease-wood. Here Anderson called a halt, and the crew piled out of the car. Prop men rushed around setting up silver reflector boards to throw shafts of light into the faces of the actors, or anyplace else where unwanted shadows formed.

By lunchtime it seemed to Jack and Stanley that they had already filmed almost half of an entire "Broncho Billy" episode. They had played posse to the outlaw gang, and the camera car had cruised along beside the riders, catching all the action of the chase. At noon another car appeared from nowhere and a man began distributing box lunches to the riders and crew. Jack took his lunch and, after loosening Cowboy's cinch, lifting his saddle to cool his back, and giving him a shot of oats that he carried behind his saddle, he sat down to eat. It was the same kind of box lunch he had seen old Dave Curry serve the vacationing schoolteachers up at Yosemite Valley, during a brief spell when he had driven a horse-drawn sightseeing stage.

Inside was a hard-boiled egg, a dry, white bread sandwich of sliced yellow cheese, some Fig Newton cookies and a California orange.

Anderson strolled by, having already finished his lunch while Jack had been taking care of Cowboy.

"Pretty dry lunch, eh?" he joked.

Jack grinned. "Well, it sure don't measure up to sow belly, sour dough and beans back at the Chowchilla chuck wagon," he admitted, "but then they didn't pay your kind of wages, either."

"You and your friends are a good bunch of riders," Anderson observed. "I've got a stunt and fall comin' up I'd like one of you to do. Since you seem to be their spokesman I thought I'd ask you first."

What Anderson had in mind was something Jack couldn't quite figure out until it was too late to say no.

"We call it a Dead Man fall, or a Stationary W," Anderson explained. "You'd be dressed to look like that man over there. He's a stage actor, and doesn't know the first thing about riding. Neither do I, for that matter," he admitted sheepishly. "Anyway, we've got a heavy bay horse that's done this stunt before, and he's built to take it. I figure you know enough about how to bail off a horse if he's goin' down to handle yourself."

"I've topped off broncs most of my working life, and done some bronc-riding in Calgary, Flagstaff, and Merced rodeos. I'm no Bill Pickett, but I can keep him from landing on top of me, if that's what you mean."

Jack was trying to reconcile Anderson's description of this stunt with the simple falls he had seen the other riders executing on the soft bottoms the day before.

"You're a member of the posse, and the outlaw is in the band you're pursuing. He turns in his saddle and shoots you dead. You've got to go down real hard. I'll show you how we do this sort of thing to make it look real."

It was all too real, Jack discovered. A prop man buried a post deep into the ground, to serve as the "dead man." Another prop man wound piano wire tightly around the post, coiled up the remaining several hundred feet and laid it beside the post. Anderson ordered someone to bring over the "stunt bay" and, while they waited, he explained to Jack. "The bay has a leather hobble attached to each fetlock, and through a ring in the hobbles we attach two ends of this long piano wire. It's invisible to the camera. The two wires run up the animal's front legs, and form a single line that runs back under his cinch and then all the way back to the 'dead man' or post.

"The trick is for you to measure off as many feet of ground as there are of wire and mark that spot, 'cause when you reach it you'll have hit the end of the wire and the bay is going to have both front feet pulled out from under him while he's going at a dead run. You may have heard of a Running W? Well, a Stationary W is a lot harder to pull off and not get . . ." Jack guessed the implication of Anderson's unfinished sentence: "And not get killed?"

"Well, injured is more like it. I'm sure you'll have no problems."

Obviously there was no learning how to do it, no rehearsal, no practice run. Nothing was going to give, either. When the horse hit the end of the wire, Jack figured the ground would come slamming up to meet him almost before he could see it coming.

Jack paced off the distance and tied a swatch of cloth ripped off his bandanna to a bit of sage. Meanwhile, Stanley and the other boys were being instructed to ride in as close to Jack's bay horse as possible.

"Bunch up around him, so the camera car ahead can catch all of you. Of course when he goes down, you want to watch out you don't ride over him."

After getting into the costume of the actor he was doubling, Jack checked the cinch on the big bay, who was edgy as hell. He fought back when the prop man threaded the wire through the leather hobble on each foot. It was obvious the bay had been put through this stunt before, and didn't take a shine to it. His muzzle and the white blaze on his face were crossed with scars where the hair had grown back a different color.

"I guess you've noticed we don't shoot many scenes more than once," Anderson said. "We work on a pretty tight schedule of five days a picture. So judge your distance well and we can make this in one take." It seemed obvious to Jack that one take would be more than sufficient for both himself and the wall-eyed bay.

Anderson stood off to one side. The camera car crew started

up their motor and the Chowchilla cowboys bunched their ponies up close behind the bay.

"All right. Action!" Anderson cried from the sidelines. Jack's spurs hit the bay's flanks, the camera car sped ahead, and the cowboys behind him surged forward as the bay lunged into a long lope that accelerated with every stride. By the third stride the bay was wide open and so were the fourteen other ponies in the posse at his back. Jack scanned the ground as it streamed past him in a blur of speed, mentally calculating the distance and trying to catch the flash of red bandanna cloth tied to the sage before he was right on top of it. It seemed he had just been able to get his seat for the chase when he saw the marked sage dead ahead. In one movement he kicked free both stirrups and pointed his right shoulder at a spot beside the trail where he hoped the bay would not follow him. There was a body-wrenching moment of separation when the bay was sent crashing to earth and Jack bailed off. After the initial impact with the ground, he bunched his arms up against his chest and shut his eyes tight against the clouds of dust and shattered sage, and tried to keep his body rolling. He heard Anderson shout, "That was great!" and then opened his eyes to a forest of horses' legs that seemed to multiply in numbers as their riders set them down hard on their tails, or whirled them gently to a stop in an effort to avoid running over the downed bay and his rider.

Through a cloud of sunlit dust, Jack pulled himself to his feet in time to see the bay lunge to all fours and indignantly shake the dust from the entire length of his body, as a dog would shake off bath-water.

Jack picked up the trailing reins and patted the horse's neck. The dazed bay looked at him with baleful brown eyes, as though surprised to find himself alive after still another Stationary W. "That's one helluva way to treat a good horse," Jack apologized as he led him, dragging yards of piano wire, back to the rope picket line.

"I'm sorry we don't have more work for you boys," Anderson told Jack and his companions at the end of the second day. "But we've got this picture in the can, and the next couple of 'Bronco Billys' call mostly for indoor stuff — saloons, a railroad train, a dance hall. We'll go back to the studio for those." Eager as the cowboys were to break their bones for Broncho Billy's princely wages, it was clear that they were once more out of work.

"Maybe someday when picture people settle down and agree on one central place to make movies, there'll be steady work for you," Anderson speculated. "But only God knows if movies will last at all. Maybe tomorrow people will get tired of flickers and want the circus back again, or the old Tom shows."

As the future of moving pictures seemed almost as chancey as the business of making them, Jack and his companions congratulated themselves on having gotten through with good pay and all their teeth intact. But they had also ridden far enough to realize there were no longer any ranches of a size to take on fifteen cowboys. They decided to split up and head in different directions. Jack and Stanley stayed together, worked a full summer driving stage in Yosemite Park, and then with the first frost drifted back down to Livingston, not far from the old Chowchilla, to visit Mrs. Danley.

"Mother" Danley was the plump and kindly wife of a Kansas farmer. The couple had migrated out to central California from Lawrence twenty years before. She liked the cowboys, and was always reminding them of the kind of families they came from and how their mothers would expect them to behave. It was easy to see how she earned her nickname.

Over homemade rhubarb pie she listened as these two favorite "boys" of hers discussed their slim chances of getting work punching cows. She fussed about the kitchen, patted her upswept steel-gray hair and fidgeted with the cameo heirloom brooch at her throat, trying to get up enough nerve to say what was on her mind.

"Jack, you know how I feel like a mother to both you boys," she began; and Jack grinned and said, "All right. Keep on nagging and I'll believe it."

"Well, there's something I must tell you. I took the liberty of writing your folks, back in Chicago, this summer while you were up in Yosemite . . ."

"You wrote my folks?" Jack's tanned face turned white as he stared at her. "You had no right to take that information I gave you — and do something underhanded with it — that was only in case I got killed, or . . ."

"Now, Jack, let me finish," Mother Danley put in stubbornly. "Your mother was really overjoyed to know you were alive. After all, don't you think you've punished her enough? She loves you and it's been ten long years since you left home."

It seemed there was a conspiracy to get Jack back home that year. Stanley had met a girl in Modesto and now he decided to get married and settle down. There just was no ranch work anymore, and Jack would die before he'd ask the new Chowchilla owners to take him on. Then, too, after he thought about it, his anger toward Mother Danley cooled a little. Maybe it *was* time he went back and took a new look at his family. He was fond of his sisters, and it was easier every day to remember his mother in a more kindly light. He wasn't thirteen anymore, and his stepfather could no longer take a cane to him. He had left home a miserable and bewildered kid who weighed just a little over a hundred pounds — green as grass, knowing nothing about the outside world. Now he stood six feet, one inch, weighed almost two hundred pounds, and had thousands of miles of trails, hard knocks, and yes, maybe even wisdom, behind him.

It might be good to go back and measure that experience against his own background.

2

West to the Waterhole

On a soft April morning Jack Montgomery stepped off the train in Chicago, and found himself one of hundreds of travelers hurrying in and out of the depot. Long-forgotten constrictions of city life pinched his mind, like a mail-order cinch crimping a green bronc's belly. This sense of confinement increased when he passed the ticket window and recognized the same clerk who had taken his fare for Calgary eleven years before. My God, Jack thought, that poor old man has never left his cage in all the years I've gone, and done, and seen so much! Without understanding what was ailing him — for twentieth-century man had not yet found labels for his unique emotional traumas — Jack was suffering severe cultural shock.

But his decision to return put steel in his spine. He had accepted the fact that he would never be cured of trail fever, nor did he care to be. It was not an altogether disagreeable affliction, but as with any other itch, there are times when it is salutary to stop scratching. The spring of 1915 was one of those times. More than mere sentiment underlay his decision to return to his family. The stockyards and packing houses of Armour and Cudahay cast a powerful aroma of prosperity across Chicago skies.

Respectable people might wish the stench away — just as ladies in his childhood had pulled down the shades and pretended they weren't at home the day the Blue Barrel men came to clean out and renew the outside privy. But Jack knew it was precisely that expensive "cow perfume" that had given many a Chicago family a high place on the city's social register. Unemployment and plow jockeys might stalk the open range, but as the cowboy saying went, "There's more ways to skin a cat than stickin' his head in a bootjack." The "catskin" Jack was after was independence from ranchers and ramrods. He would work at the stockyards until he had cached enough savings to buy his own little spread, and then to hell with both homesteaders and ranchers alike!

Alighting from the trolley that took him out to the suburb of Villa Park, he took a familiar street leading to the handsome two-story house with "J. G. Montgomery" on the mailbox. Pausing, valise in hand, he struggled to make the past and present come into focus. The same two hydrangea bushes flanked the front steps, clouds of lilacs still ranged along the veranda. Everything was exactly as he had left it, as though it were a picture in a stereopticon which he had briefly laid aside. Now it was up to him to make it come alive once more. But on his own terms.

The family's initial shock, excitement and joy at the prodigal's unannounced return were genuine and even overflowed into a sincere, if somewhat restrained, welcome from his stepfather. Jack's older sisters, Florence and Marcella, were now young women on the threshold of marriage. His baby brother, Ed, who had still been wearing sailor suits when Jack left home, was now a rising young broker on the Corn Exchange; "going places" was the way people described his ambitious younger brother. Florence added approvingly that he was also courting a delightful young lady who had recently moved to Villa Park from Wisconsin, and Florence hoped it would blossom into a serious romance.

Scarcely a week after his return, Jack scored his first goal by landing a good job with a meat packer. Hurrying home to break the news to his mother, he burst through the front door and almost ran over a young woman who was standing alone in the spacious foyer.

"I beg your pardon, ma'am!" he apologized, backing off like a colt from his first encounter with a porcupine.

"I was just waiting here for Florence to return," the girl explained. "She had to run across to a neighbor's house for a minute."

As she spoke, Jack found himself tallying up an astonishing list of outstanding features that seemed deserving of a blue ribbon at any county fair: large, delft-blue eyes, wide apart, a perfect nose and mouth, all set in a heart-shaped face. Above her flawless skin were coils of sorrel-tinted chestnut hair, and all ninety pounds, five-foot-two of the rest of her was clad in cool, white organdy that fell discreetly to the toes of white, high-buttoned shoes.

"Why, you must be Ed's brother Jack, just home from the West!" she burst out, and then, with a bashful smile, she added, "I'm Marian Baxter."

"*You're* Marian!" was Jack's astonished reply. So this was the beautiful neighbor girl brother Ed had been squiring about town for the past few months.

As they waited for Florence to return, Jack enthused over his new job and Marian seemed more than eager to hear about his adventurous life in the wild and woolly West. It sounded as exotic as the Taj Mahal to a seventeen-year-old girl who until recently had lived all her life in the little town of Lancaster, Wisconsin. When Florence returned ten minutes later, Jack had already made a date to accompany Marian to White City the following evening. As they strolled through that quite proper amusement park, he obtained her promise to be his partner at the spring ball, the entertainment event of the season in Villa Park. Ed, unprepared for competition from any quarter, had not bothered to ask Marian in advance and so lost her by default.

That evening, as they waltzed to the strains of "You Wore a

Tulip, a Big Yellow Tulip, and I Wore a Red, Red Rose," Jack fell hopelessly in love with the girl who looked as if she had just stepped off Howard Chandler Christie's drawing board. He could hardly believe he was here, all duded up in a dark suit and boiled collar, turned out like some carpet knight from Kansas City. But somehow, it all made sense, for Marian had turned his past and future upside down. The cowboy who had managed to dodge every "pretty heifer" from Calgary to California had been roped and tied at last by a girl who summed up everything that the term "a perfect lady" had always meant to him.

As for Marian, the quiet companionship she had known with Ed simply evaporated before the dark good looks and romantic charms of his dashing brother, Jack. If anyone reminded her that Ed was "going places" while Jack was a black sheep, fresh in from the range, she chose not to listen. On June 16th, exactly six weeks from the day they met, Jack and Marian were married at her Grandmother Baxter's mansion in Lancaster.

Marian had lived in that comfortable home since she was five years old, when her parents were divorced. Life had made few demands, and now as a bride of seventeen, she felt she was fully prepared for whatever the future held. Although she had been greatly attracted by her young husband's adventurous background, when she weighed it against the solid middle-class family from which he came, she felt certain their values would prevail. Their circumstances were safe, the kind she understood and knew how to deal with. She had no intentions of going West herself.

The following June a daughter, named Jack-Louise, was born. If Jack was disappointed at not having a son, this was soon dispelled by the new joys of parenthood. The event was also somewhat overshadowed by persistent headlines predicting imminent American involvement in Europe's war. When that threat became reality, Jack immediately tried to enlist in a

mixed battalion of National Guard groups called the Rainbow
Division. (This Division was decimated a few weeks later in
France.) But a wise recruiting officer dissuaded him, suggest-
ing he break horses for the cavalry instead.

Taking the officer's advice, Jack applied for a job as horse-
breaker and the family moved to Rockford, Illinois. A few
months later the army offered a better paying job as a construction foreman on Coronado Island, and Jack moved his
family to San Diego, California. There, two weeks before the
1918 Armistice, I made my entrance as a member of the Montgomery family. The nun in the Catholic hospital where I was
born gently corrected my mother when she said she wanted to
name the new baby Peggy-Jean.

"The Christian form is Margaret, my dear."

"I like Peggy better," Mother replied firmly. (Years later I
changed it myself to Diana, when being Baby Peggy forever
seemed too difficult a prospect to live with.)

With the war's end, Father found himself out of a job. Fortunately California was practically home range to him after his
years at the Chowchilla, so he bought a secondhand car and
we drove to the San Joaquin Valley, where he surprised
Mother Danley much as he had his own family, by appearing
on her front stoop, unannounced.

Leaving Marian and the babies at the Danley farm, Jack
contacted Stan, who was now married and living in Merced.
Stan knew about a job in Yosemite Valley, where he and Jack
had driven stage. That had been back in the days when the
army was still in charge. Now, it seemed, they were turning
control over to the National Park Service, which was recruiting
men to serve as rangers. Jack was interviewed and promptly
hired by Stephen T. Mather, the man who later became famous
as the Father of the National Park System.

Marian thought the news unbelievably good, but was dubi-
ous about how and where they would live with two tiny babies
in a place so removed from civilization as Yosemite Valley.

Jack dismissed her worries as groundless, and assured her they would be given a fine, snug cabin. The main thing, anyway, was that the Valley was beautiful. Packing their few belongings for the move he told her convincingly, "Don't worry! You'll love it!" The move was the first of many times when Marian would follow blindly where her husband led, with no more certainty or description of her destination than the familiar, "Don't worry. You'll love it!" ringing in her ears.

Yosemite in the spring was indeed beautiful, a fact that somewhat sweetened the bitter pill of learning there was no cabin for the "temporary man." The only such structure was in possession of the chief ranger, until such time as the service could get things together. Meantime, Marian called home a shelter made of canvas and slab, with a wooden platform for a floor.

Jack's duties were varied and ranged from dry-nursing the few tourists wealthy enough to possess automobiles, to spotting and fighting forest fires. Trapped in one such holocaust he and a companion lost their uniforms, their eyelashes, and all their hair, as they threw themselves to the damp forest floor and let the flames surge over them.

Marian helped man the station, and occasionally broke the monotony of housework and child care by visiting a neighboring ranger's wife. Such visits involved a horseback ride of from three to six miles, her infant daughters seated fore and aft the saddle. By this time Jack had begun her acculturation to the West by outfitting her in a riding habit and boots, a costume that managed to be jaunty as well as practical.

Before Marian had time to begin worrying about wintering in the Valley, Jack came home one afternoon with great news.

"Stephen Mather has just promoted me — I'm to be the new permanent ranger at the Grand Canyon!"

Marian reeled slightly, but was hardly dismayed at the prospect of wintering in Arizona's sunny clime (the finer points of geography and climate not having been covered in the Lancaster High School). Once again she began to covet the longed-for log cabin, and this time she saw it clearly in a cool, tree-shaded oasis on the sun-drenched Arizona plain.

In September, 1919, the new park ranger, his twenty-one-year-old wife and two baby daughters alighted from a Sante Fe Pullman and stepped into a new, if not entirely perfect, world. Here at the end of a thirty-mile spur running from Williams to the South Rim of the Grand Canyon was a sprawl of still raw buildings, known collectively as Santa Fe Village. Virtually all of these structures were owned by, or formed some vital part of, the famed Harvey House restaurant operation, which was the combination Howard Johnson–Hilton hotel of that era. Across from the depot was a big garage, while to the east loomed the imposing battlements of the El Tovar Hotel, and to the south lay Bright Angel Camp. Assorted stables, corrals, bunkhouses, a cookhouse for construction workers, and the residences of several supervisors of the operation rounded out the settlement.

An official of the Park met the newcomers at the depot, and proved to be an eager young Stephen T. Mather convert. To him each present inconvenience was merely one more step leading up the pyramid that was the "park service of tomorrow." As he led them to a waiting car, Marian's eyes lighted upon the log cabin of her dreams. It was spacious, its window sills were painted forest green, the walls were neatly chinked with lime, and from the pitched roof rose a handsome chimney of river rock, which spoke of a fireplace or oil-burning stove within. Unable to stand the suspense any longer, Marian interrupted their guide.

"And where will *we* be staying?"

As he handed Marian, the children and suitcases into the back seat, the young ranger smiled. "Well, that *does* pose a problem. The only cabin is that one over there, where the Superintendent lives."

As he started up the motor and turned the car toward the

emptiness of the South Rim, he added, "We'll all pitch in to make things as comfortable as.possible, before winter."

They found themselves traveling over a bumpy half-trail, half-wagon track, neither of which added up to one good un-paved road. The passing landscape looked nothing at all like the Arizona desert as Marian had imagined it, except that it was empty and obviously on the outer periphery of civilization. About a mile from the Rim, the car stopped in front of two tents, set side by side on wooden platforms. Cheerily the driver leaped out, and, with as much optimism as he could muster, presented them with their new home.

One tent doubled as parlor-bedroom-bath, the other served as kitchen, or cookhouse, the term in use out West. Here, Marion discovered, Arizona offered a fascinating variety of surprises not listed in schoolbooks back home. Just to keep her babies alive, she found herself killing scorpions, centipedes, Gila monsters and tarantulas as routinely as Grandmother Baxter used to swat flies. And although Jack knocked together as many helpful additions and "conveniences" as possible be-fore winter set in, the hard truth was, it *snowed* here on the South Rim!

Life in a tent was a relentless round of getting up in the morning and knocking either a scorpion or two inches of snow off the children's cots — depending on the season. Freezing temperatures were kept at bay by a cocksure little kerosene stove, blissfully innocent of its own limitations. To break the monotony there were pushy, stubborn bears, which had to be discouraged from raiding the cookhouse tent by having the meat and other tempting victuals kept safely out of reach.

Jack's duties proved far more hazardous than anything — short of fighting major fires — he had been called upon to do in Yosemite. Routine chores included taking mules loaded with lumber and dynamite down the crumbling Mormon and Indian trails to the canyon floor. The park service was trying to improve these time-ravaged routes so that tourists might one day make the descent in reasonable comfort and security. Meanwhile, despite all Jack's skill and caution, even sure-footed mules plunged to their deaths from eroded sections of trail. Others were trapped in the treacherous quicksands of the Colorado. More than once Jack plunged in beside his downed animals, cut away their loads and tried to snake them out with lassos and a saddle horse, but eventually had to see them go under.

Understandably, Marian worried about Jack. As for her little girls, she soon learned the Grand Canyon offered count-less more opportunities than Yosemite Valley for children to be lost, poisoned, crippled, drowned or killed. Louise was two years old, Peggy eleven months. Resourcefully, Marian rolled up her sleeves and started each day by staking Louise out on a long picket rope tied to a sapling in front of the tent. This kept her from toddling off to the Indian reservation or falling over the canyon rim while her mother was occupied in the kitchen. For Peggy, Jack fashioned a combination high chair and baby corral out of a Campbell soup carton. (Playpens had yet to be invented.) Indoors or out, the baby amused herself by banging spoons on saucepans and greeting passing Havasupai Indians with cries of delight.

The tent was devoid of *all* conveniences. Light was pro-vided by a hissing Coleman lantern. Water had to be hauled a quarter of a mile from nearby Rowes Wells. When Jack was home he brought in two buckets each morning. When he was off on his own duties — which was more often than not — Marian made do with the single bucket she dragged in with great difficulty from the well. This she rationed as carefully as if she were adrift in mid-Atlantic on a raft. First it was used for cooking and drinking. What remained was used to sham-poo her own luxuriant hair; then came the babies' shampoos, their baths, and her own. Lastly, this much-recycled water served to scrub the planked tent floors, after which it was consigned to the arid earth just outside the back door.

The distances were something she tried not to think about. Three miles to the village, for such necessities as food. For luxuries like clothes, medicine or a doctor, one went by horseback to Williams, *thirty miles*, or took the train. A government nurse made regular visits to the reservation Indians, and if a person was smart he chose that time to be sick, and no other.

But through all these difficulties of living, Marian felt her sacrifices were not in vain. Jack seemed to like the park service. It allowed him to work out of doors, and on horseback — the two absolutely indispensable requirements if he was to be happy on a job. This much she had learned in her three eventful years as Jack Montgomery's wife.

Yet one thing more remained for her to learn about her husband. He was too individualistic to make himself over into an organization man, whose loyalties to the system outweighed his own independence. A certain colonel, who had remained behind when the army pulled out, and had been incorporated into the park service, believed in authority and subordination to one's superior officers. One evening when he rode in, he had the poor judgment to order Ranger Montgomery to "cuff off my horse and bed him down in a clean stall before you check out tonight." Stunned, Jack had obliged, but not without fury.

"I've hated army brass ever since I met my first officer in Yosemite back in 1910!" Jack raged that night when he reached home. "I'm no stable boy or groom! And why are *we* living in a tent while he has that big house in the village?"

Marian sat mending socks by the light of the Coleman lantern, and when Jack had simmered down somewhat, she suggested he take his complaints about the colonel directly to Stephen Mather. Jack acted on her advice, and Mather counseled patience — and advancement in due time. Meanwhile, Jack would have to deal with such martinets on their own terms.

Jack tried, but a second run-in with the colonel unraveled what little patience he possessed. This time, in spite of

Mather's protestations, Jack refused to capitulate and handed in his resignation from the park service.

Jack temporarily resettled his family in an apartment in downtown Los Angeles. Thanks to the many skills he had mastered as a cowboy, he was once again able to take up hammer and saw, and find work as a carpenter on a new building going up on Olive Street. It was an honest job, and it provided for his family, but he was miserable doing it. Torn between his longing to go back to the old days of punching cows, and his remorse that things in the park service had gone sour, there now seemed to be nothing ahead but more of the same. On the second day of work the crew was let off early, and Jack found himself walking idly down Fifth Street, lost in his depressing thoughts, when suddenly he was roused by a voice from behind calling his name. Turning, he saw a familiar figure striding toward him.

"Goddammit, I knew that was your walk, Monty!" the man shouted.

"Handlebar Hank Bell!" Jack cried. "Why, you alkalied old sonofabitch!" Never had Jack been so overjoyed to see any man in his life, and his greeting said it all.

"Hell, I haven't laid eyes on you since that winter we was cuttin' poles together for old Felix McHugh up in Alberta! What in hell are you doin' in a dude trap like L.A.?"

The two old friends stepped into a nearby café to continue their reunion over coffee, but instead of good news it seemed both had only hard luck to share. Hank Bell was a seasoned cowhand, about thirty-five at that time, who hailed from a tank town near Waco, Texas. He was tall, rawboned, with startling bright blue eyes and a high-bridged nose. His russet hair was set off by a huge handlebar mustache that drooped well below his chin. The mustache not only softened the hard line of his long, lantern jaw, but it had given him his nickname.

"I just come in from Cheyenne," Hank explained. "I sold my horse here in Los Angeles, for city prices, but figured I'd best keep my saddle. Ranch I was workin' for in Wyoming went under. I'm clean out of a job, but by God I got a few sawbucks to spend on drinks. Where can we go?"

"Hank, this town's as dry as a canteen in hell," Jack told him.

"Yeah, I heard that from a native over at the livery barn. But he was tellin' me about a place up in Hollywood where they still serve tequila, whiskey and mescal. Said lots of cowpokes hang out over there, and maybe we'd run into some old friends."

Hank dropped by the barn to pick up his saddle, and the two men caught the trolley that ran into Hollywood. Hank paid an extra nickel for a seat for his saddle. "Hell, Monty, a Herman Heiser hull is the only insurance I got left," he confided, running his knuckles fondly over the mahogany patina of the saddle's worn cantle-board.

When the conductor announced Cahuenga, Hank hefted his saddle onto his shoulder, and the two men climbed off the red car. They felt out of place in this sleepy resort town of retired Easterners, transplanted Midwestern farmers and ardent prohibitionists. But when they saw a small hole-in-the-wall store with "Joe Posada, Hand Made Boots" painted in gold letters on the window and several sample boots on display, they began to feel more at home.

"The barn man told me this owl hoot saloon's directly across the street from the bootmaker's shop," Hank said. And there it was, the Gay Nineties lettering on the one-story gray frame building assuring them they had made it to the Waterhole.

3

Camera Range

I⊤ was late afternoon and the café was crowded. Some men sat at small round tables, eating or playing poker, while others stood lined up along the old-fashioned bar, a seasoned relic of pre-Prohibition days. Those at the bar had coffee cups set conspicuously before them, but coffee was not what most of them were drinking. Shot glasses and tumblers twinkled briefly as the man behind the bar paused before each customer to replenish the forbidden drink in his hand.

When Jack and Hank entered, everyone in the place glanced up, interest or suspicion ready to be kindled, depending on which side of the blanket the patron might be — Prohibition or free choice. Immediately the distrust melted, as two men at the bar recognized friends in the newcomers and came forward enthusiastically to welcome them to the Waterhole. Slim Whittaker was a former Chowchilla hand who had quit with Jack and ridden briefly for Broncho Billy. Old Bill Gillis had known Hank Bell "since he was knee-high to a grasshopper." Jack quickly saluted two other less-familiar but recognizable acquaintances, Shorty Miller and Ed Hendershot, both brief ranch and rodeo companions. Slim stood the new arrivals to the first round of drinks to celebrate their reunion, and old Bill Gillis bought the second, while they launched into the distinctive ritual of the Waterhole: recounting what each one had been doing since the last outfit they rode for went under.

Hank Bell told how he had just brought a trainload of steers west to L.A. as his last chore for a Montana spread selling out to farmers.

"I can savvy your situation," Bill Gillis offered sympathetically. The white-haired Gillis was already a legend at the Waterhole, and was, as the gentle jest of younger men had it, "older than God." Still, they respected his age, and behind his back paid him the ultimate tribute, referring to him as "wiser than a tree full of owls." They also used the rare term "alkalied" — meaning someone who was bone-seasoned to the desert, and with good reason as Jack would learn. Although he was thin as a bobcat's whisker, he was also as indestructible as a Gila monster.

"Hell, I know what it is to be busted down to nothin' but your saddle," Gillis recalled. "I come out here two years ago, already sixty-five years old. Me and my tiny Pima wife set out alone from Tucson a-horseback, her on the saddle skirts behind, and no pack mule even, just what we was wearin' on our backs. We made it clean across the burning Yuma desert, sand dunes and all, landing here with a used-up pony, a dry canteen and twenty-five cents to our name."

The men shook their heads in silent praise, and then Gillis turned to Jack and asked how he had come to Hollywood. When Jack had finished his recital of downhill events that terminated in a carpenter's job on a building in L.A., Slim Whittaker brought his glass down sharply on the polished bar in protest.

"Hell, Monty, you can't go out there and do that! No need to, either, even if you *do* have a wife and two kids to keep in fodder!"

"Slim's right, Jack. You and Hank oughta hear what we've all been doin' of late," Ed Hendershot put in.

"That's right," Slim responded expansively. "Me and the boys have been working almost regular as riding extras in pictures, and there's good money in it, too. Not like that time

in Niles Canyon, Jack — two good days with Broncho Billy and
then the well run dry. No sirree! Out here there's lots of big
stars makin' Westerns all the time — Tom Mix, William S.
Hart . . ."

". . . And out at Universal City, just yonder in San Fernando Valley," Gillis interrupted, "why, you couldn't untrack
out there without runnin' head-on into three or four big stars
turnin' out Western serials, five days to a chapter. Sure, it's
forkèd riding, no two ways about it. Those Stationary and
Runnin' W's can break your neck so fast you couldn't get your
hat off first."

"Yeah, but they pay three-twenty to five dollars a day for
doin' it, and a box lunch thrown in!" Hendershot exclaimed.

Hank stood hip-shot and happy at the far end of the bar,
studying each man's face as he talked. Jack turned his shot
glass slowly in his hand and listened hard to everything they
were saying.

"Almost sounds like a 'windy,' " Jack said with a grin, and
then added quickly, "but if you all say it's true, I know it's
true."

"Damned betcha it's on the square, Jack," Ed Hendershot
assured him. "Look at me! I couldn't find a ranch to hire me to
do what I do best, gentlin' mean and spoiled broncs. So I had
to hit the rodeo circuit. But hell, I quit bustin' my guts that
way three months ago, and haven't been out of work but a few
days at a time since. Ain't no long-term contract, but still it
pays three times what any of us earned punchin' cows. Besides, you're *workin' in the saddle, not on your feet!* And who'd
go back to dry-nursin' cows inside some barbed-wire pen anyway, when you can ride your tail off just as easy out here and
for better pay?"

Bill Gillis nodded agreement. "I'll say that paycheck at the
end of the day looks as pretty as a spotted pup."

"It sure beats hell out of diggin' wells and cuttin' poles!" Slim
laughed. And then, more earnestly, he added, "Why don't you

two come out with us to Mixville tomorrow? We'll prove it to you!"

"But can a stranger get on just like that, on another cowboy's say-so?" Jack asked, as Hank's blue eyes challenged Slim's ability to produce hard-and-fast results.

"You just meet me there tomorrow morning," Slim enthused. "I know everybody from the castin' director on down."

Without saying anything to Marian, Jack called the building foreman and told him he had a bad toothache and wouldn't be able to make it to work the following day.

When he arrived at the Edendale studio about ten o'clock the next morning, he found Hank and Slim waiting for him. True to his boast, Slim led his two friends through the gates and into a small office. A young man sat at a table, a ledger open in front of him.

"Hi, Sam," Slim greeted him. "I've got two good men for you. We've ridden together for years and they're both good, all-around hands with horses and stock."

"Well, we can use lots of good riders out here right now," the casting director replied sunnily. "Would you be available for a job tomorrow?"

Hank and Jack nodded in unison, and watched as the man wrote their names in the day book before him.

"All right. Be at the gate at five tomorrow morning, weather permitting — rain, that is, not just fog. And be sure to dress in Western costume, such as . . ." Glancing up he paused, and then, as if seeing Hank's garb for the first time, he added sheepishly, "Well — wear exactly what you're wearing." He further explained that if they wished to ride their own horses they could be stabled right there at the studio barn. Otherwise, a studio wrangler would cut them a mount for the day.

"You'll be paid five dollars for the day, either way, and the company gives you lunch. You'll be working on location out in the Valley, so meet me back here tomorrow night and I'll hand out your paychecks."

Jack and Hank were astounded at how easy it was to get hired on at a studio. All the mystery and difficulty that their own ignorance of Hollywood had built up in their minds had been instantly dispelled by Slim's confident recommendation. In a mood to celebrate, Hank and Jack made their way back to the Waterhole, where Hank stood everyone to a round of drinks.

"By God," he announced optimistically, "the way I see it, for that kind of pay I'd ride a horse through hell as a double for the Devil!"

"You sure wouldn't need any make-up for the part!" Gillis shot back.

Jack took the trolley back to downtown Los Angeles, stopped by the Olive Street project and turned in his resignation to the foreman. The Waterhole had worked its magic: Lady Luck had revealed the bonanza that lay waiting only twelve miles from where he stood. Of course, behind his willingness to throw away the security of a steady job for what was at best still a gamble lay the promise that he could ride again, with men he knew and could trust, men who respected and understood him in return. There was absolutely nothing more degrading to Jack — or to any other cowboy — than a job that must be done on foot. It carried a stigma bordering on shame that only another cowboy could fully appreciate.

Still, Marian was stunned when he returned to the apartment and announced that he had quit carpentering and was going to ride, stunt and double in Hollywood Westerns for much better pay.

"But the work is so dangerous!" she protested.

"What of it?" Jack replied lightly as he unpacked his worn steep-heel boots from the trunk where they had languished ever since before his marriage.

"But dear, be reasonable," she pleaded, as she watched him pull on his boots and buckle the spur strap over the arch, the big, Mexican rowels making silver music at his heels. "Why, you could be hurt — crippled for life — even *killed!*"

"Hell, Sharkey," he said, using the pet name of a famous Mexican fighting bull, which he had given her during one of her spunky Grand Canyon battles with a scorpion, "what about fighting forest fires and pulling pack mules loaded with dynamite out of quicksand?"

He looked at her for a long moment and then reached over and patted her hand gently.

"I know how you feel, dear. But hell, I could just as easily have fallen off the damned building on Olive Street and broken my neck. Besides," he added, striding toward the hat rack to pick up an old Stetson Ed Hendershot had loaned him, "if a man's going to get killed, the only decent way to go is wearing spurs."

✳

"Mixville" was the cowboys' name for the studio where Tom Mix made his films. It was a very practical spread, comprising indoor and outdoor sets, a cookhouse, bunkhouse, blacksmith shop, barns and corrals. A riding extra's day working out of Mixville was long and brutal, judged by modern Screen Extra Guild standards. But compared to the grind of a round-up or trail drive, it seemed mild indeed. Some Mixville hands, without any other ties but picture work holding them to Hollywood, even lived there in the bunkhouse Mix provided for that purpose. Before sun-up, hands were roused from their sleep by one of their own company bellowing the same familiar command that had raised them from their prairie beds for decades: "Roll out or roll up, you sons-o-bitches!" ("Roll up" meant to pack your bedroll and look for another job.) After breakfast in the cookhouse, they saddled up and, strung out single file along the edge of the road, they headed for the location of the day.

Their destination on that first day was Newhall, a ride of fifteen miles. Although it was a gray, foggy dawn when they reached their location, the producers seemed undeterred by the lack of sufficient daylight. The cowboys were ordered to push their horses up the opposite side of a steep, small knoll all the way to the crest, from which they were scheduled to descend at top speed. Meantime, the director ordered half a dozen stand-by cars to back up in a long row, with their rear bumpers flush against the base of the knoll. Directly in front of the parked cars, prop men set up a solid wall of silver reflectors. When the director cried, "Action!" through a short megaphone, the stand-by drivers switched on their headlights, which empowered the reflectors to cast a bright glow of instant daylight on the slope down which the cowboys were to make their first wild pursuit of the day. Several scenes were shot in this manner, before the sun finally burned through the haze. It was employed again after sundown, in order to snatch a few more feet of film from the jaws of impending darkness.

It was late when the riders finally turned their weary ponies back toward Edendale and the Mixville barns. It had been a long day of hard riding and a few falls, but none of the cowboys admitted to being tired. Jack Montgomery, for one, had not been so contented in years. He was working beside men he had not ridden with for almost ten years, and under circumstances that in many ways duplicated the rigors of range life. For the first time he felt no remorse at having quit the park service.

If many of the cowboys were happily surprised to discover Hollywood, producers and directors were equally delighted to encounter cowboys. For a decade or more, big name directors like Thomas Ince, D. W. Griffith and Cecil B. De Mille had needed exactly what the cowboys had to offer.

De Mille stumbled upon Hollywood in 1912. Bringing a trainload of actors west to Flagstaff, he planned to film there his first motion picture, *The Squaw Man*. But the Arizona landscape did not match up to the scenery he had in mind, so he re-embarked the entire company on the *Santa Fe* and rode to the end of the line. In Hollywood he rented a barn on the corner of Vine Street and Selma, but from the outset he found himself short of one commodity which, for all its other unquestionable advantages, Hollywood seemed unable to supply. Pretty girls to play ingenues could be had by the score. Experienced actors and actresses, finally willing to risk appearing in movies using the same stage names under which they had risen to theatrical fame, were his for the asking. As for ordinary extras to mill around in the background, entire armies presented themselves at the studio door each morning, begging to be given a crack at grease paint and glory.

But what De Mille and his counterparts had to have to stay in business was a sizable band of expert horsemen. Moreover, these riders must be wholly without fear, nerveless enough to execute the most perilous stunt, fall, chase or battle scenes the imagination of a De Mille or Griffith could conceive. Assuming directors might locate such a singular group, there were two more conditions still to be met: one, the men must be *chronically unemployed* and thereby employable at a minute's notice, and two, willing to gamble their lives, on a day to day basis, for whatever the studio heads decided they could afford to pay.

But where in this hamlet of only five thousand souls, most of whom were Iowa farmers and retired millionaires, could the great directors hope to find men to match their manuscripts? Fatefully, De Mille's barn and the Waterhole's back door were less than three blocks apart. Gradually it became known that a small colony of genuine cowboys, floating free or drifting through Hollywood, gathered in a small café they had made their headquarters. Studios began finding ways to get the word to the Waterhole when they needed the services of seasoned horsemen. Some, like Thomas Ince, sent around a stand-by car to the Waterhole, knowing riders could be found there at almost any hour. It worked out well for both sides, for that way the cowboys could put their otherwise idle hours to profit, playing poker, and still be on hand if a job should materialize.

Universal came up with another primitive but ingenious way of holding cowboys in an available labor pool. They installed a large pen, fenced with wire, just inside the studio gates. Here, riders looking for picture work could pass an hour or an entire day, as they wished, awaiting the momentary appearance of a director in need of them.

"You just stake out your claim early in the morning," Bill Gillis told Jack when the Mixville job ended. "And you wait 'til some director finds out the script calls for cowboys. Hell, Monty, some of these people shoot with no script at all — or with just a vague notion. They don't even know they're goin' to need riders until they get right on top of a scene."

Slim also told Jack about the Sunset Barn, which was located on Sunset Boulevard just a block or so from the Waterhole. It was the place where picture people, and especially cowboy stars, stabled their favorite horses.

"You'll get tagged a 'corral buzzard' for hanging around over there, but nobody ever died of it. Besides, if you're perched on a rail when somebody important comes 'round to pick up his horse, there just might be a job for you — as a double or stunt man. Happens all the time."

Jack dropped around the Sunset Barn to get acquainted, but it was Universal's hiring tank where he was picked to stunt in a Neal Hart serial. That job opened to him the marvels of Carl Laemmle's fabled Universal City. If Mixville had seemed a functional little spread, Universal was impressive beyond any other Hollywood studio.

The lot covered two hundred and thirty acres (more than twice the size of Mr. Wilcox's original Hollywood) and it was a city in more than name alone. It boasted its own police force, fire department and street-cleaning crew, all nattily uniformed with "Universal City" emblazoned on tunic and helmet. There were libraries, greenhouses, schools, a hospital, mills, shops, forges, and an immense reservoir. A special spur of the Southern Pacific ran right onto the lot. The two great restaurants could serve twelve hundred people between them, and the barns and corrals seemed endless. The tack room had enough gear to put the entire U.S. Cavalry in the field, together with an Indian army to fight it. In the big actors' lounge, cowboys could be seen at all hours, playing cards at the round tables before the red brick fireplace.

There were three or four mammoth stages, eighty dressing rooms, and vast prop departments. Behind the stages and wardrobe sprawled the outdoor sets. Here were the sad-eyed brownstone fronts and brick tenements of the New York street. Beyond were the narrow lanes and slate roofs of Paris, where Lon Chaney was to make *The Phantom of the Opera* and *The Hunchback of Notre Dame*.

The Western street lay farther still, and then miles of open country beyond. Here Universal's great herds of horses, mules, sheep and cattle by the hundreds grazed when not being used for picture work. The big buff-colored knoll that formed a backdrop for the lot also doubled as a handy location for Westerns, less than ten minutes from the front office. It was an everyday occurrence to look up and see a band of outlaws in hot pursuit of a careering stagecoach, or Indians chasing a lumbering covered wagon, around the flanks of this little hill.

Unlike Mixville, where only one Western star reigned as king, Universal was an empire with half a dozen white-hatted heroes dividing the honors and the profits with owner Carl Laemmle. And out here the stars as well as the riding extras were genuine cowboys rather than showmen like Mix.

Neal Hart, whose "Blue Streak" serials had won him the title "America's Pal," had been a cowpuncher in Wyoming before coming to Hollywood. Jack found Neal a stocky, fearless all-around hand, who had broken into movies via a brief stint with the Wild West Show circuit. He had gotten his first big break at Universal in 1916 in a Jack Holt Western. Later he became a star on his own. Jack's job as double for the heavy in this serial was the start of a lifelong friendship between the two men.

Ed Hendershot was out at Universal, too, working with Hoot Gibson. Gibson was himself a holder of the coveted title of World Champion Cowboy, won at the Calgary Stampede at a time when that title still meant a good deal. After a brief stint at ranch life in Nebraska, Hoot had cut his theatrical teeth on the rodeo circuit. He was a fantastic horseman and trick-rider, and showman enough to realize the importance of making his stunts look every bit as dangerous to the patron in the last row of bleachers as they actually were close up. He was among the greatest of the so-called "Roman Riders" — a man who could stand astride the backs of two horses racing at full speed around the arena.

Hoot eventually landed a job with Dick Stanley's traveling circus that, when the troupe played in Los Angeles in 1910, accepted a studio offer to appear as extras in a Western sequence. Upon completion of the job, the seedy little circus moved on, but Gibson decided to remain with the studio, and Westerns were never the same again. People at Universal told the story of a director who offered the fearless Gibson an extra five dollars if he would allow himself to be dragged by a running horse. Hoot shot back, "Make it ten and I'll let him kick me to death!"

But without question, the roughest of them all was Art Acord. He was Universal's top star at that time, and the one whose background qualified him to be rated as the cowboy's cowboy. Born in Stillwell, Oklahoma, in 1890, when it was still known as Indian Territory, he was a seasoned ranch hand who had worked all over the West. He was considered — even above Hoot Gibson — as the greatest all-around rodeo champ who ever lived. He was equally expert at trick-riding, bulldogging steers, and calf-roping, and was one of the three men who had ever stayed aboard the notorious bronc Cyclone past the timer's gun. Acord made an early series of Westerns under the name of Buck Farvin; then in 1912 De Mille gave him a leading role in *The Squaw Man*, which catapulted him to fame.

Jack quickly became friends with both Neal and Hoot, but had not had the opportunity to meet Acord until one day when Neal's company finished shooting early. As Jack started to leave the set, he was hailed by old Bill Gillis.

"Hey, Monty! You've been wantin' to meet Art Acord. Well, I'm workin' on the Western street with him and a Mexican knife-thrower, Ortega. I just never seen any man so quick and true with a knife as that chili-dipper, and I've seen plenty in my time."

As they strolled over to the Western street, the conversation turned to Art's character and it turned out that Gillis had known him since he was a green kid on his first ranch job.

"Absolutely no man quite like him," Gillis told Jack. "Why, I once seen a bronc take him right through a six strand barbed-wire fence, and I mean they was wrapped up together like a Christmas package. But damn if Art didn't stop that bronc, get them both unwound, and when he got back to the barn he did as good a job of patchin' that poor pony as any vet could have done."

Warming to his subject, Gillis continued, "Why, I've seen him without no clothes and I swear there ain't a patch of hide on him bigger 'n a silver dollar that don't have a knife wound or gunshot scar, or some other kind of brand. Art packs a mark of violence for every one of his thirty-one years."

They found the company between scenes, but just as Gillis started over with Jack to introduce him, three bus loads of tourists pulled in and a horde of chattering women from some out-of-state convention piled out and descended upon the set.

"Holy cats!" Gillis groaned. "Here comes another herd of them heifers in high heels. Art hates them studio tours like the Devil hates Holy Water. We better wait 'til they leave. He'll be in no mood for meetin' anybody while they're on the set."

Jack was already familiar with Universal's studio tours, which the tourists loved, but everyone else on the lot found terribly annoying. Everybody had at one time or another complained to "Uncle Carl" Laemmle, but to no avail. Universal's creator was not a man to be argued with: people in Hollywood called him "Uncle Carl" because an astonishing proportion of his employees were related to him either by blood or by marriage. He had come to America from Germany, a desperately poor youth, but even after becoming many times a millionaire, he still knew the value of a nickel. Recently he had come up with a scheme which at that time was without precedent in Hollywood. He installed runways or suspended viewing ramps on every stage where, for twenty-five cents a head, visitors could tour the studio and "actually *see* movies being made." "Besides," he crowed, "people will pay me to publicize my own pictures!"

The tour guide would come barging onto a set without warning, followed by a gabbling crowd of sight-seers, and launch into his spiel: "And here on the left you see the Neal Hart company making a Western movie . . ."

"The tourists are driving us all crazy!" Neal had protested to Uncle Carl. "The tin horn guides yelling at the top of their lungs, and the tourists calling out for autographs right in the middle of a scene . . . How can we work?"

Even Universal's bus system was enlisted to transport visitors to outdoor sets. But since the tours were Uncle Carl's brainstorm, good-neighbor policy and sugarbowl combined, there was nothing anyone could do to rid the studio of them. Nothing, that is, until this day when Art Acord took to the warpath.

Jack was surprised to find Art Acord considerably shorter than he appeared on the screen, but he was as solidly built as a brick wall, and he had the typical cowboy's squared eyelids, pistol-butt nose and sharply defined jawline. He was dressed in authentic Levis and blue work shirt, with a .45 slung, butt forward, on his left hip. Sizing him up, as he lounged against the entrance of the saloon, Jack could see why Bill Gillis had once described him as "a man who's packed a gun so long he stands slanchways."

While he waited for the cameraman to get set up, Acord strolled over to a false-front sheriff's office where he had a bottle stashed behind one of the uprights. The Mexican, Ortega, dressed in tight *vaquero* pants and a sparkling white *guayavera* shirt from Yucatan, was shorter than Acord by a good three inches, and much stockier. He killed time by practicing knife-throwing at impossible targets and scoring a bull's eye every time. Between these practice sessions he joined Acord in the serious business of killing the quart. Although the two men seemed friendly enough at first, suddenly a quarrel erupted between them. Old Bill Gillis, knowing Art's violent temper, smelled danger and decided to step between them before real trouble began.

"Say now, how about a round of poker with me and some of the boys while we're waiting?" Gillis chimed in cheerily. "Got my cards right here in my shirt pocket under my Durham."

Acord released a steam of carbolic language and then the director came over and tried to calm him.

"Come on, Art," he said. "Settle down and be sensible. Besides, there's visitors on the set. You don't want to give them a bad impression."

Nothing could have angered Acord more.

"I don't give a good goddam if Saint Peter himself is leadin' that bunch of Rhode Island Reds. I'm goin' to run this chilidipper off the lot or kill him tryin'!"

Ortega spun around, and, pushing the director out of his way, he strode angrily up to the cowboy star.

"No feelthy yellow gringo bastard calls me that!"

"Maybe I was wrong," Acord drawled, sizing up his opponent with a contemptuous glance. "I reckon you're just a bucknun Mexican sheepherder!"

The swarthy Ortega went white and jerked his long knife out of the red sash at his waist. In the same instant Acord's right hand whipped out his .45 in a cross "border draw."

"Now, Art — " Gillis said, backing off.

"Everybody get the hell out of my way," Acord snapped, his voice as sharp and level as the drawn knife in Ortega's hand. "I'm gonna fill this greaser so full of holes he won't even float in brine."

Instinctively Jack and Bill Gillis took semi-shelter behind a folding reflector, hypnotized by the sight of the two men standing stock still in the sun-flooded center of the Western street, nailed to their own long shadows.

Ortega took two dragging steps toward Acord, and then made a quick, catlike leap forward, the blade flashing in his hand. Acord fired, and the slug plowed into Ortega's shoulder. As the Mexican clutched the wound, a crimson stain spread across the front of his white *guayavera* shirt. But by a superhuman effort he sprang forward again, grappling with the cowboy star and plunging his knife repeatedly into his chest and arms until Acord's shirt was dyed in his own and Ortega's blood.

A chorus of screams went up from the ranks of the tourists as it dawned on all of them at once that this was no movie, but a real old-time Western "corpse and cartridge" affair. They scattered like turkey hens in a hailstorm, running, screaming, fainting and falling over each other in their headlong flight for cover. Some took shelter behind or underneath the buses, others crawled inside.

Incredibly, Acord still had enough strength left to hurl Ortega from him again and fire three more shots into the Mexican's body before his pistol fell from his nerveless hand and he pitched forward, sprawling face down over Ortega's already lifeless form. For the space of a breath, no one moved; then the tour guides and their charges piled into their buses and roared away. Slowly, crewmen, actors and extras crept out from their various sanctuaries, converging on the center of the street where the two lifeless bodies lay.

Bill Gillis, his face as white as his hair, said huskily, "I always feared that boy would end up this way!" Stetsons in hand, he and Jack respectfully approached the gathering circle of witnesses who hid the grisly corpses from view. And then, above the low murmur of men speaking softly in the presence of death, a laugh rang out and someone yelled:

"Hell, it was the only way we could think of to stampede that bunch of broomtails and their wranglers!"

Jack and Bill Gillis looked on speechlessly as the knot of mourners simply fell apart, every one of them doubled up with laughter, while from its center emerged Acord and Ortega, rising from the ground like two blood-drenched ghosts. Their arms were clasped across each other's shoulders and tears streamed down their cheeks as they rocked back and forth in an agony of mirth.

"When you busted that fist-full of blood capsules we stole from the prop man," Ortega gasped between seizures, "I didn't know which of us was goin' to drown in gore first!"

Acord was wracked anew. "And you — flashin' your god-dammed rubber knife! I thought you'd finish me off before I dropped you with my roll of blanks!"

As the full import of their words sank in, Bill Gillis and Jack were also caught up in the general hysteria of relief which came like a thunderclap upon the realization that the whole tragic episode had been nothing more than a magnificently staged hoax to rid the set of tourists.

When the guides got wind of the macabre joke played on them and their charges, they were incandescent with rage: they marched en masse into Uncle Carl's office to deliver their ultimatum:

"We will *never* take another tour onto an Art Acord set!"

Not even Uncle Carl could persuade them to change their minds. When word of their boycott reached Acord he put on a suitably solemn face and sighed, "I guess the punishment fits the crime!"

Acord and Ortega had not "died" in vain.

4

Windfall

LESS THAN THREE WEEKS after his first day's work in pictures, Jack found himself once again back at Mixville, and this time Mix himself was on the set. It was Jack's first introduction to the great cowboy star, for on the Newhall location job he had not appeared. But in those three weeks Jack had heard a good deal about Tom Mix, from the Waterhole cowboys' viewpoint, and it was not an entirely warm and friendly appraisal.

On a Hoot Gibson, Neal Hart or Art Accord set there was absolutely no gulf between star and riding extras, because these men considered themselves cowboys first and movie stars strictly by accident. It was not his star status, then, that put the cowboys off when it came to Mix, but a deep-seated conviction that he was somehow alien, even hostile, to their breed. They respected his horsemanship, and even believed the studio's legend that he *always* did his own stunts and *never* employed a double. Still, to them, he simply did not possess the authentic Western ring, and no amount of studio publicity could change that fact.

While not exactly shrouded in mystery, Mix's background had certainly not been clarified by publicity writers who supplied his fans with a dizzying assortment of biographies from which to choose. Most were agreed on the place of his birth, Pennsylvania. Some claimed his father had been a cavalry officer and accorded him the now-dubious distinction of having fought at the Battle of Wounded Knee. At some point, all

stated that young Mix had been taken to Oklahoma in childhood, where he grew up in the Indian Territory.

But when the cowboys discussed Mix among themselves he
was "that Pollack from Pennsylvania," or "coal miner's son from
around Pittsburgh." Indeed, the story that circulated in Hollywood for many years was that Mix had not left Pennsylvania in
his boyhood, but rather had to flee from there as a grown man
because of a "killing back in the coalfields." "Knifed a nigger
in a bar" was the phrase the cowboys used when the subject of
Mix's origin arose. But rumors both good and bad surrounded
Tom Mix.

During one action-crammed five-year period, his biographers
claimed, Mix had fought in the Spanish American War,
been involved in suppressing the Boxer Rebellion in China, saw
action in the Boer War (first for the British and then on the
side of the Boers). He had subsequently signed up with the
Texas Rangers and ridden against Pancho Villa during the
border war, served as Sheriff in Montgomery County, Kansas,
been employed as a guide to Theodore Roosevelt on an African
safari, served as town marshal somewhere in Oklahoma, and
toured in Miller's 101 Wild West Show.

When Colonel William Selig, pioneer filmmaker, discovered
the much-traveled Mix in 1910, he was still only thirty, and
working as stock foreman for the Miller show encamped at
Fort Bliss, Oklahoma. Selig hired him as incidental performer
and technical director on a low-key documentary entitled
Ranch Life in the Great Southwest. Selig, who claimed to have
used Mix's own Oklahoma ranch as location for this film,
brought him west to Hollywood where he attained fame in a
series of very short modest Westerns. These initial efforts were
light on plot but very heavy on the kind of action and stunt
work that became synonymous with Tom Mix.

In 1917, however, William Fox lured Mix away from Selig
by offering him more desirable feature-length films, a long-
term contract and a truly astronomical salary. Mix had been
under the Fox banner for about three years when Jack and

Hank Bell worked for him in the early spring of 1920. But it appears that Tom Mix was by then producing his own Westerns and merely releasing them through Fox, thereby achieving more freedom in the choice of scripts and tailoring them to fit his flashy style of showmanship. This would explain the fact that Mixville was located on the old Selig lot at Edendale, near modern Eagle Rock. Mix was apparently leasing studio space from Selig, where the bunkhouse and barns had served him well during his Hollywood apprenticeship with the colonel. Whatever the explanation, in later years the cowboys always insisted that Mixville was out at Edendale and not in Hollywood at Fox headquarters.

Of all the cowboy stars up to that time, Mix was by far the most spectacular in his personal life. He dressed in flamboyant purple or white tuxedos with matching boots and Stetson, lived in a $40,000 Beverly Hills mansion and drove a white Rolls-Royce with the initials "TM" in 14-karat gold on every door. Divorced in 1917, he remarried a year later, and his annual alimony payments were rumored to be enough for a rich man to live on handsomely for the rest of his life. His salary was said to be $20,000 a week, and when he was producing his own pictures it may have gone above that figure.

But fame and luxury had not softened Tom Mix. If he lived high, he also worked hard and played rough. At a party celebrating the christening of one of Tom's daughters, he tangled with Art Accord after both had drunk too many toasts to the new Christian. Mix rode his horse up a flight of stairs and the fight began. Neither man ever bragged about winning that battle, or apologized for losing, so it was assumed to have been a pretty disastrous draw.

There was always a lot of rough and tumble on a Tom Mix set: breakaway barroom chairs and tables, collapsible bannisters and stairs, chandeliers triggered so they could be easily shot down. Mix had evolved his own brand of Western hero, the invincible loner, who fought single-handed against hordes of outlaws or Indians and always emerged after reels of combat without a bruise or even a smudge on the brim of his Stetson.

Jack's return to Mixville was highlighted by just such a barroom free-for-all, a scene that also prompted a heated disagreement between the director and Mix. The director insisted it was simply too risky for the star to execute a particularly difficult leap from a collapsing stairway into the center of the saloon. "Why take a chance on crippling yourself in an accident that could tie up production for weeks and cost a fortune? Why not let a stunt man do it for you?" was the director's reasonable argument.

Mix, however, was proud of his hard-won reputation for personal bravery, and stubbornly refused to consider changing the filming tradition that had built his legend. But finally, after considerable haggling, the director won him over, possibly by reminding him that there was more at stake than his screen image — namely, a large slice of the production profits, which might go a-glimmering for nothing more serious than a broken ankle. Whatever the star's real reason for agreeing to the change, it prompted the director to cast about immediately for someone on the set who resembled Mix enough to serve as double. To his own great astonishment, the choice was Jack Montgomery.

"Hell, I don't look like Mix!" Jack protested.

"Yes, you do. You're almost the same build — just a little lighter, maybe. You've got the same dark eyes and hair, and even your profile looks a good bit like his. From a distance you're really a dead ringer for him."

The dashing star with his patent leather hair, collar-ad profile and ornately tailored clothes seemed a far cry from the drably dressed cowboy extra, but Jack was not one to let opportunity pass.

"Is there any more money in it?"

"Yes, it pays seven-fifty against your five." And then, as if expanding on this windfall, the director added, "And you still get your lunch free!"

But that additional two dollars and fifty cents a day made a great deal of difference to a man with a wife and two children back in 1920. Looking at it another way, it was forty-five dollars a week, and promised to be much steadier work than the average random riding job. Besides, Jack hoped soon to be able to move over into Hollywood, because it was exhausting to come home from the studio or a distant location after dark, and still have to make the long streetcar ride all the way back to downtown Los Angeles.

When he appeared the next morning for his first day as Mix's double, the director approached him and apologized.

"Monty, I forgot to tell you, you'll have to wear make-up today, as well as being costumed like Mix."

The wardrobe man was already on the set with the required costume, but there were no official make-up men in those early days. Jack turned to a veteran stage actor playing a character part in the picture. This old gentleman was glad to teach him the ropes, and quickly produced his own make-up case. One by one he introduced the novice to the mysteries of make-up: the cylinder of solid pink grease paint, wrapped in oil-skin paper, which had to be drawn across the face, violet eye-shadow, black pencil marks on the brows and a good strong black line all around the eyes to hold their own against the kliegs. Even male actors had to use lip-rouge, applied with a little finger from a small round rouge can. Last of all, to make sure the grease paint did not run or shine from the heat of the lights, an outsize velour puff was dredged in a large electric-blue can of Stein's make-up powder. This was pressed rather than spread onto the actor's face, to help seal the pores and keep the surface dull. Repowdering had to be repeated many times during the day's shooting, usually before each scene, until the face felt heavy with the considerable percentage of lead contained in that primitive brand of powder.

When his first day's work as double ended, Jack returned to the old actor for further instructions. "Okay, you got it on me. Now, how in hell do I get this damned bear-grease off my face?" The actor smiled. "Don't worry. Just pick up some cold cream on your way home, spread it on your face and it will wipe off easily with a face towel."

Jack stopped by a store on his way home, where he asked for and got his cold cream. Reaching home, he locked himself in the bathroom, embarrassed to have his wife and children see him in all that war paint and powder. The next twenty minutes were spent following the actor's instructions, but failing to make even a dent in the leaden mask. At last, in desperation he called Marian.

"I had to wear this goddammed bear-grease today, see, but . . .!"

Marian took one look at him and burst out laughing. "What in the world are you doing?"

"Well, what does it look like? I'm trying to take grease paint off with cold cream — this stage actor told me . . ."

"But not *that* kind, you idiot!"

Knowing she was risking an outburst of "Montgomery temper," Marian still couldn't suppress her laughter as she calmly took the half-pint bottle of chilled whipping cream into the kitchen. Returning with a small jar of Stein's Professional Cold Cream she ventured, "Here, dear. Try this. I'll bet *this* is the kind he meant."

Hardly a day as Mix's double went by without its share of sprains and bruises. In the silent Western, when hero and heavy faced each other, tortuous harangues between them were unknown. The children in the audience couldn't read the titles, mothers didn't want to bother whispering them aloud, and the other grown-ups were anxious to get on with the shooting. There was precious little time for airing psychological traumas in the middle of a Tom Mix Western street. They were expected to be long on action and short on talk, so naturally a stuntman at Mixville could run through nine lives in no time at all.

It worried Marian when Jack came home with a different

kind of gimp each night. Once it was a cracked collarbone, then a fractured wrist from a leap off a barroom balcony. Even the famous cowboy star's horse, Tony, had to have a double — something on which Mix himself insisted — and Jack was riding this horse one day when his most serious injury at Mixville took place. Tony's double trotted under an overhanging tree and the villain's double dropped down on horse and rider from above. Jack could almost feel his spinal column crunch under the impact. After the ensuing scuffle with the heavy's substitute, Jack had trouble getting to his feet, but he was finally able to walk away. The self-diagnosis usually ran, "Feels like I busted a gut," or "I must have popped a vertebra that time!" But for none of these injuries was he ever X-rayed. The collarbone was taped, solely so that he could get through a similar stunt the next day without doing any further damage. (As for the vertebrae, it was discovered years later that they *had* been cracked but had apparently healed themselves.)

Despite these hazards, Jack felt there was a temporary future for him as a double and stunt man. There were lots of heroes and heavies to double, and if he kept it up and survived the falls, he might not have to wait too long for that windfall the cowboys were always praying for. Maybe in only a couple of years he could have saved enough to buy a little spread of his own, where he could run maybe a hundred cows, and raise steers for market. On the trolley in the early morning and late evening ride to and from Hollywood, he found himself speculating on where the ranch would be. He remembered isolated, idyllic spots he had come upon, as though the first man to discover them, choice mountain meadows in Wyoming, Arizona and Montana. He would, of course, have to talk Marian out of her bad experiences at the Grand Canyon in order to get her to try frontier life once more. But she wasn't nicknamed Sharkey for nothing. He knew she had the kind of spirit required to pioneer a wilderness, once she made up her mind.

Things might have worked out exactly as Jack planned, had he been living anywhere else. But this was Hollywood at the very outset of its most dazzling era. And this time Lady Luck was waiting, not at the Waterhole or the Sunset Barn, but two blocks away, at a clapboard studio on the corner of Sunset and Gower.

*

The original settlers, siphoned off a flood of sunseekers from 1880 to the turn of the century, pouring into California by the trainload every day, were sober, industrious folk. They envisaged their fledgling city as the nonpareil of California's several touted Edens. Hollywood combined the delights of a balmy climate and vacationland setting with the down-to-earth advantages of productive soil. The citrus industry, for one, lured Eastern money to the coast, and investors discovered that here, indeed, one could enjoy the best of both worlds simultaneously.

On verandas of great stucco piles set in the midst of prospering citrus or avocado groves, one could in good conscience take one's ease, secure in the knowledge that all the while Mother Nature herself was satisfying the inexorable demands of those twin Yankee virtues — hard work and maximum yield. These enthusiastic developers even introduced pineapples to the region, and blithely expected the tropical plants to survive winter's killing frost (a native villain whose presence land-developer Wilcox failed to mention in the fine print.)

A Saratoga-type resort hotel, on what became Hollywood Boulevard, put the tourists up in style, while tracks extended the services of electric cars all the way to Pacific Palisades. There the unbelieving rustic could see with his own eyes where America's westering trail ran out at last in a blown-up picture-postcard sunset the color of tangerines. The countryside was lush and seductive, wild poppies pouring molten gold over thousands of acres of virgin grassland. In April the lupines spread their widening stain, like violet ink across blotter-green hills and valleys. One of the obligatory "rites of Spring" was to drive out from town on a Sunday afternoon to see and gather wildflowers. And once out there, what blizzard-broken sod-buster from Nebraska could have dreamed there were *that* many orange groves in the world, their shade-dark aisles going on endlessly, cool, hushed and scented as a cathedral, with snow-crested mountains against the cobalt sky, the whole spectacle of contrasts rising like stained-glass windows on every side.

Understandably, these transplanted Hoosiers and Buckeyes viewed the invading bands of camera gypsies with mounting alarm. Over tall glasses of lemonade or orange juice — every backyard in Wilcox-land boasted at least one citrus tree — they speculated on how soon these former denizens of Satan's Palaces (Presbyterian for theaters) would move on. "Picture people," as they were called, must certainly prove as transient as they were already known to be improvident and immoral. Movie-making was notorious for being a fly-by-night industry, what with the Edison interests and the so-called "independents" warring to the point of violence, smashing each other's cameras and burning reels of film. It was, in fact, quite discomfitting for the inhabitants to learn that one of the major attractions their village held for the embattled moviemakers was its proximity to the Mexican border. If set upon by enemy bullies or barristers, all the independent had to do was throw his camera and film into a stand-by car and find sanctuary in the nearest Tijuana bar.

While inventor Edison and the film titans fought among themselves, a dozen or so of yesterday's penniless immigrants rose inconspicuously to the stature of robber barons, the new-rich peers of Carnegie, Rockefeller and the formidable Astors. One-time furriers, glove makers and cloak and suit merchants from the garment factories of such centers as New York, Chicago and Oshkosh, Wisconsin, they had invested modestly in movies. An idle store-front was put to use as a penny arcade or "electric theater" and the deluge of nickels swept them into a new merchant prince aristocracy — that of the nickelodeon millionaires. And yet, while they donned some of the graces that money could buy, most never lost the shopkeeper's view of life. Uncle Carl Laemmle, for one, at the height of his power as head of Universal, was asked to interview a famous Broadway actor for a leading role. Walking around this prospective studio property with the keen eye of a cloth merchant, Uncle Carl examined him carefully and said to his agent as though the actor himself were deaf to his words, "Good-looking he is, act he can, maybe, but my God, *who made his buttonholes?*"

When Thomas Ince and D. W. Griffith closed down their East Coast studios and followed Ben Turpin and Broncho Billy to California, the Hollywood gold rush was on in earnest. Every young man with a profile, a plot in his head or a knack for exploiting other people's talent, decided to go West. Every aspiring ingenue with a well-turned ankle, a marshmallow-pretty face and the courage to accept the consequences, did the same.

Directors, long resigned to shooting everything from Westerns to the life of Queen Elizabeth in New Jersey's Essex Park, were ecstatic at the possibilities Hollywood offered them. Why, within a dozen miles or so of this town they could find reasonably accurate facsimiles for every type of world topography. The Pacific beaches were still unphotographed and unspoiled, the Hollywood hills had yet to see their first bulldozer. Nearby Pasadena, haven of the richest retirees, provided half a hundred august mansions and estates, referred to in studio jargon as "classy backgrounds." San Fernando Valley, almost as wild as when the Cahuenga Indians foraged there in pre-Hispanic times, was rich in canyons, valleys, leafy glens and oak-studded knolls. The century-old Spanish mission of San Fernando Rey, splendid even in decay, stood ready-made for movies on early California or the perennial siege of the Alamo. The Mojave Desert doubled for Arizona, nearby Vasquez Rocks the Khyber Pass, and Griffith Park for Nottingham Forest. Farther to the north lay the blue, snow-powdered sierras of Lone Pine, whose scenic grandeur would serve as ubiquitous backdrop for every Western hero from Neal Hart to Audie Murphy. For the more affluent producer, there were the awesome splendors of Yosemite and Sequoia, although notably difficult to cast as anything but themselves.

When these precursors of the industry were first spotted skulking among the palm and pepper trees of Hollywood's lanes and parks back in 1910, the population of dry, decent folk numbered less than three thousand souls. Now, scarcely a decade later, the barbarians had in fact taken over the town. In so doing, they introduced an American social phenomenon — movie starism — to the world. Hollywood's citizens were the first to feel its impact, and the last to bow before the changes it ushered in.

Formerly it had taken good family, money, education, political pull, native talent — or at least the immolation of self on the altar of Hard Work — to gain admittance to America's elite circle of notables. One, if not all, of these qualifications had to be submitted before an applicant was even considered eligible to compete in the game of social climbing, a game in which the well-born or wealthy few dictated the rules and doled out the prizes. But overnight the star system rendered the old credentials not only obsolete but absurd. Now, when a member of the deserving rich whose fortune stood above six figures visited his banker, he found himself next in line behind a former Little Mary of *Ten Nights in a Barroom*, a cowboy, or a low comic from the music halls of London.

Nor could one accuse these parvenus of having obtained their wealth and universal recognition through fraud, theft or bribery. It was, in fact, the other way round; they had been given their present power gratuitously, by multitudes of adoring filmgoers, whose origins were quite as humble as those of their screen idols. The pooled wealth of millions of nickels and dimes had given them an unprecedented mandate from the common people of the entire world, and there was nothing for the ordinary socialite and common citizen to do but accept their inevitable rise to fame.

A movie star did not need the prestige of family, even in those rare instances where one did, indeed, possess it. Stars notoriously had little taste for true aristocratic living, being by their very nature rolling stones who felt at ease only among others of their kind. As the silver kings and stagecoach barons had done on other frontiers before them, movie stars instinctively threw together, with scarcely anything more than raw money, a boom town of vulgar, ornately overblown pleasure domes, created more in the image of Denver and Virginia City than Newport.

This Hollywood was a far cry from what founder Wilcox and his fellow-boosters had in mind — a kind of Kansas-by-the-Sea, exotic in externals, perhaps, but every bit as dry as the main street of Lawrence. Back home they had known what to do with riffraff like this. Run them out of town. If visiting cowboys got drunk on payday they were thrown in jail. When that proved ineffective, they had, by superhuman effort and a war abroad, put the booze forever out of their reach by proclaiming Prohibition the law of the land.

But final as that had seemed, it had not really worked, for here they were, the likes of Mary Pickford and Douglas Fairbanks proclaiming themselves virtual King and Queen of the movie capital. Not to mention Tom Mix, who accepted as his due the title "King of the Cowboys," and who was rich beyond imagining because he had hit pay dirt in their California Comstock!

And still they came, young and old, wise and foolish, rich and poor, on the rise, broke, retired, but hopeful all. They flocked from every city and town, and the saying went that in

Hollywood it took seven years to realize you were starving to death because no one ever winter-killed out here. Their coming together created a potpourri society, as diverse as any to be found anywhere on the face of the earth: con men, chorus girls, drummers, cowboys, barkers, Siamese twins, midgets, animal trainers, vaudeville comics, high-wire artists, prostitutes, playwrights, bootleggers, believers, free thinkers, dream merchants and the cloak and suit men. These latter, who had entered by the back door at Ellis Island, were now the masters of the house, telling native-born Americans what kind of movies they wanted to see.

On the heels of this herd came the predators, self-appointed prophets and preachers in every stage of dress and undress, peddling their version of heaven and nirvana without logic or shame. East Indian gurus preached other-worldliness, while their eccentric (but rich) devotees drowned them in hard cash and real estate. Soon Lotuslands and onion-domed temples sprang up everywhere, like mushrooms after a heavy silver rain. Here between the temples and the tent shows the unsaved hopefuls and has-beens fought to the death in a desperate struggle to wrest their share of gold from the Hollywood mother lode.

In a community such as this, even alkalied old Bill Gillis was, in a sense, still wet behind the ears. And into this roaring camp of boom or bust in the first year of the twenties came my parents — young, innocent of city life, credulous, small-town-America incarnate, with their nineteenth-century wonder at the side show and trust of the shill, disastrously blind to the snares and pitfalls that lay everywhere in that deceptively halcyon-looking hamlet called Hollywood.

✳

Marian had been married nearly five years, but so far she had never stayed long enough in any one place to even meet people, let alone make friends. Her only close childhood friend, Martha Jordan, had married and moved to Winnipeg, and aside from Mother Danley in the San Joaquin Valley, Marian had not a single acquaintance to turn to for counsel or companionship. Now, after nearly two months cooped up in a small apartment in Los Angeles, she had what the cowboys would have diagnosed as a rampant case of "cabin fever."

Across the hall in the Beaudry Arms there lived a white-haired widow named Mrs. Campbell and her daughter Margaret. Mrs. Campbell was a seamstress, with a steady if modest income, while Margaret worked as a waitress in downtown hotels and restaurants. Margaret was a plain young woman, about twenty-five, tall, angular, with a lean face and black modish bobbed hair. Like everyone else in the area, Marian's neighbors had come West from some Midwestern town in search of a warmer climate and a new beginning after the death of Mr. Campbell.

While Margaret could scarcely be called a beauty, she did have a certain spirit of adventure that sparkled in her eyes and animated her otherwise plain features. As evidence of her determination to carve out a new life, Margaret often quit waiting tables at the Pig 'n Whistle, and took a job working extra in Hollywood movies. It was Margaret who loaned Marian the can of Stein's Professional Cold Cream the night Jack was trying to take off his make-up with whipping cream.

"I enjoy the excitement of the studios," the neighborly Margaret confided to Marian one day over coffee. "Why, there's always something new and unexpected happening. Maybe I don't make as much as I would in tips hustling tables, but I don't care. In Hollywood there's always that one chance in a million that something really big is about to happen to you."

Marian smiled sagely, the wisdom born of five years of kicking Gila monsters off her front steps, packing and unpacking, hoping and being disappointed, moving and moving again.

"Well, the main thing is to have enough to pay your bills," said the seasoned wife and mother.

"You ought to get out more," Margaret replied. "The studios are great places."

"Jack says they aren't really safe — I mean for decent women." And then flushing in sudden embarrassment Marian added, "You know what I mean — he works out at Mixville, and I'm sure that's a much rougher environment than the studios where you've been working."

"None of it is all that wild," Margaret said. "Besides, Jack is just old-fashioned. He's always telling you a studio is the same as a saloon or a corral — no place for a lady. Well, working in movies hasn't turned me into a woman of the streets, although," she added, making a spit curl with a lock of black hair and punctuating her meaning with a broad wink, "I still have hopes!"

Marian laughed, although she knew that was a pretty risqué way for a young unmarried girl to talk. Still she liked Margaret, and even if she hadn't, she was at least someone to talk to. Moreover she had an instinct about the girl. She knew she wasn't interested in a wicked sex life or anything off-color, but she simply wanted an escape from boredom. And you certainly couldn't blame a lonely spinster-aged girl for being influenced by the countless stories of how yesterday's Cinderellas had been transformed by Hollywood magic into the biggest stars of today.

One morning after Jack left for work at Mixville, Margaret knocked on Marian's door.

"I'm going over to Hollywood to pick up a day check they owe me at the Century Studio. Would you like to come along? I'll bet you could do with a change of scenery."

Marian hadn't been farther than the corner market and a dry-goods store in the two months since they had arrived there. She was ready to leap at the chance to get out of the apartment, but still she hesitated. "Oh, I'd love to, Margaret. But you know I couldn't leave the children."

"Why not bring them along?"

"Oh, but they're both so little, and they'd be a bother."

"Forget it," Margaret countered with her usual directness. "They're the best-mannered kids I've ever seen. I hate to admit it, too, 'cause you know I think Jack is too strict with them, but he sure has turned them into the best-behaved pair I've ever seen. Come on, Marian, why don't we just make a day of it?"

Marian had still another hurdle before she could allow herself the luxury of consenting.

"But what if Jack finds out? You know how he feels about me even going near a studio."

"Who's going to tell him? Peggy can barely talk and if you told Louise not to tell him, I'm sure wild horses couldn't drag it out of her."

"I guess I could simply go and just not — not tell him anything about it."

"Now, that's using your head," Margaret said approvingly. "You get yourselves ready and I'll be set to go in half an hour."

A total stranger in a strange town, Marian felt as giddy as a child at the prospect of actually setting out to see Hollywood. Jack had practically taken over where Grandmother Baxter left off in the upbringing of little Marian, and he was every bit as Victorian and conservative in his views when it came to what a lady could or could not do. It was his duty to protect his wife from the dangers and evils of a world whose wickedness she scarcely dreamed existed. If he did his duty, she would never have to learn about the seamy side of life, except as he deemed it wise to tell her, from time to time, as a means of further protecting her and their children.

But little Marian was more observing than Jack gave her credit for. She was anxious to see something of the world he talked about every day, and to form her own firsthand opinions of it. She was anything but submissive by nature, and now she felt a certain exhilaration in being able to disobey his wishes, embark on her own private adventure, at the same time making sure that he would never be the wiser.

She dressed her small daughters in their best, which dated back to a general store in Williams, Arizona, and looked pretty countrified. She put on her best and favorite outfit, the gray suit in which she had been married. Pinning a straw hat atop her upswept chestnut hair, she surveyed her flawless complexion and cameo-shaped face in a mirror. Yes, Margaret was right, she *did* look like a cross between Marion Davies and Corinne Griffith . . . Satisfied that she looked her best, she gathered Peggy in her arms and shepherded five-year-old Louise before her.

Out of the gray-frame Beaudry Arms the entourage swept, and strolled briskly to the Olive Street station. There they boarded the trolley, and Louise was delighted over the straw seats, which could be moved back and forth depending on which way the car was going.

Disembarking at Hollywood Boulevard and Gower, they walked the two blocks south to Sunset Boulevard. The studio that was Margaret's destination occupied several sprawling acres of a once-loved farm, and it hardly impressed Marian as a movie studio at all. It was a cluster of several small, faded California bungalows, with the paint peeling and the awnings, half rotted out by the sun, hanging in long, weathered shreds. By way of apologies for the disappointment, Margaret explained, "It's just a little independent outfit, but they make a lot of movies here."

They entered a corner bungalow, the former living room of which had been fixed up into a front office of sorts.

"I worked on the dance hall scene last week for director Fishback," Margaret told the girl at the desk, "and I've come to pick up my check."

The girl glanced up disinterestedly. "The director will have to pay you himself."

"Is he in his office?"

"Oh, he hasn't got an office. Just go on the lot and ask

somebody which set he's working on today and he'll take care of it."

Even Margaret seemed surprised at the informal way they had of running things at this studio, and emboldened by it she asked, "Is it all right if we *all* go in?"

Without glancing up, the girl said, "Through that door," and waved the entire parade toward a narrow door that opened onto the inside of the lot.

The set where the director could be found proved to be a huge, gray, made-over barn with a door conveniently ajar. Inside there were several quiet, darkened sets, but in a far corner of the gloomy interior shone a bright island of light. Here was a group of people, surrounded by cameras, reflectors, spotlights, kleig lamps and the usual paraphernalia of movie-making. At last Marian was going to see a movie made right before her very eyes!

Encumbered as she was by two small children, Marian quickly decided to leave her mind clear for the enjoyment of the moment. Parking Louise in a chair close to the door she told her "not to make a sound and not to move until Mother comes back." A high stool, closer to the action, was singled out for the baby, whose tender age required a somewhat shorter tether. The same strict orders were impressed upon Peggy, who had lived long enough to know that her father had a way of materializing out of thin air the minute she disobeyed explicit orders. She was prepared to sit motionless on that stool for five minutes or five years without a murmur. It was the way she had been raised.

While Marian stood entranced watching the company shooting a love scene between a beautiful girl and a handsome collarad-type actor, the director Margaret was looking for appeared. He peeled a five dollar bill from a roll in his pocket and thanked her for coming by. Softly, so as not to distract the actors nearby, he added, "By the way, who does that child over there belong to?" Margaret pointed to Marian.

Fred Fishback stood a long time studying the child. Finally

he strolled over for a closer look. The nineteen-month-old baby perched high on her stool was anything but a pretty child. Her black hair was cut in the briefest bangs across a wide forehead, just touching the tops of her ears on either side. She had an almost square face, large brown eyes topped with whimsical questioning eyebrows, a short, turned-up nose and the overall happy expression of a very contented clown. The director tried to get the baby to talk, but she kept silent and smiled back, as if in possession of some secret wisdom. He tried to coax her off the stool, but she shook her head and fixed him with the same polite, enigmatic smile.

As the scene before the cameras ended, Fishback approached Marian and tapped her on the shoulder. "I beg your pardon, but does that little girl over there on the stool belong to you?"

Marian's blue eyes opened wide and she shot a startled glance at Peggy. "Yes, that's my little girl. Why? Did she do something wrong? Is she bothering someone?"

"No, not at all," the director reassured her. "But I'm really fascinated by her powers of concentration and her obedience. She has been sitting there without moving or talking to anyone for almost half an hour. How do you get her to do that?"

"Oh, *that!*" Marian sighed with relief. "Well, I just tell her to do something and she does it."

Almost to himself the man mused, "She isn't pretty at all — but she *is* cute." And then turning back to Marian he said, "I wish you'd leave your name and phone number with the girl at the front desk as you leave the studio. You see, I'm Fred Fishback and I've been looking everywhere for a small baby like that for a comedy I plan to make soon. I'd like you to bring her in to the studio for an interview later this week."

Marian blanched, started to say something about its being impossible, but she couldn't find words. Instead she watched helplessly as he smiled and walked away, giving the immovable baby on the stool an affectionate pat on the head as he passed.

When they got outside the barn Margaret could hardly keep from shouting with joy, and she launched into an endless stream of hallelujahs.

"Why Marian, that's fantastic! Just think, Fred Fishback himself! He's a very important director. And he hasn't even seen how well-behaved Peggy can be! Imagine, just like that, discovered sitting on a stool! See, I told you how exciting movies are!"

Marian was not even able to hear Margaret above the pounding of her heart and the flood of panicky thoughts. She was the victim, not of exaltation, but fright, guilt and remorse.

I knew I shouldn't have gone! Jack will be furious. He'll swear I did something awful to get the man's attention. And that thought unleashed long conversations in which Jack had told her about those most shameless of all Hollywood women, movie mothers, who dragged their offspring from studio to studio, even offering themselves to casting directors if they would give their child a "break." "No better than sporting women, that's what they are!" she could hear Jack saying as clearly as though he were standing there beside her now.

"Oh, Margaret, I couldn't possibly bring Peggy. You know what Jack would say!" And then, as if warding off any possibility of today's events ever reaching her husband's ears, she took this moment to impress upon Louise the importance of silence. "No matter what happens, you're not to tell your father a word about today!" Louise nodded solemnly.

"But Marian, you're acting crazy," Margaret protested as they hiked across the open lot in the hot spring sunlight. "You can at least do what Mr. Fishback suggested, and it would be perfectly wonderful for Peggy. Why, Mary Pickford started out as 'Little Mary' and Ben Alexander became famous playing that kid in *Hearts of the World*, remember? Think of Peggy's future — she could earn enough to travel around the world, or go to college when she grows up . . ."

"But Jack . . . !"

"You can't throw everything away because you're afraid of

what a man will say. He'll get over it. Until then, he doesn't have to know anything about it. He'll be jumping out of trees over at Mixville while you're taking Peggy on that interview. He doesn't need to know until it's all settled."

By the time they reached the front office, Margaret had sufficiently worn down Marian's resistance so that she agreed to leave her name and phone number at the desk. But she did so with a kind of superstitious finality, that by so doing she was really insuring herself *against* any possibility of a call.

But the call came anyway. Margaret answered the tenants' phone in the hall upstairs, and as Marian peered out through her own half-open door, Margaret began signaling frantically. "It's the studio!" she hissed. "It's for you!" Marian took the receiver as if it were a live hand grenade.

"I'm calling for Mr. Fishback," the voice on the line informed her. "Will you please bring Baby Peggy in to see the assistant tomorrow morning at ten o'clock?" Marian managed a barely audible "Yes," and hung up.

The next day Marian and the little girl to whom Mr. Fishback's secretary had offhandedly given the name "Baby Peggy" approached the assistant's office at ten o'clock sharp. He was a thick-set man with glasses and was smoking a long cigar.

"Hmmmmmm," he observed rather dubiously, circling the child slowly and scrutinizing every detail of dress and comportment. "She had any acting experience in pictures or on the stage?"

"Naturally not," Marian flashed back, inwardly indignant at his insulting tone. "After all, she isn't even twenty months old!"

"Scared of dogs?"

"I don't know. We don't have one."

The man grunted, laid his cigar carefully in an ashtray on his desk, and then stepped to a rear door of his office. Opening it he called to someone in the adjoining room and a second later a short-haired, mongrel dog bounded into the office. Since the child's head was exactly on a level with his own, the dog raced over to her and licked her cheek enthusiastically. Peggy let out a shriek of terror and backed off. The dog backed off, too, still wagging his long, white-tipped tail slowly.

"Well, she's afraid of dogs, that's sure," the man said, as though he were quite pleased over this discovery. "She'll never work with Brownie."

"Well, really," Marian protested, "she hasn't even had a chance to get used to him."

The man shrugged disinterestedly and Marian snatched up her handbag, grabbed Peggy by the hand and walked out. She was furious, but at least her anger permitted her to enjoy the cold finality. This had settled the question once and for all. She had given Peggy her chance at world travel, college and all the rest, and it hadn't worked. Best of all, she thought with merciful relief, Jack need never know a thing about what might have been. It was all over, ended, sealed forever in her memory, something she could tell her grandchildren someday. But just as she reached home the phone rang and Mr. Fishback himself asked to talk to Mrs. Montgomery.

"I'm sorry about the interview," he told Marian gently. "I'm sure Peggy will get used to Brownie, and we'll pay her five dollars a day for the five days she will be working. I *do* hope you'll reconsider. I'd like to see her again myself tomorrow."

The director had such a persuasive manner that Marian was completely undone.

"Yes, Mr. Fishback," she stammered uncertainly. "I'll — I'll see that she gets there."

Marian was in a state of panic, but instinctively she did what she had learned to do on black days back at the Grand Canyon — bake one of Jack's favorite cakes. It usually served her well as insurance against a really bad Montgomery rage.

That night, when the devil's-food cake was put before him, Jack was in a genial mood. "Sharkey," he told her, "I don't know how you manage. Out of the little money we can afford you really put on a first-rate spread." Marian decided now was the moment to take aim and squeeze the trigger.

"Oh, by the way, dear," she began as nonchalantly as she could, "remember that studio where Margaret's been working lately? Well, you'll never guess what happened. We went with her the other day, and the director noticed Peggy — of all things — and then he called here — and . . ." her courage began to ebb.

With a forkful of cake halfway to his lips Jack froze, and his dark brows came together in the warning cloud that always presaged the tempest.

"And?" he asked.

Marian flashed her most innocent smile. "Well, they want her for a picture job next week. I told them — that is, I really *promised* Mr. Fishback — he's an awfully nice young director — that I'd bring her to the studio tomorrow for a final interview."

Jack's fork came down on the plate like a pistol shot. "You're not going near that studio again, do you understand?" he exploded. "The next thing I know this 'nice young director' will be *seducing you* — trying to put *you* in pictures!"

Seldom in their married life had Jack's latent jealousy played into Marian's hands, but this time it couldn't have served her cause better.

"Oh, but I'd really much rather that *you* took her anyway," she put in, taking swift advantage of this favorable wind, "because with me she seemed afraid of the dog, and maybe you'd be able . . ."

"Afraid of a dog?" he stormed. "Hell, she's not afraid of a dog or anything else that wears hair. Wasn't she riding a horse when she was three months old?"

Marian kept prudently silent while Jack strode about the living room, engaged in a kind of monologue. He had been caught in an embarrassing dilemma. As a stunt man he simply couldn't have a baby daughter that registered panic at the sight of anything so harmless as a dog. It just didn't make sense. Quieting down, he slipped into an almost philosophical mood. "Well, after all, it isn't as though she was going to spend the rest of her life in a studio," he mused. "God knows how they found even *one* part for a baby her age. There'll surely *never* be two!"

In the last analysis it was the dog episode that rankled with Jack, and the possibility of proving to the people at the studio that his daughter had not backed down out of fear, but surprise. He felt absolutely certain that had he been with Peggy rather than her mother she would have stood up bravely to the movie dog's rude greeting. The following morning he took Peggy on her third ride on the red trolley into Hollywood.

"Mr. Fishback," he told the director across a desk at the studio, "I'm a very outspoken man. I've got a good job doubling Mix that pays me seven-fifty a day. My wife says you only want to pay the baby five. Now, I won't permit my wife or anyone but me to work with Peggy at the studio. So if I have to be laid off my own work for the week this picture will take to shoot, I've got to make at least what I'm losing at Mixville."

"I appreciate your situation, Mr. Montgomery." Fishback smiled and his blue eyes shone with understanding. "But the owners of this studio wouldn't pay more than five dollars a day for the baby if she were the original Alice in Wonderland. But because I really want her, I'll pay the additional two-fifty out of my own pocket to get her. Is that fair?"

"It's a deal," Jack said, and the two men shook hands on it.

"Oh, just one more thing," Jack added. "That dog, Brownie — can you bring him in?"

"Of course. I'll send for him."

As they waited for Brownie's arrival Jack turned to Peggy and said, "Brownie is bigger than you, but he's a good dog. He won't hurt you. Don't be afraid, do you understand?"

Peggy nodded cheerfully.

A moment later Brownie trotted into the office. Peggy looked him over distrustfully, but boldly stood her ground when he licked her face, and even mustered up enough courage to pat his neck as a show of good faith. Jack beamed, even more satisfied than Fishback. He knew he had been right.

What he didn't know until a week later when the first comedy, *Playmates,* was completed was that he had embarked on a course from which there was no immediate way out. The Stern brothers who owned and operated Century Studio called him in and announced that the dog and baby team had proved to be "a natural" and they wanted to co-star Brownie and Baby Peggy in an entire series of comedies. Brownie was already studio property, under a long-term contract with his trainer. In order to secure Peggy's services they were willing to offer a seven-year contract at what was for them a very high salary indeed — seventy-five dollars a week!

Jack and Marian were stunned by this turn of events. They had never trained their daughters to recite little pieces, exploited baby talk or in any other way instilled in them a sense of cuteness or performance. Pushing either child into the theatrical world was utterly beyond the realm of anything they had ever dreamed of or discussed. And yet here they were, their world turned upside down, and the dazzling sum of three hundred dollars a month for the next seven years theirs for the asking if they consented to let Peggy perform.

"It wouldn't be fair to Peggy to refuse," Marian said, almost as if the child had ceased to belong to her but had suddenly been turned into a changeling by some unseen fairy godmother. Jack, with his dream ranch always a mirage on the margin of his mind, could almost see it begin to take shape before his eyes. At Mixville it would take him twice as long to rack up the same amount as Peggy was now being offered, and for far less hazardous work.

"Besides," Marian added, "it would mean you could quit

breaking your neck doing stunts. I wouldn't have to live in fear every day that you'd be brought home crippled or dead!"

The contract was signed. But Father was not through doing stunts. The only difference was that he and I would do them together for the next few years.

5

The Stardust Trail

CENTURY STUDIOS occupied the southwest corner at the inter-
section of Sunset Boulevard and Gower Street. Tall palms
lined the boulevard, wooden bungalows and an occasional
stucco manor comprised the quiet residential neighborhood.
But despite its halcyon appearance, these four corners housed
the film industry's booming factory district. Tucked away in old
barns, stables and newly built sheds (to house the indoor sets),
a dozen or more filmmakers churned out hundreds of low-
budget movies every month.

Westward on Sunset one approached respectability and near
grandeur at Warner Brothers' white-pillared studio, rising
amidst plantation-sized lawns. Beyond at United Artists,
movie royalty reigned in the persons of Mary and Doug, while
Chaplin's La Brea headquarters symbolized the very heights of
majesterial isolation from the Hollywood hoi polloi. But if
prestige was measured by how far west one moved on Sunset,
status virtually ceased to exist immediately east of Gower.
There, for a stretch of almost two blocks, lay the leper colony
of the industry, already anathematized as "Poverty Row."

This chain of two-story pseudo-Spanish baroque buildings
housed the shabby offices of fly-by-night independents, compared to which even Century would rank as a major company.
Occasionally these seedy outfits rented sets and lot space from
the more reputable studios, but for the most part necessity,
lack of cash and their own unsavory reputations forced them to

work in league with each other. They shared a few ramshackle stages and outdoor sets on the lots behind their offices, and were infamous as the Scrooges of Hollywood. "We get our actors cheap," was their universally recognized but unwritten motto, "on the way up, or on their way down." To a reigning star, Poverty Row was to be viewed with genuine horror, and, one hoped, only from afar. I cannot remember a time when I was not keenly aware that with a single misstep on the tortuous stardust trail, one could end up laboring in the sunken mines of Poverty Row forever.

Father and I drove a secondhand Franklin car to work each morning and parked it in front of the imposing wall surrounding Christy's Studio, directly across Sunset from Century. The studio where I would spend the next eighteen months of my life sprawled over about two acres. Formerly a farm, the corner had been pioneered for movies by an early filmmaker named Nestor, who set up shop there in 1910. His operation foundered and he was fortunate to find a buyer in Carl Laemmle when the latter moved his entire organization West in 1915. Uncle Carl later turned the Century lot over, either by sale or lease, to his brothers-in-law, Abe and Julius Stern, the brother-producers who were responsible for my comedies.

Every five days (sometimes only three), a new Baby Peggy comedy was canned, and on the sixth day we started shooting its successor. Only by keeping such a schedule, and working often at night and on weekends, were we able to rack up the grand total of one hundred and fifty two-reelers in that relatively brief period of time. But that was pretty average at Sunset and Gower. Compared to our shot-from-the-hip scriptless satires, even program Westerns were esteemed *haute cuisine* in the entertainment kitchens of the world, but no matter. The fry cooks who threw them together were millionaires just the same.

When I went to work with Brownie, the Wonder Dog was already an established contract player at Century. He was also more than four times my age, but — as with many studio prop-

erties where youth meant value — the studio concealed
Brownie's age. Instead, they focused upon his remarkable
comedy sense and his quite astonishing repertoire of tricks.
But one morning, about six months after I began my career,
Brownie's trainer was unable to rouse the gray-muzzled old
trouper, and sorrowfully brought word to us on the set that
Brownie had died in his sleep.

Brownie's unexpected demise created a temporary crisis, but
it also freed me from being forever type-cast as straight-man
for a dog. At Fishback's insistence I was allowed to develop a
natural gift for pantomime and satire that my directors felt
would prove unique. Beginning with broad parodies on familiar fairy tales like "Little Red Riding Hood" and "Jack and the
Beanstalk," I quickly graduated to really savage spoofs of such
movie greats as Valentino, Harold Lloyd, Theda Bara and Mae
Murray. These two-reelers were designed to be run immediately after the serious films they lampooned, as part of a package program. They were so successful that we followed them
up with still more sophisticated and irreverent comedy versions of De Mille's greatest melodramas — Carmen, The Girl of
the Golden West and his 1915 re-make of The Squaw Man.

As a consequence, my comedies were not child-oriented (as
were the "Our Gang" series produced by Hal Roach in the later
1920's). I not only played most of the leading roles, whether
male or female, but was surrounded by an all-adult cast, including Jake Earle, a giant at nineteen who stood nearly eight
feet tall. In this manner Fred Fishback was able to exploit the
many comic possibilities of having a lustful Sheik, a hapless
Indian maid, a resolute Canadian Mountie and a villainous
matador, all played by a two-and-a-half-year-old comedienne.
As a result, I rarely worked with other children, and it was in
my miniature two-reel Westerns and mimic melodramas that
most of the cowboys who had worked with Father at Mixville
and Universal now found additional riding jobs.

With my entry into movies, Father moved the family into a
small rented house on Franklin Avenue, just above Hollywood

Boulevard. Although my seven-year contract postponed the realization of his dream ranch, even while my salary made it possible, Father compromised by buying three horses, which at first we had to keep stabled at the Sunset Barn. Redwing was a pretty blood bay mare for Mother and Louise. For himself Father bought a big, seventeen-hand high gray horse named White Man and then, from a Mexican trader he met through Joe Posada, he picked up Chapo, a magnificent, spirited black. But finding a suitable mount for me was as difficult as it was necessary. Since I was scheduled to parody grown-up Western stars, I could hardly be shown astride a Shetland pony. On the other hand, I was so little that aboard even a small eight-hundred-pound cow pony I looked like a peanut on top of an elephant. Posada's friend made a trip into Mexico and discovered Tim, a perfectly proportioned jet black midget horse, bred especially for size by his owner. Tim looked exactly like a full-grown horse except that he stood just under thirty-six inches high.

One afternoon, Father drove me over to Selma Avenue to visit Joe Posada. The slim, dark Mexican bootmaker, with the long narrow face, high cheek bones and quick, bright smile, sat me down in one of the three folding theater chairs he kept for customers in his tiny store across from the Waterhole. The whole store was rich with the smell of freshly tanned, unseasoned leather.

After a brief conversation with Father, Joe brought out a tape measure, a pencil and some brown wrapping paper. As I stood on the paper in my stocking feet, he carefully traced the outline pattern for the smallest pair of steep-heel boots he had ever been asked to make. Then he measured me for a pair of elkskin chaps, a leather gunbelt and a set of spurs with tiny Mexican rowels. For Tim he fashioned a finely tooled miniature saddle and bridle, and a Mexican *reata*, which was a perfectly balanced lasso made entirely of hand-braided rawhide.

There was only one flaw in Century's creation of the smallest cowhand in the West, and that was Tim himself. The horse trader from Sonora had forgotten to mention that Tim was a spoiled horse who cow-kicked, bit and was as cold-jawed a runaway as any Hollywood chase horse in the business. For the first three hundred yards he was faster than most horses twice his size. But Father and the cowboys quickly taught me the rudiments of staying aboard Tim, not overlooking such basics as checking the cinch before mounting and swinging into the saddle with only one hand on the horn.

"No better time to teach a horse who's boss than when he explodes under you," the cowboys used to say, and one Sunday morning, as Father and I were taking our regular Sunday ride together, my time came to either show Tim I could handle him, or resign myself to the fact that he was a bad horse I would never dare ride again.

Father, wearing a white Stetson and white batwing elkskin chaps, cut a fine figure on the high-stepping White Man, while beside him on the tiny black horse I looked like a miniature version of himself. Tim had to take five steps to White Man's one. As we were trotting past the Hollywood Hotel out to the bridle path that ran down the center of what is today the Sunset Strip, a passing trolley startled Tim. Laying his pointed ears flat against his head, he took the bit between his teeth and bolted east on Hollywood Boulevard.

I lost my seat on the very first jump, and would have lost my reins as well had Father not always tied them above Tim's neck, as a precaution against that very danger. I realized Tim was stampeding, but I was too preoccupied with trying to stay in the saddle to think of how to stop him. Suddenly Father and White Man drew up beside me. With a sweep of his arm Father could have lifted me from my saddle and onto the safety of his own, but according to the cowboys' reasoning, that would have taught me nothing. Typically, he valued experience above theory and Father decided that now was the time to show Tim his rider would not back down.

"Don't just pull back on the reins," he shouted at me as we

continued to streak down the Boulevard. "Plow-rein the cold-jawed sonofabitch!" Father's voice and presence both calmed and put the fight back into me, and I began carrying out his commands as he shot them out.

"Take a rein in each hand . . . that's right . . . now wrap them around your palms . . . good! Now SAW HIS MOUTH with everything you've got . . . take the goddammed bit away from him!"

Seconds later, by bearing down with all my strength, I managed to turn Tim sharply onto a side street and finally planted him on his tail almost in the laps of a couple who were reading their Sunday paper on the ivy-covered porch of their bungalow. My hands were blue from leather burns, but I was unharmed and ecstatic at having won control of Tim. The cowboy philosophy was valid, for I never forgot what I learned from that runaway — nor did Tim, it seemed, for he turned into a very honest horse.

Except for such strictly movie-star duties as interviews, fund-raising functions and cross-country personal appearances with one of my new films, our lives during the five-year period that I was in pictures gravitated around the cowboys' Hollywood. After I moved out to Universal when I was about three and a half, Father was able to lease an ersatz dream ranch in the almost unpopulated San Fernando Valley. The Spanish-style stucco house sat in the middle of three acres of apricot orchards, and here we maintained our own stables and had endless miles of open country to ride in. Our nearest neighbor was Edgar Rice Burroughs, author of *Tarzan,* who was engaged in making movies of his jungle hero's adventures. Louise and I felt sorry for his three children because they only had a wicker pony cart to ride in, while we had our own horses.

Unlike other children of our generation, my sister and I did

not have to go to Saturday afternoon matinées to see our
cowboys — they came to us. Those I didn't see at work we
caught up with on Sunday at the nearest rodeo, for we attended rodeos as religiously as other families went to church.
There were competitions at Newhall and Saugus, over at Vic-
torville or up at Lebec where the "grapevine" began twisting
down toward Bakersfield. Hoot Gibson held a show at his
Saugus Ranch almost every weekend, with primitive board
bleachers surrounding his converted corral. Father would
settle Mother, Louise and me on the shady side to watch the
day's events, and then he would join his friends at the bronc
chutes to work the gates, or haze calves and steers. More than
once as we watched bronc riders or bulldoggers plowing up the
deep, golden dust of the arena, an empty bronc would bolt into
the crowd or a runaway steer climb through the bleachers,
while spectators scattered to safety. Mother became an expert
at judging which bronc or steer was likely to make for the open
country almost as he charged into the arena.

At home our tiled patio and corridors rang to the chime of
time-mellowed spurs. The hatrack in our hallway was strictly
a Stetson tree, blooming nightly with the big beige, black,
brown or pearl-gray hats that were palpable extensions of their
owners' distinctive character and history. I learned early in life
that those costly Stetsons spoke a silent language all their own,
for each crown was pinched and creased in a special way that
wordlessly proclaimed the region and often the individual state
from which its owner hailed.

Even the cowboys' names seemed to have the ring of an old-
time silver dollar on a hardwood bar: Buck Bucko, Kansas
Mooring, Morgan Flowers, Slim Whittaker, Cloud Smith, and
Vinegar Roan (who got his nickname from a particularly ugly
desert insect). There were also the regulars, like Handlebar
Hank Bell, Shorty Miller, Ed Hendershot and Jack Padjan.
Jack was a tall, strikingly handsome cowboy from Montana,
whose proud bearing and rich sense of humor combined the

best of his half-Blackfoot and half-Black Irish heritage. He was employed by the Del Monte properties around Monterey, working with their extensive cattle herds in the virtually un- inhabited Carmel Valley. Jack would not settle permanently in Hollywood until the early 1930's, but in the twenties he would take a good riding job occasionally, as a break in the monotony of life at the ranch.

Dinner table conversations ranged from old-time ranch reminiscences to the day's activities on studio lots. It was a good school at which to learn the tribal values that a small group of men could bring from the outside and set up within a totally foreign culture, one that was already notorious for demolishing the values of less independent souls.

To the cowboys who worked, rode and played with men like Gibson, Accord and Neal Hart, a Western star was just another man who had to step into his pants each morning. They were neither awed by his fame nor dazzled by his wealth, although certainly the genuine cowboy stars who had made it big were more than generous. In our own home gimpy cowboys out of work or otherwise in need were commonplace, and Father never sent them away empty-handed. A five- or fifty-dollar loan was given as a gift until circumstances permitted re- payment.

Their evaluation of Western stars was the key to how they would survive their years in Hollywood. Those White Hats who claimed authentic range backgrounds might fool girl friends, the front office and fans, as Hank Bell used to say, but the cowboys who rode in their shadow could read them better than anyone else alive. They observed the hero under fire, confronted by the daily challenge of the job and the nightly pitfalls of fame. They would pursue generations of such big names, eating stardust as they followed each new White Hat's fortunes from his first big break to the last fade-out in the final frame of a long and precarious career. Pressured by producers, directors, bad horses, leading ladies and ex-wives, a cowboy star might appear to hold his own, but there was not one whose boot was so fancily stitched it could hide its owner's clay feet from the men in the posse. They had only one yardstick by which to judge any man, from the greenest juvenile to the most powerful director, and that was: "Is he the kind of man you'd want to ride the river with?"

That seemingly poetic phrase was loaded with significance, for it summed up all the probing questions to be answered if one were to learn a man's true character. Was he trustworthy, or would he dry-gulch you in some arroyo for your horse, your saddle or your poke? How did he treat his horse? On a long trail was he a hazard or an asset, a gunsil or a good hand? Would he stand by you, or quit when the chips were down?

Not surprisingly, very few Western stars over the years measured up to this code, or were accepted into the ranks of real cowboys. I remember Hank Bell's distinctive appraisal of William S. Hart, who was then regarded by everyone outside the small coterie of cowboys as a genuine frontiersman.

"Bill Hart's all ham, and melodrama is his middle name. He can put on that dome of a hat, and deck hisself out in a bandanna as big as a Harvey House tablecloth, but he ain't no hand." Actually, Hart had been discovered by Thomas Ince when he was playing the villain Messala in a road-show version of *Ben Hur*. "He's got the conscience of a Puritan elder," Hank opined one day after working on a Hart movie. "And about as much sex appeal as a Joshua tree. Besides, he's always suckin' on a stick of alum between takes, and that's how he gets his face all puckered up and solemn-lookin' come shootin' time."

Among the later stars, John Wayne was universally respected and liked by the cowboys, not because he was one of them, which he never claimed to be, but because he never pulled rank on them, fraternizing sincerely on the job and over cards. Conversely Gene Autry, alone of all Western stars, emerged with no points at all. This was partly due to his attitude toward the cowboys, but mostly because of his seeming contempt for horsemanship as an art to be learned; he appeared to take pride in the fact that he could barely stay in the saddle for the close-ups. Hank summed it up in his comment "If horses was dollars, Autry could ride." It is an interesting and little-known footnote of movie history that when Autry went to war after Pearl Harbor, and young Leonard Slye was picked from The Sons of the Pioneers singing group to replace him, the cowboys found the boy responsive to their advice. As a result they went out of their way to impart all the horse savvy they could to the green novice. Not surprisingly Slye emerged as a competent and believable horseman and rose to stardom as Roy Rogers.

Similarly, famous directors were popular or not, depending on how their performance measured up to the cowboys' code. James Cruze, Raoul Walsh and John Ford were unanimously respected and admired by the group from the very outset of their relationship. But one director whom the cowboys would start out disliking and end up despising was the man on whom, ironically, they were most dependent for their livelihood throughout their decades in Hollywood. His name was Cecil B. De Mille.

The historic disaffection between De Mille and the cowboys was rooted in their antipodal attitudes toward life, men and horses. It was Hollywood's oldest, deadliest and yet least-publicized feud, for I have never met anyone outside of the cowboys' intimate circle or families who were even aware of its existence. But Hank Bell and Jack Padjan were on the set that day in 1923 when the opening shots of the long battle were fired, and Father and Neal Hart would work on the same location spot, many years later, when the smoldering fuse finally came to flash point.

The silent version of De Mille's famous *Ten Commandments* may evoke pious memories in the minds of those who first saw it shown at a church festival or impressively premiered at a major theater. To me it brings back the scene of Jack Padjan and Hank Bell at our dinner table, rejoicing over the fact that they had just landed a picture job that promised to last for weeks, perhaps even months. De Mille planned to make his religious spectacle at an unheard-of cost and would employ thousands of "atmosphere players" in the course of the lengthy production. Already the call had gone out for so many riders that Hollywood alone was unable to meet the unprecedented demand. But the cowboys' initial jubilation over this Biblical bonanza would curdle into hatred before many weeks had passed, and we heard the events recounted, chapter and verse, as the shooting progressed.

A barnstormer, born forty years too late for the nineteenth-century road-show grind, De Mille was nonetheless a true believer in its stage-worn moral props. For him the sinful excesses of the rich, and the ultimate triumph of virtue, were absolutes: divine plots in which God Himself, if need be, put the record straight with a storm or some other such heaven-sent calamity at the end. Some of these simplistic themes he borrowed from his playwright father, who had staged them long before Cecil brought them to the screen. Henry De Mille, a frustrated actor and preacher, instilled in his sons, William and Cecil, a respect for the Old and New Testaments as thundering good drama. Henry's daily scriptural stint was followed by reading aloud — in stentorian tones cultivated to be heard in the last row — the popular romantic stories and novels of the day. In these he dwelt lovingly upon lavish descriptions of balls, sumptuous banquets, coronations and overblown funerals.

Cecil pursued his own private obsessive interest in Biblical drama by paging through the family's *Bible Gallery*, a volume published in 1891 and illustrated by French artist Gustave Doré. Featured were larger-than-life paintings of *The Prodigal Son's Return, The Judgment of Solomon* and *The Sermon on the Mount*. As a director, Cecil would later decry the simpering, effeminate Jesus of Sunday School and Holy Card, and supplant that image with Doré's version, which had formed and set his tastes in boyhood.

As a fledgling theatrical figure, Cecil found the physical limitations of the standard stage constrictive to his wider vision, but after 1914 and *The Squaw Man* all that would change. When talkies first came in, De Mille was quoted as saying, "Oh, God, what I will be able to do with sound!" and one can only speculate on his words when the first camera loaded with film was placed in his hands and a thousand hungry extras were heard pounding on the door.

Once in Hollywood, the formerly hesitant De Mille became a combination of Billy Sunday, Flo Ziegfield and Jay Gould. Moralizing, showcasing sex and performing financial wizardries, he blossomed into an ego whose self-confidence was overshadowed only by self-righteousness. Some critics of "the Old Man," as the cowboys called him in their more charitable moments, accused De Mille of hypocrisy, but they misread his character. A hypocrite must deceive himself. De Mille, having become convinced his was an evangelistic mission, had no more need for self-deception than the Deity Himself.

Possibly because of his impoverished childhood, De Mille empathized with shopgirls (every other movie seat in America was warmed by one) and their burning desire to know what really went on in the gilded cages of the rich. To satisfy this curiosity he staged scenes of socialites selecting Paris gowns in dazzling fashion salons, while exploiting the opportunity to reveal a bare bosom or thigh through lacy lingerie. The same logic inspired his famous "bathtub scenes," which he justified as a salutary means of underscoring the decline and fall of various overripe empires — and actresses.

The mindless "modern" plots enmeshing his filthy-rich characters were spun out of the envious daydreams of plain, hardworking scriptwriter, Jeanie McPherson, and her "Bertha the Sewing Machine Girl" values. But Jeanie is more to be praised than faulted for taking the public pulse and discovering that it pretty much matched her own. And she was plucky, too, utterly undismayed by any subject, however outside her ken, that "the Chief" might hand her, from *Joan the Woman* to *Madame Satan*.

For every bona fide sophisticate in the audience who recognized the time-worn road-show plots and treatment, millions more were seeing lust and virtue dramatized for the first time in their lives. What matter that forthright Miss McPherson named one femme fatale "Satan Synne," dubbed a heroine "Charity Cheever" and forced a self-respecting actor to perform believably for five reels as Schuyler Van Sutphen? If the modern theme meandered, De Mille and Jeanie could salvage their dead horse by hitching it to a Biblical flashback. (De Mille put the same faith in togas that small-time vaudevillians placed in the flag.) Without warning, audiences would be hurled backward in time, as hordes of wildly athletic and nearly naked extras charged down upon them, arms and legs flailing, in an orgy to end all orgies. Grapes, goblets, and presumably a coliseum full of wine soon reduced these lustful, writhing bodies to limp limbs dangling from parapets, king-sized beds and thrones, fortuitously overcome en masse by strong dark drink, just as Will Hayes reached for the scissors.

Hank Bell defined De Mille's formula as "a mixture of the Roman Empire, God's truth and mare's milk." Certainly C. B. possessed a snake-oil vendor's instinct for what the rustic will buy, and over the years bottled and marketed his elixir so successfully he became convinced it was the certain cure for what ailed mankind. Not only was it more efficacious and sweeter to down than admonitions from the pulpit, it also made millions, and so he set about converting moviegoers as zealously as a Calvin overhauling the morals of Geneva. By simple logic, anything that altered or slowed the master plan was treason; resistance or rejection became heresy, which in turn transformed an outrageous De Mille tantrum into a truly righteous rage.

A few outriders of the Hollywood cowboys had worked for
De Mille in his earlier, less flamboyant days. Others had put in
some light riding in his subsequent Westerns, but the first time
they were ever hired by De Mille as a distinct group was on
The Ten Commandments. This initial encounter between the
intransigent tyrant and the fiercely independent cowboys could
hardly escape being historic.

De Mille needed crack riders, and at least six hundred of
them, to bring to life his version of the pursuit of the Israelites
by Pharaoh's armies. But Hollywood at that time did not yet
have even a hundred men to put into the field, so De Mille
hired every cowboy available, and then picked up another two
hundred riders from the San Jose area. Through his military
contacts he was able to obtain three hundred field artillerymen
from a San Francisco army post, plus two troops of Eleventh
State Cavalry and a battery of field artillery from the Presidio
at Monterey.

The field artillerymen were, of course, famed for their ability
to deploy horse-drawn caissons over parade grounds and execute intricate drills in which teams and caissons performed
flawlessly at a dead run. Most professional horse shows and
rodeos of that era featured just such exhibitions by trained drill
teams, which were marvels of precision and timing.

By contrast, the cowboys were masters of independent
action, capable of split-second decisions and instant reaction in
any dangerous free-for-all where men and horses mixed. Besides their totally divergent approaches to similar situations, it
was common knowledge that ever since before the West was
won, the wild, unfettered frontiersman and the strict, order-
bound trooper had gotten along about as cordially as a bull and
a bear. They went at riding, fighting and even living from
completely antipathetic points of view. De Mille, however,
had an instinctive affinity for the army and its system. An
authoritarian himself, he admired and adopted its style. He
dressed in army fashion, favoring the military's sand-colored

breeches and shirt, their boots and puttees. On *The Ten Commandments* set he surrounded himself with military personnel and advisors.

To be fair to De Mille, getting his long-cherished dream of *The Ten Commandments* before the cameras proved almost as demanding and time-consuming as had acquisition of the original tablets themselves. Jeanie McPherson was experiencing more than her usual quota of problems making the contemporary and Biblical sections of the story hang together. De Mille's financial backers were stunned and dismayed at the whole concept of putting well-known, drawing-room actors in beards and bathrobes to play "dead Biblical characters." Modern moviegoers could never be made to identify with ancient Israel and its problems, Adolph Zukor warned, unless massive injections of love interest and sex were forthcoming from Jeanie's not always passionate pen. The wrangling heightened the tensions between De Mille's New York bankers and his ardently loyal "palace guard" surrounding him at the studio. To make matters worse, once Zukor had given his grudging consent to shoot this first Biblical Western, "with everybody wearing bedsheets," De Mille went completely overboard mounting his masterpiece. In a matter of weeks, the original budget had evaporated and a price tag of one million dollars was presented to his bankers — a quite stupendous sum, even by Hollywood standards at that time.

Still the spending continued, while all of Hollywood watched, savoring the spectacular events behind the making of the spectacle. Thousands of dollars were spent researching everything from Persian armor to recent archaeological discoveries of Tutankhamen's tomb. Designer Claire West was given a free hand to conjure up thousands of costumes. C. B. ordered three hundred chariots constructed for the great pursuit of the Israelites by the cruel Pharaoh's hosts. This, the publicity office stated unequivocally, was "the largest order placed for chariots in 1,700 years!"

De Mille dispatched a studio scout to find the finest team of

horses money could buy to draw Pharaoh's chariot. The scout
picked up a magnificent pair of matched black stallions in
Kansas City, and C.B. sent the bill — for five thousand dollars — to his bankers. They screamed. When he announced
his grandiose plans for location sites they screamed again. But
De Mille defended his expenditures with unassailable argu-
ments. For example, he had passed out Bibles to every member of the company, saying, "As I intend to film the entire Book
of Exodus, the Bible should never be far away from you." He
also listed as indispensable the orchestra, under direction of his
childhood friend, Rudolph Berliner, which he had hired to
play suitable religious and martial airs on the set, inspiring the
necessary sentiments of piety and valor in the breasts of some
seven thousand extras.

From March until late April, De Mille helped Jeanie complete the fusion of the two stories, ancient and modern; he
attended to countless time-consuming details of costume, casting, selection of cameramen and sets — all of which were meat
and drink to him.

At the last minute, Adolph Zukor, who held the purse
strings, flatly refused to accede to De Mille's request that he be
allowed to film the Exodus in Egypt and use the original
Palestinian background for the pursuit of the Israelites
through the Red Sea. A dreary expanse of sand dunes at the
beach in Santa Maria, California, was quite a comedown as a
location site, but De Mille was determined to make it every bit
as authentic and colorful as the real thing. Here on the windswept, gritty dunes he created a vast, teeming tent city that he
named Camp De Mille. Twenty-five hundred people and some
fifty thousand animals were reported to have gone by train
from Hollywood to Camp De Mille by the beginning of May,
1923. Everything was run army style, under the coordination
of one Captain Barton, whose credentials for the job were
nothing less than six years' experience with the American Army
of Occupation in Europe.

Dozens of tents housed the extras (men and women slept

and ate in separate quarters), bootleg liquor was banished, swearing was forsworn and Bible-reading became the order of the day. There was a special tent set up where only kosher meals were served to the more than two hundred Orthodox Jews hired to work as extras. Other tents housed the enormous wardrobe, and a schoolroom where some sixty luckless extra children were obliged to attend classes before dawn in order to be ready for work at seven. A corps of magazine and newspaper reporters set up their own field unit, covering this gargantuan historical reconstruction for the news services of the world.

But of all the razzle-dazzle side-show elements that went into the spectacle behind the spectacle, no sight so stunned the cowboys — and disgusted them — as the one that met their eyes when they looked up to the highest sandhill, commanding a total overview of the encampment.

"At first I thought it was a part of the set for the Pharaoh's palace," Jack Padjan said, "but then somebody told us what it really was. Jumped-up-Jesus, if there didn't stand an Oriental-style pavilion, as splendid as Saladin's, that De Mille called a marquee. To keep out the sand he'd spent fifteen hundred dollars on havin' gardeners plant acres of blue lupines all around it. And flyin' from a staff on top was a banner, with a background as blue as the sky and white letters, all personally designed by the Old Man, spellin' out 'De Mille' so clear not even God Himself could miss whose tent it was."

About the second day on the set, and before they had done any riding at all except to sit their ponies in the long shots, it began to dawn on the cowboys that a kind of conspiracy was afoot among the army men. The San Francisco contingent had been used in a few flashy scenes and De Mille had gone out of his way to butter them up about their performance. Already grown self-important over this, their first crack at immortalizing their horsemanship on film, De Mille's extravagant praise had gone completely to their heads.

"Hell, I hadn't been on the set five minutes," Jack Padjan said later, "before I hear the Old Man telling all the newspaper and magazine people what fine and fearless riders the artillery-men were, and how his experience with cowboys proved *they* tended to be timid in the saddle." Jack's Blackfoot and Irish blood came to a boil, but Hank laughed it off. Then, during a lunch break, an artilleryman strolled by and one of the Israelite extras pointed him out to Hank.

"Have you heard what those army boys plan to do to you cowboys when the big scene comes?"

"Cain't say I have," Hank replied.

"Well, the artillerymen from San Francisco figure they're just going to ride you down when De Mille shoots the big battle scenes."

During their years in Hollywood the cowboys had learned to treat picture riding exactly as they had range work. It was an honest job, a job to be done fairly and well. "The idea that this bunch of gunsils on their goddammed flat saddles was so set on makin' a big show of themselves for posterity they was willin' to bust up good men and horses just didn't set with us," Jack said. But what neither Jack nor Hank knew at the time was something that De Mille would admit only years later in his autobiography. He not only identified with the military con-tingent but, like them, he held the cowboys in what he called "supreme contempt." When he got wind of rumors that the artillerymen hated the cowboys and planned to show their superiority by running them down in the course of the scene, he secretly rejoiced. Rarely was he able to wring genuine or even believable emotions out of his extra people, although he never ceased trying. Here, however, was a ready-made animos-ity he could exploit on screen to achieve convincing results beyond even his own wildest dreams. Casting the artillerymen as the Egyptians and the cowboys as Israelites, he could set up the two camps to fight out a petty feud, hoping the hatred would shine through realistically.

Before the big battle scene, however, the artillerymen had to stage a solo charge of their own. Days had been consumed in careful preparations for this spectacular scene. When De Mille took up the megaphone he exhorted them "to charge like hell!" The orchestra, on its wooden platform, struck up a stirring martial air and the artillerymen were ready for their first big moment in the sun.

"They was ridin' like they didn't give a damn for horses or men," Jack said. "But even so, nobody could blame the army men for what happened next. The lead chariot, driven by Pharaoh's double, simply crumpled up like a goddammed lunch-box on wheels. Then the whole charge just seemed to telescope into a massive pile-up of horses, chariots and riders."

Hank chuckled as he recalled the funny side. "And all the time them duded-up musicians in their tuxedos and flowin' gowns just kept right on sawin' their fiddles and blowin' their horns like they was back at the Ritz-Carlton ballroom where they come from! Until finally a regular twister of horses, wheels and busted-up chariots just plowed right through their plank oasis, tore up their harps and hymnbooks and charged straight on out the other side."

Injured horses ran loose everywhere, screaming pitifully, some with their flanks so badly ripped they seemed to be trailing scarlet bandannas instead of their own torn flesh. The Pharaoh's magnificent team of blacks, which had cost the studio five thousand dollars, were smashed up and permanently lamed.

Hank and Jack marveled at De Mille's apparent satisfaction with the footage obtained out of this debacle, but then a rumor swept Camp De Mille that someone had seen the axles of the lead chariot before the charge began, and he swore *that they had been sawed almost in half!* The newspaper people picked up the story and it was headlined in Hollywood, but De Mille laughed away the entire incident as "studio gossip."

The following week the company moved from Santa Maria to Muroc Dry Lake in the middle of the Majave Desert, for the

long-awaited Egyptian-Israelite battle scenes. By that time the
climate was ripe for a confrontation between the cowboys and
cannoneers.

One hundred Hollywood riders and the San Jose band
gathered on the hard-packed white sands under the rays of a
rising sun that felt like molten lead. Their bodies had been
painted from head to heel with brown body make-up. They
stood in their chariots or sat their restless mounts waiting for
De Mille to give the signal for the charge. But instead, he
pointed out the steep bluff down which he wanted the cowboys
to race their teams and chariots, as they fled before the Egyptian host. The cowboys sized up the job and objected.

"Hank and I got up a delegation," Jack said, "and we went
over to the Old Man and told him we thought it was too
dangerous — especially in the light of what had happened the
week before and the useless slaughter of good horses."

" 'Mr. De Mille,' I says, 'you just can't put that many chariots
hub to hub down that bluff and not lose somebody or bust up
some horses.' "

De Mille listened to the cowboys' objections and then (as he
himself told the story over the years) he decided to shame the
cowboys into carrying out his plan. Calling to his eleven-year-
old daughter Cecilia, who was riding her pony on the same
hill, he ordered her to gallop down the slope at full speed.
Complying delightedly, she made the descent at breakneck
speed and without injury. Turning to the cowboys with a
disdainful smile, De Mille said, "Well, if a little girl like Ciddy
can do it, why can't you?"

"It's one thing to bring down a single rider, Mr. De Mille,"
Jack told him respectfully. "Any one of us could do that blindfolded. It's somethin' else to have fifty to a hundred men pile
off it, with chariots and teams."

Jack then went on to inform De Mille that, not only was the
situation itself dangerous, but the artillerymen intended to use
the occasion to make good their own claims to superior horsemanship by riding over every cowboy in their path.

"When I finished talking," Jack recalled, "he looked right through me and said, 'I must confess, my sympathies are with the artillerymen.'"

Furious, the cowboy delegation went back to their companions, climbed into their chariots and saddles and waited stoically for the order to charge. De Mille stood on his raised platform scanning the spectacle through eyes slitted against the glare from the hard-packed white sands.

"Ready! Action! Camera!" came the familiar commands, and, as one man, three hundred eager, brash artillerymen uncoiled their spring-tight horses and bolted toward the enemy. But in their path only a handful of San Jose cowboys picked their way down the bluff and made a stand against their assault. The main body of two hundred and seventy-five God-inspired, fearless, fighting Israelites sat quietly on the sidelines, their teams and fretful horses tightly reined, their gleaming chariots motionless. The San Jose boys scattered and Pharaoh's hosts, unopposed, kept right on going toward the shores of the Red Sea.

His mighty spectacle ruined by the cowboys' willful insubordination, De Mille's rage was apocalyptic. Grabbing a megaphone, he addressed the entire hushed company of several thousand actors, extras and crewmen, denouncing the cowboys as cowards who were afraid to face the superior horsemanship of the "Egyptians" from San Francisco. In his memoirs he remembered fondly that no Pharaoh had ever used stronger language than he unleashed on the cowboys that day, but that they preferred being verbally skinned alive to taking their chances with the artillerymen.

What De Mille did not realize was that his public denunciation and groundless assumption of the cowboys' cowardice had cast the die for a bitter feud with them that would plague him for the next three decades. One day they would even seek his life as the price of keeping their honor.

6

"Meanwhile, Back at the Ranch . . ."

CENTURY may have been a catchpenny outfit, but the Stern Brothers managed to make millions by keeping Baby Peggy light and laughable. But after a contract disagreement with them, Father moved me to Universal, where Uncle Carl decided to make me over into a serious actress, leading a full-scale studio assault on First National's woebegone Jackie Coogan. In three major features, I matched Chaplin's erstwhile protégé anguish for anguish and tear for tear — real ones, too, not glycerine. These torrents of tears were produced by an internal emotional mechanism as reliable as an electric pump, aided only by the string quartet which Uncle Carl provided to supply "cry music" on my set, playing such selections as "My Buddy," "Roses of Picardy," and "Danny Boy."

Unfortunately, major studios did not yet maintain script-writers to provide a steady flow of suitable vehicles for their stars, De Mille's Jeanie McPherson being one of the few exceptions. This shortage was particularly acute for juvenile stars like Jackie and myself, and accounted for some of the very poor features both of us made after our initial success. However, in a perfect case of Jack Sprat's lean and fat, Sol Lesser found himself in Uncle Carl's plight, only in reverse. Lesser, as producer of some of Jackie's more successful films, had exhausted his meager stock of childhood classics featuring a boy hero, but left over were three literary plums — *Captain January*,

Helen's Babies and *Heidi*, — each requiring a female child star. Metro promptly took Jackie off Lesser's hands to star in a series of maudlin films, while Sol Lesser relieved Uncle Carl of his four-year-old — but aging — tragedienne.

The six years between my fourth and tenth birthdays, when I was at the zenith of my popularity as a child star, were among the most demanding and eventful of an already pressured childhood, but this is not the proper place to relate that part of the story. What was of crucial importance at the time to my parents was that my career — unlikely in the beginning and unpredictable in its subsequent skyrocketing — placed them in a dilemma that was unique even in Hollywood. They vacillated between playing it as it lay, with the aid of so-called business advisors (whose turnover and personal take was phenomenal), to withdrawing me entirely from pictures and sinking what was left in a ranch. A third possibility, of course, was to do what dozens of other stars were doing, invest in blue-chip property in the golden crescent around Hollywood — Beverly Hills, Santa Monica and San Fernando Valley, the new California mother lode.

Throughout the prosperous and virtually tax-free 1920's, many silent stars piled up respectable fortunes in real estate, an abiding source of great wealth that would very often survive all the vicissitudes of age, talkies, and Depression which lay ahead. Father bought and sold the requisite number of expensive properties in all the right locations — San Fernando Valley, Beverly Hills, Laurel Canyon — but his timing was wrong. He was far less fortunate in these gambles than others, like Hoot Gibson, for one, who by merely hanging on to his original Newhall ranch found himself a millionaire by the close of the decade.

But while Hoot and William S. Hart preferred to hold on in Hollywood, other cowboy stars began an imperceptible movement away from the movie capital. When his contract at Universal came up for renewal in 1928, Neal Hart asked to be dealt out of the game of being "America's Pal," cashed in his chips and withdrew from show business. He purchased an expensive guest ranch in a spectacular setting in British Columbia where he and his wife and son planned to live out the life that Neal felt had been interrupted and postponed by his Hollywood career. Tom Mix kept his fabulous Beverly Hills mansion with his name in neon lights atop the roof, but, with an eye to a possibly different future, he also invested in a huge place in Arizona called the TM Ranch. Similarly Jack Hoxie, weary from his many miles on the stardust trail, tossed in his cards and, with his brother Bob, bought a spread of his own in Oklahoma where he hoped to raise cattle.

While the unknown cowboys-turned-riding-extras did not have the options open to them that the big stars did, even they began to admit that Hollywood had never held much charm for them. From the start it had been merely a spot to "noon the wagons" on the trail to someplace else. Once the pinch of hunger and the insecurity of being jobless and dispossessed wore off, the cowboys felt increasingly bored with the sameness of silent Westerns, and uncomfortable in the alien theatrical environment.

By this time, too, I was ten, and if there were few stories for young children, there were none for adolescents entering the awkward age. Father was affected strongly by the prevailing mood — a feeling that now was the time to get out before it was too late. Things had never been more prosperous for most Americans. It seemed an ideal moment to make his decision.

In the fall of 1928 Father left on a trip, and a few weeks later he telephoned long distance to announce his good news to Mother.

"I've just bought the most beautiful ranch this side of Paradise," he exulted. "Fifteen hundred acres of good pastureland and native hay meadows lying along three miles of the Big Laramie River. There's a fine log house with fourteen rooms, all the equipment, barns and harness needed to run the place, outbuildings and bunkhouses that we can remodel and turn into guest cabins. Believe me, this is going to be the most fabulous dude outfit in the entire country!"

When Mother put to him a few such pertinent questions as was there electricity, running water and indoor plumbing in Paradise, he replied impatiently, "Not yet, Sharkey, but there will be by fall. The ranch itself was a pretty expensive investment, even at the rock bottom price I got it for. I'm forming a corporation with three Eastern investors and that way we can develop the property. By the end of summer they'll put in $75,000 more and then we can install all the improvements."

The stark realities of her year in a tent on the rim of the Grand Canyon coming vividly alive once more, Mother persisted, "But what about this summer?"

"Sharkey, don't worry! Believe me, you'll love it!" As she put down the phone, Mother thought that phrase had a strangely familiar ring to it.

The J-Flag Ranch and Recreation Center hardly lived up to its impressive title when in June of 1929 Father turned the sand-colored Lincoln off Highway 66, just thirty-two miles south of Laramie, Wyoming, and drove down the bumpy, unpaved private road to the ranch house. The Big Laramie River had risen to the highest level in memory, so the natives told us, and had flooded the place right up to the dooryard of the log ranch house. The grounds were littered with drowned mice and dead bloated chickens, while the debris left by a Portuguese sheepman, who had leased it briefly prior to our occupancy, floated up from flooded root cellars and in and out of bunkhouse doors.

To distract Mother from the temporary horrors of the flood, Father enthusiastically pointed out the beauty of Sheep Mountain to the north, which towered like a long, high wall above our extensive pastureland on the opposite side of the highway. Behind the ranch buildings rose Jelm Mountain to a height of 13,000 feet, a virgin wilderness of aspen groves, cottonwood, and pine. The ranch itself lay tucked away by the river and sheltered on every side by sharp ridges falling away from the high, windswept expanse of the Great Laramie Plains.

But despite the bad beginning, the place proved indeed beautiful, and all was optimism and excitement that first summer. We camped out in a tent while a crew of carpenters set about remodeling the handsome old log house that had been built, entirely of hand-hewn logs, by a Norwegian homesteader named Jake Lund back in 1880. Father bought two milk cows, a flock of laying hens, and a herd of twenty-five fine work and saddle horses. For two girls, thirteen and ten years old, the ranch was really a paradise. Louise and I lived in the saddle, and never donned skirts except when we made the thirty-two mile trek into town to shop or see a movie. Although we were hardly ready to accept guests, Hank Bell dropped by for a drink and stayed a month. He, too, was on his way back to the land, headed for Cheyenne to see if his old outfit was in any better shape than when he had left nearly ten years earlier.

Hank and Father soon found some stray cows and steers that had drifted through downed fences during the several years that the property had been abandoned and up for sale. These they delighted in pursuing, rounding up and, when permissible, marking with the J-Flag brand. One Sunday, after a couple of rounds of mint juleps, they decided to stage a home-made rodeo with their captured herd.

Father had just bought a new cutting horse he wanted to try, and Hank was considering buying another horse he fancied, to ride over to Cheyenne. But before they could mount, a sharp-horned old cow went on the prod and, taking after Father who was standing beside his horse, forced him to jump over the feed rack to escape being gored. Landing on the hard-packed feed lot just beyond, he felt an excruciating pain in his right arm and realized that he had dislocated his elbow.

As Mother wrung her hands and wondered if there was a doctor in town who would come this far on a house call, Hank led Father out of the corral and, through a rose-colored haze of bourbon, assured him, "Hell, I'm as good as any doctor. My old man used to practice out in the country and I seen him treat this sort of thing lots of times." With that he told Father to sit down on the ground with his back against the hard log wall of the chicken house.

"That's right." he muttered knowledgeably. "Now, then, I'll sit down right here in front of you, take your wrist in my two hands, put my foot like this against your chest and — p - u - l - l . . ." Father leaned back while Hank pulled, and sure enough, the elbow popped right back into place, but as it did so, the patient suddenly bent double with pain.

"Now what's wrong?" Hank asked, almost petulantly.

"What's wrong?" Father echoed, beginning to laugh, although it made him wince with pain. "Hell, Handlebar, you just drove your goddammed boot-heel right through my ribs!"

For a moment Hank was stumped, then said grandly, "Oh, well, the doc ain't goin' to be in his office on Sunday anyway. Let's go on up to the ranch and have another round of juleps!" With that, he threw Father's good arm over his shoulder and, with Father alternately laughing and swearing, they marched up to the veranda for another drink.

But there were many sober moments, and Father proved he possessed unerring judgment where horses and other livestock were concerned. His management of the huge property, with the help of a hired man, was firm and wise. Although we were hopelessly rushed and unprepared for haying season that first summer, he made sure the ancient horse-drawn rakes were cleaned of decades of rust, and the blades on the mowing machine were sharpened and oiled. A full crew was at work in the fragrant meadows of timothy and clover by mid-July, and the hay cured slowly under a burning August sun, before an early rain could sour it. Well ahead of the first frost, the hay was in the barns or stored neatly in several field stacks, of two or three tons each, which he knew how to top off to keep rain and snow from seeping through.

Mother did not find the rugged life too unpleasant. She had a seemingly bottomless fund of energy, and most of all she possessed a sparkling sense of humor that knew how to make light of such inconveniences as Coleman lanterns, an indoor pump instead of running water and bathing in a round laundry tin set before the oven in the kitchen. It wasn't really hard to be patient when she knew the discomforts would soon be memories as distant and amusing as her Grand Canyon battles with tarantulas had since become.

Then, too, the heavy work load was broken almost every day by a swim in the icy waters of the river, or a night ride under an unbelievably big and brilliant moon. There were wild gooseberries to pick and preserve, black chokecherries to strip from trees that grew in profusion along the flanks of Jelm Mountain just across the river. There were neighbors to meet (the nearest one lived three miles away), with hayrides and picnics providing the excuse for such strangers to get acquainted.

Father was in his element at last. Sitting on the screened veranda in the aquamarine mountain twilight, or sipping drinks on a summer afternoon, he could admire the spring colts as they frolicked in clover that was belly-deep to the mares. He and Neal and a few others like them had finally escaped the tyranny of weather-permitting calls, and leather-lunged directors bellowing, "That take was no good. Let's shoot it again, and this time let's get some *action* in it!" What were three cracked ribs and an out-of-joint elbow to a man who was sitting on his own ranch, realizing at last the dream he had feared might never come true?

By autumn the remodeling was complete. Jake Lund's original fourteen small rooms had been reduced to ten more spacious ones, including a main lounge and large dining area, facing opposite sides of an enormous fireplace fashioned of mottled brown and gray river boulders.

In mid-October it was time for Father to return to the East to collect the promised $75,000 from his three trusted investors. This money would bring old Jake Lund's homestead out of the nineteenth century and into the twentieth — replete with electricity and indoor plumbing.

Father climbed behind the wheel of the Lincoln and turned its aristocratic nose toward the highway.

"I'll be back in two weeks," he said cheerily as he kissed us goodbye, "and I'll be bringing home the bacon. Now, Sharkey, you and the girls be sure and get the apples picked and in the cellar before the first snow hits."

Jack Lund had planted the only apple orchard in Albany County, and possibly the only one ever to survive forty years at the elevation of 7,500 feet. The orchard, numbering about fifty trees, lay directly in front of the ranch house, and it was a joy to sit on the porch and watch the apples turn from yellow-green to a deep red-gold. Now that they were ripe, Louise and I and a hired man attacked the two-week-long job of harvesting the crop while Mother was kept busy in the kitchen putting up applesauce and apple jelly. As we were winding up our chores, Mother came out to help us pack the last of the harvest into barrels to be stored, when she noticed a small, Model-A Ford jolting down our private road.

"Do you think we could be getting more dudes this late in the season?" Mother asked as she shaded her eyes against the warm autumn sunshine.

As the Ford drew closer, Mother lowered her hand and allowed an apron full of apples to slide unnoticed to the ground.

"It's your father!" she exclaimed incredulously. "I didn't recognize the car. I wonder what happened to the Lincoln?"

What had happened to the Lincoln was only the first chapter of the long and harrowing story Father had to tell. The rich, gem-encrusted oil heiress who had often clasped me to her bosom in my Baby Peggy days had remarried, and her new husband had pledged $25,000 to the J-Flag Recreation Center. But a week before Father arrived at their apartment in Chicago, her husband had been found in his bathtub, dead, with a shotgun by his side. He had been wiped out in the stock market crash of Black Friday, and his widow was left penniless. The second investor who had been counted on for $30,000 was destitute, pauperized by the catastrophe. The third man had jumped from his broker's office, twenty stories, to his death. Father was ashen with shock and sorrow as he related the events that had turned his trip into a nightmare.

So much for what the crash had done to our Eastern friends. As for the completely modernized and equipped J-Flag Ranch, it existed now only on paper. The cold reality was a ten-room house built to last until Judgment Day, a bunkhouse that was still a bunkhouse, acres of native hay and the only apple orchard in Albany County. The apples, at least, could be sold to neighbors, Father observed philosophically. It beat selling them on street corners as he had seen former millionaires doing back East.

Father added another five-thousand-dollar mortgage to the ten he already owed the bank in Laramie, in a determined effort to ride out the Depression. He invested in a 30.30 rifle and a box of shells, and, thanks to the fact that he was a crack shot, for the next three years we lived off the land, enjoying a diet of blue grouse, sage hen, cottontails, venison, elk meat and even bear. Mother cold-packed the venison as it was killed, and preserved everything from chokecherries to wild rhubarb. The cows gave us milk and cream, the chickens gave us eggs and more chickens, the garden provided greens. The neighbors traded horses and harness for apples and milk, and the feed store in town gallantly extended our credit for oats, chicken feed and cow bran.

The summer of 1930 brought us a few former Hollywood

friends — who had somehow come through the disaster un-
scathed — as paying guests. It also brought a steady stream of
broke or broken-down cowboys, strangers as well as friends.
One of these was Ed Hendershot, who only the year before
had been playing second-leads with Hoot Gibson at Universal.
Ed arrived in a battered car with a horse trailer behind, which
he had made over into an adequate house trailer for himself
and his wife. Even without Ed's telling him anything, Father
realized that he was desperately in need of help. But typically,
he turned Ed's plight completely around, so it appeared as
though his arrival had proved of providential importance to us
and to the ranch.

"You and Flo have just *got* to stay on here with us for a
while," he said. "There's a nice spot down by the river on a
secluded little meadow where you can set up camp. And if you
could help me breaking out these bad horses I picked up over
in Cheyenne from the army remount station, I'd really be
grateful."

The game worked both ways, of course, and Ed ventured
that he would be willing to help take the kinks out of the
spoiled horses, providing Father wouldn't consider any salary
involved. Just a place to stay the summer was all the payment
he needed.

"Hell, I quit Tom Mix after a season following him on the
Sells Floto circus route. If I wanted money I could pick up
plenty of chink riding with his outfit again, but I couldn't stand
the life — Tom's gettin' mean, and doing some really heavy
drinking."

Tom had, of course, lost everything in the Crash: his mansion, his Arizona spread, and a million dollars in worthless
stocks. The Sells Floto offer for a man pushing fifty who was
forced to begin all over again was a bitter pill for Mix to
swallow, and one couldn't help but admire his courage.

"Hoot lost over a million, too," Ed told us. "But he's managed to keep the Newhall place. If he can hang on in pictures

he'll be all right, but they say his voice doesn't come across in talkies." Then, with a wry smile he added, "Mine doesn't either."

Ed Hendershot was a short and wiry man who looked as if he had stepped right out of the pages of a Will James's illustrated story. His sandy hair, pale blue eyes, high-beaked nose and firm set mouth bespoke the typical cowboy. He was soft-spoken, slow in his movements, and a superb horseman. Most of all, he possessed the gift of "horse-talk," the ability to keep talking to a mean or spoiled horse until he actually seemed to get through to him and win his confidence. Louise and I would sit for hours on the top rail of the horse corral watching him saddle a bronc, then let him soak, then talk to him, blindfold him if necessary, slide up on his back and then step down again. He gentled two absolutely unbreakable, spoiled rodeo broncs that way, working patiently, quietly, understandingly, with them, as though he had all the time in the world to set things straight at last for those poor ponies.

About midsummer Father came upon a band of wild horses, led by a wily white mare, running free on our vast Sheep Mountain pasture. There were several good animals among the usual broomtails, and Father told Ed he could take two or three for himself, gentle them and maybe sell them in Laramie or Cheyenne, as a way of grubstaking himself. But first we had to catch them, and since chasing wild horses is about as time-consuming and ordinarily as fruitless an occupation as a rancher can undertake, we were in for a two-week marathon. Louise and I were invited to join Father and Ed, a couple of hired men, and several cowboys from neighboring ranches, because numbers were important. It was during this chase that I first became aware that my father and his band of riding-extra friends were truly among the finest horsemen in the world. Seeing them through the eyes of much younger men, themselves good riders, I recognized them for what they were, masters of their craft.

After days of vain pursuit, Father and Ed finally figured out how to foil the escape pattern used by the lead mare. Usually she bolted up a narrow canyon and holed up there where riders simply could not follow. Now the plan was to put a rider on top of each "hog's back" — the sharply rounded hill rising on either side of the mare's favorite escape route. The local men thought Father and Ed were crazy even to attempt such a thing. Sure enough, as we tried to haze the band toward the open pasture gate leading down to the ranch road, the mare doubled back and pointed her band to the dark and timbered gully. But Father and Ed were ready on the ridges above, and when they saw the mustangs streak toward the canyon, they started their ponies down at a dead run.

Father, on his favorite mount, Ginger, hit the sorrel once with his spurs and Ginger simply took flight, landing only long enough on each ledge or jutting portion of rock to gather his hindquarters under him again and make another catlike spring for the bottom. Ed, on the other side, took his long-legged bay straight down the side of a rocky cliff, until the two riders joined at the head of the canyon just as the herd streamed in. Surprised, the mare spun her bunch around and headed straight for the open pasture gate, with Father and Ed on their tails and the rest of us holding them in by riding hard on either side.

Pushing them at a dead run down the private ranch road toward the open corral, we had the wild satisfaction of seeing the whole slick band churn into the corral, ears pricked forward, manes flying and tails high. Father and Ed planted their horses' rumps flat on the ground in front of the corral gate, dismounting before the animals had stopped moving, in order to swing the big pole gate shut on their hard-won prize.

A local rider, twenty years old, who had watched the surround for the entire two weeks, shook his head in disbelief.

"I can't believe any man can stay aboard a horse the way those two can — going straight up or straight down. That kind of riding would kill any other man I know."

With infinite patience Ed broke out three of the best and youngest of the wild ones, and sold them for a good price to a neighboring rancher. By this time he had become alarmed over his wife's steadily failing health, and was doubly grateful to have the money to get her back to Hollywood and her family.

The day before hunting season opened that fall, Father, Mother, and a new hired man named Clyde decided to ride up to the open pastureland at the foot of Sheep Mountain and scout out a good spot to lie in wait for game. At that time of year entire herds of elk came down from the mountain to nibble at the tempting haystacks studding the open prairie-land belonging to our neighbor, Ole Ericson. Although Father normally favored Ginger, on this particular day he wanted to try out a new saddle horse called Keno, a big long-legged pinto he had just bought that looked as if he might develop into a good dude horse. He suggested that Mother ride Ginger and discover for herself what an easy gait he had.

"I don't trust pintos," Father said as he saddled Keno. "Every one I've ever known has had a hole in him. But we'll see if this one is counterfeit or not."

A wagon trace led across the flat prairie to the high pasture, and after going over the ground near the haystacks, Father and Clyde agreed upon the site where they would take up their vigil the following morning before dawn. As they started back along the wagon track toward the highway, about a mile from our ranch, Father turned in his saddle and shouted to Mother, "Let Ginger out and see what a marvelous lope he's got!" At that he drove his spurs into Keno's ribs and the big bay pinto began eating up the ground in long, powerful strides.

They had raced about a quarter of a mile over the hard-packed plain when, without warning, Keno plunged both front feet into a huge badger hole that was completely hidden under a clump of blue sage. The big horse went down as though he had been rigged with a Stationary W, and Father was cata-pulted over his head, sailing thirty-five feet through the air before coming to rest beside his 30.30 rifle, which had been hurled from its saddle-scabbard in the fall.

Ginger plowed into the fallen Keno's rump and Mother was almost thrown from the saddle. Throwing away the reins in her panic, Mother ran to Father's side.

"Darling! Dear! Speak to me!" she cried hysterically. Just then Clyde, who had been riding a slower horse, caught up with her, and noting the dark stain in Father's dust-caked temple, he announced gloomily, "I'm afraid he's gone, ma'am. That there's a thirty-thirty gunshot wound in his head."

"Oh, no!" she gasped. And then with characteristic decisiveness she fired orders at Clyde. "You stay here with him, and try to hail a passing car on the highway. I'll run to the ranch and phone for a doctor."

Louise and I were on the veranda, curled up on either corner of a long couch reading Zane Grey novels. We heard Mother's screams before she topped the little rise in the road, and ran out to meet her.

"Your father!" she gasped, so winded she could hardly speak. "He's been terribly hurt. Call Doc Fitch!"

Instantly Louise was at the wall phone, grinding away on the hand crank, trying to alert the operator. Getting through to Laramie, she learned that Doctor Fitch was out of town, but another doctor was taking his calls. When Louise finally reached him, he promised to come at once. "At once," of course, meant at least forty minutes, since the highway leading out of Laramie was an unpaved washboard of a road.

While Louise phoned, Mother and I started up the road to the pasture, but we had hardly gone thirty feet when a car appeared, with a stranger at the wheel and Clyde holding Father in his arms in the back seat. It took all five of us to lift and drag the unconscious, dead-weight body up the front steps and into the house.

"We'll never be able to get him upstairs to the bedroom," Mother said realistically. "Let's put him on the long sofa in the dining room." This was an oversized wicker couch, a relic from our Hollywood home, but it was more than six feet long and wide enough to serve as a makeshift bed. Coated with dust, and his eyes glazed, Father was completely unconscious and barely breathing as we stretched him out on the sofa, his boots and spurs still on his feet.

"Hear that rasping sound in his throat?" Clyde put in lugubriously. "That's the death rattle. I heard my wife go the very same way, back in Oklahoma City. She looked real nice, though, when them undertakers got through with her. I even got some nice snapshots of her in her coffin. Would you care to see 'em?"

Mother continued rubbing Father's wrists, ignoring Clyde's gruesome asides. All I could think of was how on earth we had picked up such a grave-digger for a hired man. We had had all kinds by this time, but Clyde was a real stand-out.

"If only Ed Hendershot were still here!" Mother cried. And then a moment later, "Oh, where is that doctor? Why doesn't he come?"

Almost an hour had passed since Louise had reached the doctor, and now Father's breathing seemed fainter and more irregular, when at last I heard the familiar sound of a car jolting down the private road and coming to a halt in front of the ranch house door. Relieved that the doctor had arrived at last, I ran out to greet him, but froze on the front steps when I saw him stumble out of his Chevrolet coupe. His clothes were disheveled, he had a three days' growth of beard, and his eyes could hardly focus on me. In his right hand he carried the little black bag, in his left a big cream-colored ceramic jug. As he lurched up the gravel path toward me, he paused long enough to take a sizable swig from the jug; wiping his lips with the sleeve of his coat he then asked thickly, "Okay, whersh the patient?"

"He's in here, doctor," I said, my heart turning to stone. "He's never come to since he was thrown from his horse over an hour ago."

Considering his condition, the doctor's presence was hardly a comfort to us, but I'll give him credit — as drunk as he was he seemed to know what he was doing. He was short and thick-set, with iron-gray hair and the kind of eyes one comes to expect in the West — eyes that are accustomed to gazing across great distances and skilled at reading the landscape for every signal and sign.

"All right. You womenfolk get out of here," he said, stripping off his coat and rolling up his shirt-sleeves. "First I'm goin' to force-feed him a shot of my old 'Sam Beatin' here, and that ought to bring him around. I reckon he must have busted some ribs." He felt Father's side. "Sure enough — okay — now, off with you."

As Louise, Mother and I paced back and forth in the living room, we could hear the low murmur of conversation between the doctor and Clyde. Then, suddenly, the deep country quiet was split by a scream of pain.

"Good God, Doc, *don't do that!*" It was Father's voice, and for an instant I thought the doctor must be amputating a leg. But when Mother asked through the door what was happening, the doctor calmly shouted back at her: "Nothin' to worry about, ma'am. Just settin' his ribs, and I ain't got no anesthetic."

"Not so *hard*, Doc! Not so goddammed *tight!*"

After that Father did not speak rationally again, but began babbling incoherently, bits and snatches of disconnected memories. I could think of nothing worse than that the blow on his head should have brought about insanity.

Soon the doctor emerged, his black bag snapped shut and the cork out of the jug. He took another swig of what he called his "Sam Beatin Whiskey" and said matter-of-factly:

"Well, as I see it, it's this way with your husband, Mrs.

Montgomery. Them ribs was about all I could fix. He's no doubt got a real blue ribbon concussion of the brain from that fall, and it's my guess he's got a fractured skull as well. Cain't tell about those things, though. They fool you. You just have to keep him quiet and snubbed-up close for the next few days. He may be sort of looney in the head for a time — maybe forever, *if* he lives. Cain't tell in cases like this — just have to hope for the best. Well, good evenin' to you."

With that the doctor climbed into his Chevrolet, and Mother, Louise and I stood there numbly as the yellow headlights sent two long shafts probing the darkness of the October night. I didn't know anything about medicine, but it seemed to me that the disappearing doctor's shattering diagnosis would have been more appropriate delivered some forty years back, when Jake Lund and his clan occupied the house we now called home. It was as though there were no such things as X-rays and hospitals and what people back East called "modern medicine." But the truth was there was virtually no money in our household at this time, and perhaps that is why we all accepted the old country doctor's word without question. We never saw him again, and no other doctor would examine Father.

"I'll take the first watch," Mother said as she turned back into the house. "Let's see now . . ." We followed her into the dining room where Father lay unconscious. "The doctor said to roll him some cigarettes in case he comes to — Peg, you can do that. And he said home-brew beer was all right to give him if we don't have whiskey — and we don't." Louise nodded wisely and headed straight for the kitchen where the crock of home brew was kept.

There was no sleep for us that night. Instead we all stayed downstairs, watching Father's every breath, listening in secret agony as he mumbled and raved.

"I figure Jack would want me to go hunting just like we planned this afternoon," Clyde said. "I can knock off an elk and at least we'll have meat in the freezer." The freezer was a large screened cupboard, big enough to hold the entire carcass of a deer or elk. The screen kept the flies from "blowing" the meat (maggots would have resulted) and the Wyoming winter, with a mean average of thirty-five below, took care of the freezing.

"All right, Clyde," Mother replied. "That's a good idea. Did you bring the thirty-thirty back down from the pasture?"

"Yes, ma'am, and I cleaned it. And, you know, I reckon Jack *didn't* pick up a bullet through his head like I thought, or the Doc would have noticed, don't you think?"

"Clyde, that doctor wouldn't have noticed if he had a Minié ball in his stomach!" Mother flashed back hotly. "Take the rifle and good luck."

Louise, Mother and I took turns keeping the long night's vigil by Father's sofa-bed, and finally, at five in the morning, as we were all half-dead for lack of sleep and haggard with worry, we heard Clyde's boots scraping up the back steps. I got up and let him in.

"Did you get some meat?" I asked in a whisper.

"Yes, ma'am, I got some meat — but — "

"What's the matter with you, Clyde?" Mother asked irritably. "What happened?"

It took a while to get the full story out of Clyde. Being a veteran of the First World War, he said he could shoot better lying on his stomach. He had waited long hours in that position, watching for an elk, or a herd of them, to loom onto the horizon. Something finally loomed, all right, and Clyde fired. But when he went to dress out the animal, he discovered that he had made a terrible mistake. It was not an elk, but one of Ole Ericson's prized sheep!

"Well, there's no use crying about it, Clyde," Mother snapped. "We can eat mutton just as well as venison. Unload the packhorse in the barn, hang the ram by his hind feet from a single-tree, just the way Jack does, and dress it out."

Five sleepless days and nights later, Father still had not

regained consciousness. The money was dwindling and the cupboard was almost bare when, on a sparkling November morning, a stranger came striding purposefully down our lane to the front door.

"I see by the sign on the highway that you people run a guest ranch," he began.

"Yes, we do," Mother replied, drying her hands on her apron.

"Well, ma'am, I've got a mighty peculiar problem on my hands, and maybe you can help."

"I'll try," Mother said lamely, ready to tell this stranger that he didn't know what problems were.

"I'm moving a steam shovel down the highway from Fox Park to Laramie, and the blamed thing's broken down on me. There's thirteen men in my crew, counting me, and we can't repair the steam shovel in less than two or three days. We have to get the parts from town, you know. Could you put me and my men up and feed us for as long as we're stalled here? I expect it would come to a couple of hundred dollars."

Without batting an eye, Mother flashed her most beguiling smile. "Of course we can, Mr. — ? What did you say your name was?"

The man gave his name and a fifty-dollar deposit and returned to notify his crew of their good fortune. As soon as she closed the front door behind him, Mother went into the living room and took the 30.30 down from its gun rack — a handsome, seven-foot spread of longhorns with black tips, which Shorty Miller had given Father in repayment for a fifty-dollar loan back in our San Fernando Valley days. Going to the back door, she called to Clyde, who was busy splitting stove wood at the chopping stump.

"Clyde, I've just promised to feed thirteen road hands three meals a day for a week. Now, you take this rifle and go up to Sheep Mountain tonight. I don't care if you kill Ericson's sheep or Hansen's prized Hereford bull. But just don't you come back home without meat!"

The road hands rivaled lumberjacks for appetites, and worst

of all, they had to be sitting down to breakfast at four-thirty in the morning. That meant we had to be mixing the hot-cake batter and brewing gallons of coffee by three A.M. Of course, it didn't make too much difference, because the three of us had been keeping such erratic hours anyway, trying to arrange a round-the-clock vigil beside Father's bed in the dining room.

The crew proved very helpful. While they waited for meals they rolled cigarettes for Father and stacked them, like miniature logs, in an ashtray on the end table. It was during this week when the steam shovel was parked at our gate that Father regained full consciousness for the first time since his ribs were being set. He wasn't rational, and he was far from being lucid, but at least he seemed to know who he was and he recognized his wife and daughters. After a time it came back to him who Clyde was. The hired man celebrated this event by whipping out the snapshots of his late wife, Ida, sitting up in her coffin in Oklahoma City's finest funeral parlor. Father agreed that she looked quite natural.

A week later Father sat up on the sofa and called for his boots.

"What in heaven's name do you want your boots for?" Mother asked.

"I'm going out to the corral and catch up Ginger and go for a ride along the river. It'll do me good."

Father was not a man to have anyone change his mind, and he did exactly what he said he would do. An hour later he returned, refreshed and happy. But his happiness would soon be overshadowed by the storm that had been gathering for the past three years.

As the Depression grew worse, and fewer guests found their way West to Wyoming, the mortgages grew heavier. I don't know how the rude awakening came to Neal Hart and his family in Canada, or to Bob and Jack Hoxie in Oklahoma, but I remember well that *we* were honored by having the Sheriff of Albany County call on us in person.

"Jack, I really hate to do this to you," Eugene Smith said sadly. "But I just don't have any other choice. The bank has foreclosed and ordered the ranch put up for Sheriff's sale within six weeks."

I can still see the Sheriff and Father, standing together down by the corral gate: Smith miserable with embarrassment, his head thrust forward, his toe poking at withered cottonwood leaves; Father, unwilling to believe the end had finally come, standing straight as a jack pine against a pale April sky.

As Smith took out the papers of foreclosure, he added sympathetically, "Don't feel too badly. You've got plenty of company in this county alone. I've had to do this to so many sheep and cattle ranches hereabouts I figure the bank owns the biggest spread since old John Chisholm's day."

Out of compassion, the Sheriff tacked the public notice of foreclosure on the side of the chicken house, rather than up on the gatepost at the highway entrance. Still, it was a killing blow to Father. At forty-one he saw everything he had worked and hoped for swept away. Although Mother had never really felt at home out here on the ranch, she had fought just as tenaciously as he to hold on to every precious acre.

Ironically enough, one of our last paying guests was Jack Hoxie. He said he had been driving through and heard we had a place near Laramie. At first Father could not bring himself to break the bad news, but apparently Hoxie had some equally painful tidings of his own.

I remember his visit vividly, because at the time I was just thirteen, adored ranch life, and was heartbroken over its impending loss. Mother had asked Jack to talk to me and see if he could improve my attitude.

We rode along the flanks of Jelm Mountain, over the grouse-blue sage, as a dark gray curtain of spring rain blew slowly toward us.

"You wouldn't want to bury yourself for life up here in this mountain country," he said, but I could find no conviction in the way he delivered his lines. "Your folks can find work back in Hollywood, and you can have proper schooling and all the advantages of city life."

If I had doubted what we would do when the ranch was gone, his words made it inescapably clear.

There was a long silence, with only the rising wind jingling our horses' bridle chains.

"I'm going to have to go back, too," he said at last. I looked up at him sharply but he shifted his eyes to the distant rain. "We'll all have to go back before it's over," he added sadly.

For a moment I lost my own self-pity in a wave of sympathy for him, and then he said offhandedly, "Come on, I'll race you to the river!"

7

The Men from Gower Gulch

THE HOLLYWOOD to which we returned in June of 1932 stood in shocking contrast to the little town of a dozen years earlier. From a mere 36,000 citizens, the population had soared to what seemed to old-timers a truly unbelievable 235,000. And continuing the classic tradition of most residents being from some other place, the ratio of newcomers to natives had also risen to astonishing proportions.

As we drove down Sunset Boulevard toward Gower, I marveled at the great heights to which the seemingly tall palms of my childhood had grown. But nearly all the other familiar landmarks had changed even more drastically, and many had disappeared altogether. Warner Brothers' studio with its once dazzling white facade was badly in need of paint. Streaked and graying, it had the melancholy air of an abandoned outdoor set, which in a sense it had become, for Warners' were now moving to a new Burbank location. On the scrubby and greatly reduced lawn, two ugly metal antennae rose skyward, electric bulbs spelling out the letters K F W B. These towers identified the radio station now owned and operated by the studio that prided itself on having pioneered Vitaphone. This system of sound pulled Warner Brothers out of near bankruptcy with *The Jazz Singer,* but it also was responsible for throwing Hollywood into a new industrial revolution.

The big wall around Christy studios, in front of which we

used to park the Franklin, had been torn down and the studio dismantled. The Napoli Restaurant on the corner of Gower was still there, but where Century's clutter of bungalows and barns had once been there was now a huge vacant lot. We were told a devastating fire had broken out one night and destroyed everything — including all the original prints of my comedies.

Around the formerly sleepy-looking four corners there now flowed a steady stream of expensive cars, many of them custommade, with their tops down, and famous stars at the wheel. It came as a shock to note that chauffeur-driven limousines, once the hallmark of Hollywood status and stardom, had almost disappeared. The new individualized carriages purred along Sunset or Hollywood at a leisurely thirty miles or less, expressly so that their famous drivers could be duly recognized by friend, foe and fan, as the case might be. A favorite outdoor pastime of tourists and the naive newly arrived "natives" was strolling or driving along these popular thoroughfares and counting the number of famous faces one had managed to see.

About the only chauffeur-driven limousines around anymore were those that glided up to the curb of Grauman's Chinese on the occasion of a spectacular "World Premiere." Usually these belonged to a studio or to one of the clique of movie moguls who still preferred being driven to and from work every day. After all, what was the use of becoming an American millionaire if it didn't *show?* These successful immigrant Horatio Algers may have been restricted from every WASP golf club in the area except the Hillcrest, but there were other ways to share the American Dream. One was to flaunt their hard-won status by escorting very tall, very patrician-looking starlets to very flashy restaurants like Al Levy's at Hollywood and Vine. These avid young "stock girls" could carry off the satin gown, trailing silver-fox or ermine evening wrap far better than the average short, rotund front-office wife. And during the day a canny producer could still get his money's worth from chauffeur and car alike by letting his wife use it to take her friends shopping at the exclusive new Bullock's store at Wilshire, and to lunch afterward at the Brown Derby's real "Derby" restaurant across from the still-fashionable Ambassador Hotel.

Trying to weather the twin disasters of Depression and sound, the film colony appeared to have split into two opposing camps. Perhaps it would be more graphic to say that Hollywood society now resembled two ships — one a luxury liner with her hull ripped open, heading for the bottom, the other a fast and jaunty yacht, hovering nearby.

The stricken *Titanic* was, of course, the silent film industry, with a passenger list of once youthful and beautiful talents who had embarked only yesterday on what promised to be an eternal pleasure cruise. Now deans and dowagers of an outmoded form of mute canned theater, they found themselves on a doomed ship in a sea of awful change, and aboard her tilting decks all was panic and disarray. Only a disdainful few — those wealthy enough to afford the luxury of professional oblivion — chose to go down with the ship rather than suffer the indignity of rescue at the hands of an alien crew.

The aliens were a seasoned group of sophisticated new Broadway and British actors who had responded to Hollywood's S O S, but hardly for altruistic reasons. They sailed in, full steam ahead, on a seaworthy yacht that a poet might have christened *The Talking Muse*. Keenly competitive, with well-trained voices and a far less melodramatic style than their silent counterparts, they were experts at dominating any stage as convict or courtier, heroine or harlot. While many of the silent stars (graduates of traveling companies) had let their stage techniques rust with disuse, these people were incredibly quick studies, who could commit uncounted sides of dialogue to memory overnight if need be, arriving letter-perfect on the set to deliver their lines in resonant, pear-shaped tones, only faintly touched with what would later be known in the trade as a Theater Guild accent. Their special genius was their ability to make a throaty whisper, delivered through upward curling cigarette smoke, come across on screen as far more sexually exciting to audiences than anything formerly glimpsed on Theda Bara's *chaise longue* or Valentino's couch.

The less well-heeled, if not less heroic, passengers of the dying *Titanic* abandoned ship and everything but their own egos in a desperate attempt to survive. But they soon learned that they would be allowed aboard the hovering *Muse* only if they could drag themselves out of the water under their own power. The crew made it quite clear from the beginning that their presence at the scene of the disaster was in no sense to be construed as a rescue operation. Far from it; the new Hollywood elite rather preferred to keep their yacht party pretty much a private affair. All of which posed a serious problem of survival for the ordinary Hollywood citizen, who, like a passing fisherman in an open dinghy, found himself in danger of being either cut in two by the proud, onrushing yacht or sucked under the waves by the derelict *Titanic*.

Queen Mary still reigned socially, but she and the King shared Pickfair's throne with growing disharmony between them. Her career had been mortally wounded by her first venture into sound films, and a thickening Doug Fairbanks no longer felt comfortable playing youthful, stripped-down athletic roles. Charlie Chaplin stubbornly clung to silent pantomime, as though it were a fig leaf with which to cover his sudden artistic nakedness. Perhaps more than any other silent film star, his vocal problem was compounded by a lower-class British accent, for how could American audiences be expected to accept the lovable little tramp if, when he spoke, he sounded like a Billingsgate fishmonger?

So extensive was the decimation among silent stars that a kind of stigma became attached to anyone who had risen to fame in that now defunct medium. Legitimate theater vet-

Ranger Jack Montgomery and his twenty-one-year-old wife, Marian, descending Arizona's Grand Canyon on the all but impassable Mormon Trail. The year was 1919 and the sure-footed trail horses were "Cowboy" and "Blue," rare exceptions to the usual all-mule means of transportation on these perilous descents.

A scene from an early G.M. "Broncho Billy" Anderson two-reel Western. Anderson is the man in the center, brandishing the pistols.

Jack Montgomery, left, helps cowboy hero Tom Mix shove the bad guys around in this still from a silent Western made at "Mixville" in early 1920.

Jack Montgomery in 1925 when he was doubling actor Ronald Colman in the riding sequences of *The Winning of Barbara Worth,* Gary Cooper's first film. The Mexican horse, "Chapo," later won fame as Rudolph Valentino's mount in *The Eagle.* This photo was taken in an open field that is today the heart of the city of Van Nuys in the San Fernando Valley.

Child star "Baby Peggy" in 1921, as she appeared in the two-reel comedy *Peg of the Mounties.* Her boots, saddle, bridle and hand-woven *reata* were all the work of master bootmaker Joe Posada. The midget Mexican horse, "Tim," stood only thirty-six inches tall.

Three-year-old "Baby Peggy" in one of several two-reel Western satires. Here cowboy extra Jack Dawn shares his Bull Durham and other makin's for a "roll-your-own" smoke between scenes at the Sunset Barn. Jack Dawn later rose to prominence in the industry as head of MGM's Make-up Department.

Above: Art Acord, short, stocky, fearless and a hard man to kill.

Left: Fred Burns, silent cowboy star turned riding extra, one of the most durable and well-liked of the Gower Gulch men.

Left: Neal Hart when he was starring in the "Blue Streak" serials at Universal.

Below, left: Al Jennings, sole survivor of the once deadly Jennings Gang, in his favorite portrait, which he gave to the author in 1932. Autographing his pictures as "The Outlaw" was a source of pride to him.

Below, right: Leo McMahon, playing a Western lead in the late 1930's. When his riding career was ended by a near-fatal runaway accident, he turned to a second career as a screenwriter, specializing in Western films.

Above: Director Cecil B. De Mille (in fedora hat and pointing his walking stick) in a rare publicity still for the silent version of *The Ten Commandments* filmed in 1923. The platform on which De Mille, crew and an actress are shown is set up for the filming of the flight of the Israelites from the Egyptians and the parting of the Red Sea. *Below:* Appearing like a mirage in the desert, the Egyptian horsemen and charioteers thunder across the still-wet sands of the miraculously parted Red Sea. Army riders and cowboys mixed in this dramatic sequence filmed on the Mojave desert.

The durable Hollywood Posse, this time costumed as Arab raiders,
plunges through desert sand dunes. The rider on the far right has
just kicked free of his stirrups as he gives his trained horse the cue
for a perfect horse fall.

An unidentified cowboy takes a dangerous saddle fall, as his horse
unexpectedly stumbles and goes down with him. Note how the rider
has barely cleared his left foot from the stirrup as he hits the ground.

Above: A routine but nonetheless dangerous saddle fall involving two veteran doubles and their equally experienced chase horses.

Left: A cowboy, dressed as a Mexican soldier, executes a double saddle fall with veteran actor and stunt man Yakima Canutt, in this scene from *Zorro's Fighting Legion.*

Below: In a Columbia film, a cowboy dressed as an eighteenth-century highwayman leaps from his running horse to the back of a speeding tallyho. This is probably only the first phase of a favorite triple-stunt involving a fight with the driver and a two-man fall from the moving coach.

Four cowboy stunt men simultaneously executing Running W's — causing their mounts to plunge to the ground while running at top speed. The horses have just had their forelegs pulled out from under them by their riders yanking up on a rigged wire device. Taken during the filming of *The Three Mesquiteers* series made in 1940 by Republic, this still is one of the very few in existence that shows the dangerous Running W in action.

A rare photograph of a dead studio horse that had to be destroyed after breaking its foreleg in a Running W fall. Scores of horses were killed in this manner before the cruel stunt device was formally outlawed by the courts.

He was dead. No more work on location that day. The general attitude was of men ashamed of their jobs. Among the spectators, a woman wept bitterly. She knew the horse well, for it belonged to her husband.

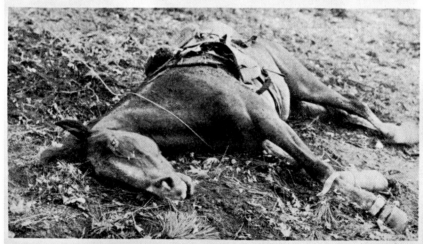

VICTIM OF THE RUNNING W

One leg was broken in the fall and the horse was shot by a representative of the Association. Notice the hobbles still attached to the forelegs and the wire running over the neck.

A blond stunt woman and her male companion throw themselves clear of an overturning buckboard after releasing their team from the doomed vehicle. (This is identical to the wagon involved in the chase described in the final chapter.)

A stunning example of the hazards involved in making a run-of-the-mill John Wayne Western at Republic. With at least four wagons and their double teams involved in this chase, the cowboy driver of the forward wagon has just executed three dangerous stunts simultaneously: tipped his vehicle to assure a spectacular crack-up and fire; released his team to assure the animals' escape from injury; and hurled himself from the driver's seat, clearing the overturning wagon only by inches and landing on his shoulder to absorb the shock of the fall. The slipshod production methods of such low-budget companies can be seen in the web of tire tracks criss-crossing the foreground where camera cars have passed repeatedly.

Cecil B. De Mille, seated on a crane next to his cameraman, lines up a scene on the set of his 1935 epic, *The Crusades*. An assistant (in white shirt and suspenders) signals instructions to the extras on the set. De Mille is dressed in his typical costume, army style breeches and boots.

Above: Saracens and Crusaders engage in hand to hand combat above a deep moat on the set of *The Crusades.* Horsemen charging over a similar narrow ramp were forced off and fell into an identical moat in a sequence filmed on this same set. *Below:* It was in this battle sequence in *The Crusades,* employing hundreds of foot soldiers as well as cowboys doubling as Crusaders, that famous archer Jack Lorenz scored his bull's eye and struck a blow for the Hollywood Posse in their longtime feud with De Mille.

Above: The famous charge sequence in the Warner Brothers 1935 spectacular, *The Charge of the Light Brigade,* starring Errol Flynn. Seconds after this still was taken, the cowboys portraying the British cavalrymen began executing some of the most dangerous group Running W stunts in movie history. *Below:* Their ranks broken by withering enemy fire, the "gallant six hundred" regroup for a second charge.

Above: In this memorable scene from MGM's *Gone With the Wind* (1939), Scarlett runs to the depot to find the doctor for Melanie. Behind Vivien Leigh can be seen the extras fleeing the horrors of war. *Below:* On the boxes of their wagons, two Gower Gulch men are seen trying to keep their panic-stricken teams from stampeding in the melee of recreating the flight from burning Atlanta. In these *Gone With the Wind* sequences, scores of extras on foot shared the dangers of fire and fright with seasoned cowboy drivers and their terrified teams.

"Slim" Whittaker, a veteran picture cowboy, dons the traditional black hat of the heavy and threatens "Buddy" Roosevelt in a typical grade-B Western.

A between-scenes publicity shot of one of the stars of the 1940 MGM action film *Northwest Passage,* together with unknowns who were handling the dangerous stunts and falls. Left to right, Jack Montgomery, Neal Hart, star John Carradine and "Buck" Bucko. The man on the right is not identified.

A successful dude rancher in 1944, Jack Montgomery sits astride his powerful strawberry roan trail horse atop a Colorado peak in the heart of the Rocky Mountain National Park. In rough country such as this, he and other seasoned members of the Hollywood Posse loved to round up stray saddle stock and wild horse herds.

John Wayne leads a band of horsemen into the ruined ranch destroyed by Quantrill's Confederate raiders in a scene from *Dark Command,* filmed in 1941.

In this scene from the fine Western, *A Distant Trumpet,* directed by Raoul Walsh and filmed in 1964, many veteran cowboys were gathered together for the very last time. Portraying the cavalry, regrouping to stand off an impending Indian attack, the old-timers could practically put the scene together without direction.

The sheriff's posse hard on the trail of the badmen — a scene from one of dozens of half-forgotten program Westerns in which the Gower Gulch men rode and rode and rode.

erans often had to put in a brief but needless stint on Broadway in order to qualify in the eyes of stage-oriented producers for starring or supporting roles in talkies. Those who had the good fortune to have spent a few years on the stage exploited that fact to the fullest in an effort to achieve acceptance by the exacting new heads of the industry.

Many New York and foreign-born actors, directors and specialists quickly displayed the same human predilection for garish ostentation as their silent film predecessors had shown for nearly two decades. But side by side with the rich old guard and the acquisitive outlanders, a great deal of highly visible poverty existed all over Hollywood. The violent shift of people who had been on the top of the deck and been dealt to the bottom created genuine destitution and near-starvation. To make things worse, there was neither state nor federal aid forthcoming for those who had not resided in California or Los Angeles for a specified period of time.

The Motion Picture Association provided the only form of welfare even remotely available to the victims of Hollywood's disaster area. Special tickets or coupons were printed and distributed to old-time picture people — stars, directors and extras alike — with which they could purchase food. Certain grocery stores were designated to honor these tickets, which the Motion Picture Relief Society redeemed. I saw both sides of the coin of Hollywood wealth and poverty during the darkest days of Depression, because I was invited to fund-raising events, where my name still had power to attract donors, while at the same time, unknown to anyone but the MPA volunteers, our destitute family was issued books of the blue and red tickets needed to purchase meat, milk, bread and eggs at the Pay 'n Takit market.

The coming of sound had wrought real havoc among the cowboy stars. Movie columnists posted what amounted to a weekly casualty list of silent Westerners who, following their initial struggle with mikes, mixers and the capricious noises of the great outdoors, were picked off by snipers in the front office. One day's rushes was sometimes all it took for a producer to determine that the career of his greatest cowboy star had been permanently spavined by the advent of sound.

Wild West Shows and the small-time circus and rodeo circuits had been crushed by the Depression. Many ranches, which had survived all previous calamities befalling the cattle industry, were dealt the final blow in 1930 and succumbed to repossession and foreclosure. Young cowboys might hang on at home, or seize the opportunity offered by the Civilian Conservation Corps to ride out the hard times on a government subsidy. But for the older Westerners there was no such federally funded holding pen. Once again, the only place that seemed to offer any real hope for beginning again was Hollywood. As a result of all these factors, the early 1930's saw a return of most of the cowboy extras and stars who had left, together with a sizable contingent of new recruits drawn from defunct ranches and rodeos.

Sad as he was over what had happened to himself and most of his cowboy friends, Father was cheered to find so many members of the Hollywood posse back in town. The Waterhole was another victim of change and progress, but John's Café, a few doors down and across the street from their old headquarters, now became the cowboys' point of contact. Close by was Joe Posada's boot shop, still in its original location. Miraculously Joe had come through the past three years in surprisingly good shape, probably because he had never made enough money at his trade to risk losing it in the universal catastrophe.

Two who had never left were Bill Gillis and Tex Cooper. Cooper was younger than Bill by a few years, but still past sixty, silver-haired, six-foot-three and ramrod straight, once a star with the Miller 101 Ranch and for some years a bit player and rider in Westerns.

For the past four years — in fact, ever since talkies had

begun to take over — Westerns had suffered more than other types of films. It was difficult enough to control inside dialogue with microphones hidden here and there on a set, but on an outside location even such simple sounds as crunching gravel, the rustle of leaves and a persistent wind produced insuperable problems for early sound experts. Although *In Old Arizona,* the first of the sound versions of the *Cisco Kid,* had held out the doubtful promise that the great outdoors might be brought under control, it was not until three years later that John Ford's *The Big Trail* proved that talking Westerns could actually be filmed on the assembly-line scale needed by Hollywood to turn the necessary profit. *The Big Trail* proved to be to the 1930's what *The Covered Wagon* had been in the '20s, and John Wayne was the first of a new crop of Western stars who would attempt to fill the boots of such fallen greats as Art Acord.

"What's happened to Art?" Father asked his old friend Bill Gillis.

"Poor old Art's gone under," Gillis told him sadly. "You'll hear folks tell how he was depressed over losing out in Hollywood. But actually, he figured it was just the way the dice fell. He went down into Mexico, and they say he was in some gold-mining scheme and it fell through and he committed suicide. No sich thing, I tell you. What happened was he tangled with the wrong *vaquero* in a bar in Mexicali, a knife artist, and this time he got it in the guts for real." Gillis shook his head. "I remembered that day out at Universal, Jack, and thought it was passin' strange. But y' know, somehow I *knew* that was the way that boy was goin' to go someday."

Neal Hart's British Columbia ranch had foundered, and Neal had come back to Hollywood hoping to pick up his career where he had left it. He made a couple of cheap Westerns on Poverty Row before it became clear to him and his fans that he simply couldn't handle dialogue. Neal was well past fifty, but he was a superb horseman, and he let it be known to producers that he wasn't too proud to do silent bits or even take day jobs riding with the nameless men in the posse. Fred Burns, another once well-known Western star who had become famous portraying heavies opposite Neal and Hoot Gibson, also traded his former status for the privilege of staying alive as a member of the growing band of permanent riding extras. Fred was fifty-four.

Hank Bell, too, had come full circle once again. The new people who had bought out the old place in Cheyenne had taken him on as a steady hand when he left our ranch in the summer of 1929. But soon after they had been forced to the wall.

"With things as bad as they were there I figured they couldn't be no worse back here at the Waterhole," Hank said.

"Is there enough work?" Father asked. "I understand the big companies are shying away from the expense and problems of shooting talking Westerns."

"Oh, the riding jobs have been kinda few, I'll allow," Hank told him. "But some of us boys been workin' pretty steady for Old Lady Ringe out at Malibu."

"Yeah, what about this Malibu place? What's goin' on out there?" Father pressed.

"Well, they say it's goin' to be a swank beach resort. Mrs. Ringe won't *sell* any beach property, but she *rents* it for ninety-nine years at — they say — fifty thousand dollars for the lease. And that don't put a shingle on the place. That's just for the sand and the view. She's into everything, that woman. She owns the Adohr Dairy, which is her daughter's name — Rhoda — spelled backwards. Got a great big tile factory down by the beach, too, with crews of Italian and Spanish workmen. She's built herself a mansion up on the hill that's got real-looking Oriental rugs on the floors — but every last one of them *is made out of tile!*"

"Where'd she get her money?"

"Actually she owns one of the last of them old Spanish land

grants that goes all the way from the Malibu Range right down to the water's edge. The state's been trying to get a coast route through her property as an alternate to Highway 101. But Old Lady Ringe, she's as tough as whang leather and she ain't givin' up one square foot of her grant for passage of no highway.

"She's hired fifteen or so of us cowboys to work as line riders, to keep the road crews off her land at the business end of a Winchester. Nobody doubts but the state will finally win out. But meantime we're makin' five dollars a day, and I must say I admire the old girl's grit. Never liked railroads or highways much myself anyway, and it's gratifyin' to look at them surveyors and earthmovers over the barrel of a good old-fashioned rifle."

Our financial situation was beyond desperate. Not only had we lost the ranch, but all of our furniture and other valuable possessions from our Beverly Hills and Laurel Canyon homes had been sold at auction in Wyoming before our departure. At first Father thought the quickest way out of our situation was to launch an all-out campaign to re-establish us on a ranch — either the one we had lost, or a similar spread somewhere else in the West. He had many Hollywood friends and acquaintances who had come through the Depression in better shape than when they started. Edgar Rice Burroughs, once our next-door neighbor in San Fernando Valley, was awash in the revenues flowing from the revival of his famous Tarzan books in a talking version. But Ed's marriage was breaking up, he had turned his brainchild into a corporation, and now real estate investments in the booming San Fernando Valley were his central interest.

Then Father approached his old friend Douglas Fairbanks, Sr., but at Pickfair the atmosphere was positively electric. The Junior Fairbanks had just married what his father considered an upstart chorus girl, and about the only thing he and Mary Pickford could any longer find to agree on was that the new marriage was a catastrophe. Father found it curious that two such formerly avid troupers as Miss Pickford and Mr. Fairbanks should have moved so far from their humble origins that they found a typically ambitious young actress like Joan Crawford an embarrassment as a daughter-in-law. To add to Fairbanks' disinterest in dude-ranching as an investment, he was seeking solace for his stranded career by traveling abroad and seriously taking up social-climbing.

Lewis Milestone, another old friend, had just pulled Uncle Carl back from the very brink of bankruptcy by winning an Oscar for his direction of *All Quiet on the Western Front*. But Russian-born Milestone was understandably less than interested in going into the dude and cattle ranch business. "Don't call me, I'll call you — " was the universal response.

And so it went throughout the summer and fall, until finally Father realized that a fully financed, all-at-once return to ranching was impossible with things the way they were in Hollywood. The only realistic way to get back the dream we had lost was for him to shed his flat shoes and city clothes, pull on his boots and begin all over again.

Getting work as a riding extra in pictures in 1932 required far more than merely knowing a friend who knew a casting director. No longer did studio stand-by cars pick up available cowboys at the Waterhole, or discover likely doubles at the Sunset Barn. Replacing these outmoded means of getting the riders to the job was Central Casting. This central clearinghouse had been set up by Bert Hampton, himself a former extra. The studio heads paid for the convenience of having a pool of ready workers at their call by funding the salaries of Hampton, who headed the organization, five full-time assistants, and a corps of operators who manned the great switchboard. For four decades it was the busiest switchboard in the Los Angeles area, Central Casting's operators putting through more than three thousand calls an hour. The organization occupied an entire floor in a building on the corner of Hollywood Boulevard and Western Avenue, and at its peak, just prior to the Depression years, there were an estimated 17,000 people registered as full-time working extras.

With the inauguration of Central Casting, the extras unwittingly shackled themselves to a ball and chain from which most would escape only at death — a few others with the subsequent death of the industry itself — the telephone. Mother would not even go outside our apartment to hang up clothes without making sure that either Louise or I stayed inside to listen for the phone. Otherwise an extra job might be missed, for Central's busy operators only took time for five full rings.

Extras could be employed one night and out of work the next. As a result, the tribal ritual throughout Hollywood consisted of sitting down to the telephone every afternoon (except Sunday) around four, and dialing the number Hollywood 3711, at five- or even three-minute intervals. If the line was busy, it meant there was a job in, and the process was speeded up to beat the competition. Often in such cases, one extra would thoughtfully call up his job-seeking friends.

"Jack, I just got a call for Paramount," Neal would say. "They need riders for a De Mille Western tomorrow morning. Better call Bert Hampton and see if you can get on before it's filled up."

"Marian, I just got a call from Warner's — street clothes, rain or shine. Better call Central right away."

The phone stayed literally hot until about eight, when the monotonous act of calling one's name over the switchboard and receiving — after a short pause — the discouraging reply from the operator, "Try later," finally came to an end. When the five or six hundred job openings throughout Hollywood's score of major studios had all been filled, it didn't matter who called their names over the board. The weary operator changed her reply to a flat, "Nothing more tonight, Jack. Everything's filled."

Nevertheless, next morning at six, Father would get up and

call Central, or the studio for whom the casting agency had been filling the job call, to check and see if there had been a cancellation due to illness. Often the reply would come, "Yes, Jack. Hank Bell's car broke down and he can't get out to MGM. Be here in twenty minutes and you can have the job. It's weather permitting, Western street clothes of the 1880's." Weather permitting meant that if the fog was too dense to shoot or if it rained the extras would be dismissed, with no more compensation than fifty cents each for carfare home. Rain or shine meant they worked regardless of the weather.

Families like ours that had been virtually wiped out moved into one of the countless apartment houses and bungalow courts scattered all over Hollywood. These were completely furnished, one-bedroom affairs with a pull-down bed in the front room for the kids, which rented for only $37.50 a month. Hollywood was still a small town, but the cowboys' Hollywood was even smaller. As they depended solely on the industry for their living, they had to live within walking distance or an easy streetcar ride of every studio in town.

Except for MGM in Culver City and Universal out in the Valley, the studio world remained a cluster of familiar baroque-style buildings, within an area not even fifteen miles square. Fox stood at Western and Sunset, Warner Brothers, Columbia, Paramount and RKO were a few blocks to the north and east. Mascot, Monogram and the rest of the Poverty Row independents lay just beyond Columbia at Sunset and Gower. Western Avenue, where Central Casting was located, represented the eastern boundary of the town. United Artists, near La Cieniga, was the western edge. Hollywood Boulevard represented the northern wall and Santa Monica Boulevard the southern barrier.

The industry had almost overnight become a highly stratified and specialized operation. Where back in the days of Biograph and Broncho Billy, actors had provided their own make-up, costumes and wigs, today there was a veritable army of experts in every field: screenwriters, hairdressers, wardrobe people (backed up by an entire department of seamstresses), film cutters, production assistants, art directors, unit directors, and make-up artists, all of whom had come into being in the brief period between 1928 and 1933. Jack Dawn, who had been an old cowboy friend of Father's and had worked extra with me at Century, discovered he had an exceptional talent for sketching and sculpture and had quickly risen to the head of the make-up department at MGM.

Fortunately for Father and the other cowboys who had now swelled the ranks of riding extras from its former seventy-five or eighty to almost two hundred, *The Big Trail* revived the Western as an entertainment staple. Ken Maynard, Buck Jones, Hoot Gibson and even Tom Mix climbed back in the saddle once more, starring in serials or major Westerns. De Mille's cast-of-thousands spectacles had fallen on hard times, and during recent years he had turned again to drawing-room comedies. But with *The Sign of the Cross*, he ushered in a whole new series of religious-oriented epics in sound, which required hundreds of regular extras and often dozens of expert riders.

But whenever the clarion call went out from Paramount's casting office for the riders required by the current De Mille script, Father and the other cowboys responded with mixed emotions. Since the Old Man was never one to take Jerusalem, Rome or Dodge City with barely enough men to do the job, they could nearly always expect a long and lucrative run on a De Mille production. On the other hand, Bible epics almost always required wearing "Bullamania" (from "bole armenia"), the despised body make-up needed to turn riders into Egyptians, Arabs, Nubians or whatever other dark-skinned hordes the sequence called for. In addition, their distrust and dislike were so great where De Mille was concerned that the majority would rather turn down the job than take it. However, this was a luxury the cowboys could rarely indulge.

"Thank God I got three weeks' work lined up over at Fox," Jack Padjan told us one night when a De Mille call was in. "I sure don't envy the boys who couldn't afford to turn the old bastard down!"

Very quickly, then, the cowboys developed into a distinctive group on the Hollywood scene. Although they were notorious for being nonjoiners, they founded in Hollywood an organization that at the time was among the most exclusive clubs in the country. Membership could not be acquired by any amount of money, politics or prestige. The sole requirement for joining was that a man had to have been a working cowboy and trailed a bona fide chuck wagon prior to 1910. The Chuck Wagon Trailers, as they called themselves, paid dues of only one dollar a year, and when their membership rolls were at their all-time high about forty years ago, there were only two hundred and forty-two members who qualified. They got together each spring and fall for an informal "round-up," where they squatted on their heels around the tailgate of a chuck wagon and bolted down the familiar fare of sow belly, sourdough biscuits and beans. Unlike other state or ethnic groups who held state picnics around Los Angeles, the cowboys avoided Griffith Park and Sunland. They favored instead the barren hills of Chatsworth or the flatlands of Newhall. It is not surprising that all but a handful of these men earned their living as riding extras.

Another mark of distinction, of course, was their dress, for they dressed off screen pretty much as they did on. Levis or whipcord straight-legged riding pants, checkered shirts, leather or wool vests, and, of course, Stetsons and steep-heel boots, comprised their daily costume. A cowboy's hat and boots were something far more than either a necessity or a luxury — they were the hallmark of his pride in his profession.

Father always paid anywhere from forty-five to sixty dollars for a genuine pearl-gray or chocolate-brown Stetson at Silverwood's. Joe Posada made every pair of boots for him by hand from 1920 onward, and not one of them cost a penny less than fifty dollars. They were of the finest leather, with a dignified last, stitching and low-keyed design, nothing resembling the *corriente*, thick-soled and square-toed rodeo red hots, that one ordered out of the big mail-order houses in Denver and El Paso. Every riding extra owned at least two or three pairs of these costly "custom-made" Posada boots for everyday and dress, and the same went for his collection of hats. Even the oldest, most battered ten-gallon hat and the most run-over pair of boots had cost the equivalent of a week's wages, and this during the Depression when a dollar was as dear as it was sound.

Like his cronies, Father always dressed from the top down. The first thing to go on as he climbed out of bed was his Stetson, the crown pinched "Wyoming" style to show from whence he hailed. The cowboys were colorful in their native garb, a costume that was as much a part of them as their skin and one they refused to shed for what they termed "civilian clothes." When a cowboy walked onto the average Western set from the street, all the wardrobe department had to provide was a cartridge belt and guns.

Most of the men even wore their sideburns long, in the fashion of the 1880's, so they would always be "in period." There were a few, like Hank Bell and silver-haired Henry Morse, who would never be parted from the long handlebar mustache and the aristocratic white goatee that were their trademarks and served to garnish the barroom background in many a Western film.

A gifted but tragic figure in this group was a one-time Nevada cowman named Curley Fletcher. Curley was tall, weatherbeaten, and in his early forties, but he was going blind from cataracts so he was no longer able to ride. He emerged as a fine natural poet and songwriter, who possessed a genius for putting the cowboys' ideas and language into words. He claimed authorship for the cowboy classic "The Strawberry Roan," and few men could handle Western lingo as well as he.

In one stanza he described in Biblical terms the cowboys'
tendency to fight among themselves.

Since the day that Lot and Abraham split the Jordan range in halves,
Just to fix it so their punchers wouldn't fight,
And since old Jacob skinned his dad-in-law of six years' crop of calves
And hit the trail for Canaan in the night,
There has been a taste for battle 'mongst the men who followed
*   cattle,*
And the love of doing things that's wild and strange.
And the warmth of Labon's words when he missed his speckled
*   herds*
Is still useful in the language of the range.

While most of these cowboys took their lives in their hands
only before the cameras, there were a few among them who
managed to live as dangerously off screen as they did on. One
of the most memorable was a man called Blackjack Ward, who
not only bore out Curley Fletcher's poetic claims that cowboys
loved to fight, but also gave Hollywood a historic landmark in
Gower Gulch.

Blackjack had already been a seasoned rawhide back in 1910
when he had joined Pancho Villa's *dorados* in raiding both
sides of the border. Blackjack got himself named the Mexican
liberator's right-hand man in one of those absurd military alli-
ances that can only happen on a wild frontier under fire. Villa
figured Ward had a lot of necessary American know-how, and
when his forces triumphed, and the illiterate Villa found himself not just a border hero but president of the whole Mexican
republic, it was to Ward he turned for advice.

"My God, Blackjack," cried the dread Scourge of the North,
as helpless as a child. "The goddammed country's bankrupt.
There's not a *centavo* in the treasury. What do I do now?"

What Ward knew about stabilizing a nation's war-shattered
economy couldn't have filled a shell of his .45, but he went at
finding a solution as confidently as a bull at a gate.

"Well, Pancho," he told Villa, "you're running the country now. Why not print your own money?"

"Ahhhh, Si!" grinned Villa. "Why didn't I think of that? No wonder you crafty *gringos* stole half our goddammed country out from under Santa Anna's nose!"

According to Blackjack's oft-told story, Villa promptly ordered the stunned officials of the Mexican mint to print up one hundred million pesos to get the stalled economy back in gear. Blackjack would start out in the morning with two gunny sacks filled with the worthless bills slung on either side of his saddle. He rode through villages inviting the astonished storekeepers and farmers to help themselves.

"My idea was to get the money in circulation," Blackjack explained. "Nobody gave a damn who got it!"

By the mid-1930's most of the cowboys were deeply disillusioned men. Those like Father, who had finally had a chance at ranching and lost it, were in danger of losing faith in themselves. Others who had never had any respite from the grind of poverty felt they had been doubly betrayed. They spent the long dry spells between picture jobs visiting with each other, which in a sense only intensified their bitterness.

After the Waterhole had finally dried up, John's Café briefly became their rendezvous. But because of its proximity to several major studios, they came to favor the corner of Sunset and Gower where, about 1934, they made the Columbia Drugstore their official headquarters. Here, at almost any time of day, one could find twenty-five to fifty of them loitering between picture jobs.

The cowboys chose the drugstore for another very practical reason. There was a phone booth inside. Either the men had no phone of their own, or it was temporarily disconnected for nonpayment of the bill. The indulgent manager of the Columbia allowed the cowboys to place their calls to Central Casting at regular intervals in order to have their names called across the board throughout the day. If one man got a job that way, it naturally started a stampede for the booth that resembled a run on a frontier bank.

Curley Fletcher captured their plight in another poem:

> There's a mixed herd in Hollywood's movies,
> They all hang around Sunset and Gower
> And brother to brother
> They beef with each other
> And belly-ache hour after hour.
> They hail from New York and Montana,
> Some are young, some are bearded and gray,
> But each sorry hand
> Wears the earmark and brand
> Of the range where he first learned to bray.

It was true; they engaged in continuous grousing, for money and jobs were scarce. They grew edgy and quarrelsome, and it was either fight with their wives or with each other. Most wives were like Mother, who preferred having Father sweat out the long periods between pictures with his cronies at the Columbia to watching him pace the floor at home, waiting for Central to call.

"I'm going down to the drugstore," Father said one morning as he took his Stetson from its permanent hat stand atop Mother's favorite floor lamp. "If the studio calls, have them ring me at the Columbia."

That morning Father found things as usual, with about fifty men on the corner, killing time and bravely jingling a few two-bit pieces in their pockets to keep their spirits up. Among them were Blackjack Ward and, as bad luck would have it, Ward's arch enemy, Johnny Tyke. The origins of this feud between Ward and Tyke were unknown to the cowboys, but it soon became apparent to Father and the others that the ancient quarrel was finally coming to a boil.

"You've been fooling around my girl again," the short and wiry Ward said accusingly as he swaggered up to the tall, powerfully built Tyke.

"What makes you so sure she's yours?" Johnny countered contemptuously. "Appears like she cottons up to me."

The babble of conversation among the cowboys died as suddenly as though an assistant director had just yelled, "Quiet on the set!" On a silent cue they formed a circle around the two men, for it was apparent to everyone there was going to be a fight and one of the two contestants was going to have "his hide hung up" in defeat.

"Julie's mine and I'm going to see things stay that way," Ward said icily.

"You better go easy, Ward," Tyke snarled. "You're grabbin' the branding iron by the hot end — "

"Johnny Tyke," Ward responded in a voice as cold as the .45 he suddenly produced from out of nowhere, "there's six steps to hell, and according to what I know of your lousy record, you've taken all six of them!"

At that, Tyke let out a roar of rage and lunged fearlessly for the gun, but Blackjack fired his first shot, catching him in the shoulder and knocking him to the ground.

"That was for the first step — lying," Ward informed the fallen Tyke. And then in a loud, clear voice that every man present could hear, he proceeded to recite his six steps to hell, punctuating each one with a shot. "Two — horse-stealing, three — woman-stealing, four — cowardice, five — double-crossing a friend, and six — MURDER!"

Father said that Tyke heard every word until the sixth and final bullet pierced his heart.

This cold-blooded killing, in broad daylight in the very heart of Hollywood and in the presence of fifty witnesses, brought about the most crucial division in the cowboy camp since the Tonto Basin War split Arizona wide open back in 1889.

"Blackjack dry-gulched Johnny Tyke," my father argued, using an old frontier term that originally meant to kill a man in cold blood and then throw his body in a dry-gulch to conceal evidence of the murder. All of Tyke's friends took up the same cry of "Dry-gulch!" but Blackjack's partisans just as stoutly maintained that he had not taken advantage of an unarmed man. "Everyone knew Tyke always carried his gun concealed," they argued, "so if he got caught that day without his equalizer on him that was just his tough luck."

The court trial was as lively as any ever held west of the Pecos, with eyewitnesses to the shooting split right down the middle as to who was the aggressor. The defense pointed out that, even unarmed, Tyke was a far bigger man than Ward, and that the latter had acted in self-defense. The Ward faction claimed that Tyke had pulled his own gun first and that after the killing his friends had cached the gun, both to pin a murder charge on Ward and to preserve untarnished Tyke's record as a cat-eyed gunman who had never lost a "Colt quarantine" to an opponent in his life. Finally, after a trial that lasted several days, the bewildered jury — which one cowboy described as being "dizzier than a blindfolded bronc being sack-broke with a new slicker" — returned a verdict of "Not guilty," presumably on grounds of self-defense.

Whatever the facts in the Ward affair, that was how Gower Gulch got its name. For many years not only the cowboys but everyone else in the industry referred to the Columbia Drugstore's corner by that name, until long after the man responsible for the colorful label had "forded the Jordan." And, characteristically, as Blackjack Ward lay dying peacefully in bed, he whispered to the old cowboy friend at his side "Bobby, you tell my friends *adios,* and my enemies I'll see them in hell!"

8

A Cast of Thousands

To THE KIDS of my generation, the Saturday Western showing at a neighborhood theater far outranked in urgency and portent any world-shaking event being served up in the headlines by our local dailies. Everything from the Sino-Japanese War to a brazen gold digger's latest breach-of-promise suit ran a poor second in our book to what fate lay in wait for Ken Maynard or Tim McCoy out on the Tonto Rim. And the hallmark of the typical loyal kid fan's devotion to his particular Western idol was his unshakable conviction that "*Nobody ever* doubles for *him!*"

Conversely, however, when it came to the black-hatted henchmen in the pursuing posse, these fans were equally steadfast in their blind belief that all *those* dangerous-looking stunts and falls were faked. "Everybody knows it's done with optical illusions and camera tricks!" ran their favorite argument.

I not only shared the average youngster's addiction to action films, but my passion for Westerns far exceeded theirs because of my singular exposure to ranch life and my having grown up around the very men who had lived the genuine Western experience. But also, having been brought up on the other side of the screen, so to speak, I simply could not remember when I didn't know all about the hazards of breakaway barroom furniture, Running W's, tilt chutes, "idiot bags," and the quite considerable difference between a saddle fall and a horse fall. I knew only too well that Westerns hardly qualified as escape entertainment for the men who made them, and that they would have welcomed camera tricks as substitutes for the hard-packed earth that came up to meet them several times a day. But it was impossible to convince my contemporaries at school that these men executed not only all their own stunts, but those of the stars and principals as well.

The Scythians, the Cossacks and the Sioux have been lauded as the most supremely expert horsemen in history, but perhaps that is only because the Hollywood cowboys have lacked a chronicler. They spent their working days riding stirrup to stirrup, or throwing leather at salty teams of two, four and six up; driving army ambulances, buckboards, Roman chariots, stagecoaches, tallyhos, caissons and Conestogas through flood, flames and over cliffs; jumping, falling, swimming, knifing, brawling, killing and being killed a dozen times a day; riding horses as no men have ever ridden them before or since. Proud, fearless, death-defying men, they went on, year in and year out, cheerfully taking falls and breaking bones, all for the princely sum of from three dollars to seven-fifty a day with a sand-dry lunch thrown in.

Today's average TV viewer does not dream that many a good cowboy was crippled for life or killed in a routine movie chase or charge that takes less than two minutes when rerun on the screen. When such suicidal devices for getting spills as the Running W and the tilt chute were still in daily use, the casualties among horses and riders ran higher in Hollywood than they ever had in the real West. Although the cowboys casually referred to their perilous occupation as mere "picture work," it is better described as Russian roulette on horseback. Probably never in history has any band of men more cold-bloodedly invited death and then outridden him so many times a day, all for pure survival when a call-back for tomorrow held out the doubtful promise of another twenty-four hours of equally precarious "job security."

On the set, these picture cowboys were men of instant, un-questioning courage. If a director asked one of them to bring his pony down off the steepest cliff and do it in an all-but impossible six jumps, he could turn any horse into a cat and bring him down in three, landing at the bottom still glued to the saddle and right on camera. Their natural genius in the saddle had been honed to a flawless edge by years of picture work that demanded split-second timing and the ability to judge speed and distance, width and depth, down to a fraction of an inch.

The cowboy's Hollywood also constituted a sort of unofficial Burial Ground of the Elephants for old-time Western figures. Pawnee Bill settled there; so did Western artist Charlie Russell. Even the original Wyatt Earp, famous marshal of Tombstone, made his home in Hollywood until his death in 1929 when he was rewarded by having Tom Mix and William S. Hart for pallbearers.

Less well-known but equally picturesque figures made life at home every bit as colorful as anything you might see inside a studio. Cowboys were always bringing visitors to our door, colorful characters such as Al Jennings, the last survivor of one of Oklahoma's most dreaded outlaw bands, the Jennings Gang. Jennings was about forty when he dined with us, having spent most of his life since he was seventeen or eighteen behind bars. He dressed in a plain dark suit with stiff collar and tie, and looked more like a visiting Presbyterian parson than a bank robber. (Later I realized it was probably the suit the prison authorities had given him and, considering the times, the only one he owned.)

He had the palest blue eyes I had ever seen, and his thick wavy hair was worn in the style of Rudy Vallee. I think he must have hoped to break into movies, for when Father or anyone else showed any interest in him he would whip out a professional studio protrait of himself decked out in full Western regalia. With a flourish he would autograph it: "Al Jennings. The Outlaw!"

He found a rapt audience in my sister and me, especially after he casually dropped the fact that he had killed his first man when he was only eight years old. This made him a veritable child star among killers. It seemed little Al had been working as swamper in a cowtown saloon, when about dawn a man came in and threatened to kill the bartender if he didn't hand over the cash. Al was behind the bar and the man did not suspect his presence. "I picked up a pistol from on top of a barrel and slipped around the far end of the bar," Al said. "I drew a bead on him and dropped him with a single shot." I gathered that Al cut many more notches in his gun before the big train hold-up that put the Jennings Gang in a class with the James Boys and the Daltons. It also put Al, and those members of the gang who had survived lead poisoning, behind bars until a compassionate President Theodore Roosevelt, pardoned him.

Another mysterious figure, known to us only as "Curley," won our admiration for his remarkable ability to weave and braid brightly dyed horse hair into magnificent bridles and hackamores. This work had to be done with his hands completely submerged under water, he explained. He was also a marvel at making fine chests and tables of inlaid cedar and mother-of-pearl. He was a kind, soft-spoken, white-haired old gentleman, and had a way with children. When I asked him how he had ever found time to master his unusual crafts, let alone fashion so many pieces, he smiled and said, "Oh, I had a lot of time on my hands back in Montana."

Mother knew why, and one evening I overheard her discussing Curley's clouded past with Father.

"I don't think you ought to allow a man like Curley around the girls," she said. "I think he's a bad influence."

"But he's not dangerous, Sharkey," Father argued defensively.

"You told me yourself he's an ex-convict who served ten years at Deer Lodge for *murder!*"

"I know, but that doesn't make him dangerous! Hell, he only killed his wife!"

As for the Gower Gulch men, they constituted a kind of second family to us as we were growing up. It was a family comprised of wise grandfathers, cool and fearless uncles and keenly protective older brothers. At home our apartment was redolent with the mixed aroma of Bull Durham, barn-ripe boots, Absorbine Junior, and the faintly rancid odor of Bulla-mania. Studios provided no such luxuries as showers, so when body make-up was the basic costume of the day, the cowboys had to wear it home and even out to dinner if they were lucky enough to be invited to share Mother's ranch chili, "Depression Special" as she called it.

Over dinner they passed on to us vital information about which chase horse to watch out for on a set — which was cold-jawed or cow-kicked, which teams were runaways. "Nugget Nell" was their pet name for me, because I was then a rangy, horse-happy teen-ager who wrote at least one Western novel a week, ranging in length from ten pages to two hundred. They displayed great patience with my ridiculous plots. Jack Padjan was enthralled by my yarn about ten Mexican *vaqueros* trapped in a gold mine who were discovered twenty years later. My illustration showed ten fully dressed skeletons, still sitting around a card table playing poker to decide how their fortune in gold nuggets was to be fairly divided. "Nugget Nell, that's got to be the goddammedest, longest poker game ever played!" was the extent of his critical analysis.

During the lean years when Louise, Mother and I all had to seek extra work or bit parts to augment Father's uncertain earnings, the cowboys became our special protectors. Being a "streetwalker" (the cowboys' term for extras who worked on foot as opposed to those who rode) was grueling work, but the walking, running, climbing or dancing in the streets dictated by the script was far from being the worst part. For a girl or a young woman, the real agony of becoming a member of the "rabble" was in being paired off by the assistant director with a certain type of male extra, sometimes referred to as a Hollywood lech. Once established in a scene as one's official companion, he was unshakable for the duration of the sequence.

This assigned bore's idea of sophisticated or amusing repartee consisted of all the old tired bathroom, boudoir and sex jokes thought up since the caves. His way of offering a girl her big break in pictures was to persuade her to sign up with his exclusive casting agency — which held interviews for new talent in a suite in the Hollywood Roosevelt Hotel after nine o'clock at night. This type of extra man worked at the studios by day and moonlighted as a pimp. The jobs he could land a girl had nothing to do with a career in pictures, although they sometimes led to more lucrative employment than extra work.

One beautiful but otherwise ungifted girl I knew had come to Hollywood at sixteen and appeared in one picture, the promised prize for having won an obscure "movie star" contest in some hamlet of the Deep South. A year later I bumped into her on a set.

"You're just crazy if you don't take Frenchy up on his offer sometime," she told me. For one unguarded, uncritical moment I thought perhaps Frenchy might be on the square. "Did he make you a dress extra?" I asked, greatly impressed by her transformation from a pretty schoolgirl to a sophisticated beauty wrapped in furs.

"Well, I sure can afford my own dress extra's wardrobe, if that's what you mean."

What she really meant, of course, was that she worked for Frenchy as a studio-employed prostitute. When out-of-town exhibitors or small-town theater owners came to Hollywood, their studio hosts usually provided them with very high-caliber call girls that would have cost them at least one hundred dollars a night without the benefits of the "group plan." Understandably, the procurer of such luscious party favors for the visiting firemen was rewarded by studio brass and kept unofficially (and cheaply) on the studio payroll by being given work as a "streetwalker" whenever a script called for extras.

When one was on the Western or New York street with someone like Frenchy, every dark corner or concealed passageway provided the excuse for a silent wrestling match. Never off the job, as it were, he could sprout four sets of hands, all of them proficient at cracking the combination of any button, zipper, snap or hook devised by Western Costumers. But once established in the background of the star's close-ups, Frenchy was assured of a long run, and no assistant could be persuaded to let a girl change partners in the middle of a job. If she raised a fuss, word managed to get back to the front office that she was being uncooperative. On many counts, it paid to do business with Frenchy.

Getting home from the studio posed another hazard. One extra girl I knew was raped by a family friend, working as assistant director, on the back lot at MGM while being given a lift home. Of all the men you could meet in a studio, the only ones I knew I could really trust were the cowboys. They were chivalrous, protective and very old-fashioned in their respect for a lady. And they had a practiced eye for the other kind. As Padjan used to say, "I can spot a sportin' woman in a crowd quick as a goat in a flock of sheep."

As soon as I arrived on a new set with the usual hordes of extra people, I went looking for a coach, a wagon or a carriage. I knew a cowboy would be on the box, and whether he was personally known to me or not, I knew how to put myself under his protection.

"May I be your passenger, or do you already have someone?"

The cowboy would size me up, jump down off the wagon seat and hand me up.

"Just step aboard, Miss. No need for you to soil them pretty hoop skirts mopping a dirty set with them. I'll just stroll over to the assistant and tell him that you're with me."

"You're with me" said it all. From that moment on it was
understood that he would keep the Hollywood lechers at bay.
When the company was dismissed for lunch, he accompanied
me to the commissary, but we each paid our own bill. If box
lunches were issued on a set, he stood in line for me, got the
boxes and brought them back so we could eat together. If any
troublesome male extra tried to get my attention with dirty
jokes, or suggestions for relieving neck tensions by a special
"studio massage," the cowboy would set down his hard-boiled
egg and listen very intently to every word the stranger had to
say. Soon the man began to burn uncomfortably in the presence of my chaperone and quickly drift away. If I had no way
to get home, my "prairie knight," be he young or grizzled,
escorted me in his car or on the bus or streetcar, and there were
no "shenanigans" on the way.

On one particularly exhausting job (a slave-ship melodrama
of the 1850's entitled *Souls at Sea*), Father drove the carriage
in which the star, Frances Dee, rode to the dock, while I was
one of the townspeople, in bonnet and skirts, watching the ship
come in.

The job wasn't much, although it did last three weeks. What
made it unforgettable to us were the hours. We had to be at
Paramount studio at five A.M., a feat only possible at that time
by taking a cab that charged two-fifty, one way. As we arrived
at the gate the assistant director handed each of us a
voucher — a little white paper slip with our name and the
name of the production company on it. With this passport we
were admitted into the inner studio, men, women and children
all pushing and straining up the iron stairs leading to the make-
up, wardrobe and hairdressing departments. There we shoved
our own clothes into a day locker, individually assigned, and
each received the costume that had been fitted to us the day
before at Western Costumers.

Then another rush into the hairdressing room where fifteen
tonsorial experts matched buns, braids and curls to the real

tresses of women extras. (On the opposite make-up bench, men received sideburns, wigs and mustaches in the same assembly-line fashion.) At five-thirty we started down the iron stairs once more, hurrying to be on time for the buses, five of which were to carry us to our location, the dock at San Pedro, twenty miles distant.

We reached location about six-thirty in the morning, and as we filed out of the bus, the assistant director once more signed our vouchers. Eleven hours later he signed them again, as we boarded the buses for the long drag back into Hollywood. Back at the studio, still another struggle began — up the clanging iron stairs to the make-up benches where, with increasing urgency, weary men and women stripped off braids, buns, sideburns and Van Dyke beards. Then into the wardrobe to peel off the hoops and petticoats, unlock our locker and re-dress once more in our own street clothes. Then the wild stampede down the stairs and toward the front gate, each extra trying to be first at the cashier's window.

The cashier stared out wearily from behind her glass booth. As each crumpled, thrice-signed voucher was pushed through the wicket, she took it and rang up the sum of seven dollars and fifty cents on the register. She stacked a five and two ones on the counter and shoved them through with a single motion, while sending a half dollar or two quarters clanging down the change chute.

After the cashier's window, the most desperate footrace of the day began, this time to be first to reach the single pay telephone booth outside the studio gate. For those who had not been called back for tomorrow, it was imperative that they be able to call their names over Central Casting's board before it closed. Some found work this way, others gave up and headed for the bus or trolley. By now it was nearly eight o'clock at night and we had all been up since four. But the seven-fifty we received covered only the hours from eight to five. The rest — cab fare, time at the wardrobe and hairdressing department, the bus ride both ways — all had been strictly on our own time. And it would be another hour before we reached home, too weary to fix dinner or even eat anything more substantial than a peanut-butter sandwich.

Tiring as the ordinary extra's day could be, that of a rider was far more strenuous and dangerous. Picture work for them was an endless cycle of "pony express" getaways (mounting a running horse), horse and saddle falls, and of course the deadly Running and Stationary W's. The Stationary version Father had first experienced when he worked for Broncho Billy back in 1911. It had been almost entirely superseded by the Running W, not necessarily out of compassion for horses and men, but because the latter was somewhat more flexible and predictable to use.

The Running W took its name from a seldom-used range method for breaking broncs — tying them to a wagon by means of a long line, which threw them if they fought it or ran to its end. It became standard equipment in its far deadlier movie form, and was employed on almost every Western, Civil War epic or any other film where riding and action falls were called for. The devilishly simple Running W consisted of a slender piano wire (invisible to the lens of the camera) threaded along the inside of a horse's two front legs, and then attached to a hobblelike leather strap encircling each foot just above the fetlock. The third end of the wire was run up to the saddle horn where, affixed to a ring that the rider held in his hand, it could be triggered at will. The sole and savage function of the W was to produce hard-hitting horse falls precisely where the camera wanted them. A saddle fall required the rider to bail off his running horse, while a horse fall meant taking his horse down with him. Today, stunt horses are trained to fall on signal, such deliberate falls giving the horse control of his action. The Running W gave him no control at all.

At some spot, predesignated by the director, the cowboy in a chase or cavalry charge triggered the W by coolly yanking up on his end of the line, snatching both front feet out from under his running mount and, in mid-stride, plunging the animal to the ground. The horse often hit with such force that his neck or his back — sometimes both — was broken in the fall. Literally hundreds of horses rigged in this fashion were killed or had to be destroyed during the first twenty-five years of movie-making.

As for the cowboy, it took iron nerve, disciplined strength and an uncanny sense of timing to save his own life when his horse went down. He not only had to clear his stirrups to avoid being crushed or dragged, he also had to dodge the hooves of the oncoming riders behind him, some of whose mounts were also being thrown by W's.

Another horse and man killer was the tilt chute, which was designed to make a jumper out of even the most reluctant horse. An animal that could be made to do almost anything else usually balked when a rider tried to force him to jump over a cliff and plunge into a large body of water below. To solve this, a low wooden chute was built and poised at the brink of a bluff. The floor of this chute was sheathed in metal and heavily greased, making it as slick as ice. A curtain was often installed in the forward end or the horse was blindfolded so he could be led in without a fight.

The chute was built atop a low rocker-type platform, and after the rider had mounted from above — bronc-chute fashion — a prop man tilted the platform forward while another crewman removed the blindfold and raised the forward curtain. Willingly or not, the horse was shot forward into space to perform the desired dive. By splicing the film, it could be made to appear that horse and rider had galloped up to the brink and sailed gracefully off the cliff's edge into the lake below. Unfortunately, a great many horses forced to jump by means of this brutal device hit the water with such impact that either their necks or their backs were broken, depending on the way they landed. Either way they drowned or had to be shot. In such cases the camera would pick up on the rider swimming to shore on a fresh horse, with similar markings to the animal that had to be destroyed.

To a body of men who prized a good horse above rubies, being forced to rig horses with these cruel devices was especially loathsome. But until the late 1930's such stunts remained a part of what every studio boss and second unit director demanded of his riding extras and stunt men.

The all-time record for carnage among picture horses was set in 1935, when Warner Brothers filmed *The Charge of the Light Brigade*. In the historic charge that gave the film its name, the gallant six hundred who rode into the withering cannonade of the enemy were — naturally — cowboys. Father was one of them.

As the charge was planned, the galling fire that was to decimate wave after wave of the attacking brigade could only be simulated by employing Running W's. Father estimated that about one hundred and twenty-five horses were rigged with W's. There were also dozens of individual saddle falls, as the cavalrymen were "shot" off their horses. When Father returned home that night, he was white with dust and hollow-eyed from fatigue, pent-up anger and grief.

"Damned savages is what they are," he exploded over dinner. "I never saw so many good men and horses smashed up in one day in all my years in the picture business — or anywhere else for that matter." Later, he sat down and tried to reckon the damages and came up with something like twenty-five horses killed in action or destroyed after the charge for broken legs. Scores were lamed, and nearly a dozen cowboys were so seriously injured that they had to be hospitalized, some of them on the critical list. Father knew every man. He also knew by sight or had himself ridden, every chase horse that was a casualty that day.

"I've always thought those Humane Society people with

their 'reps' snooping around on every set or location job were a
bunch of busybodies," he raged. "But by God, today every
cowboy on the set stood behind the rep when he set up a
howl."

✳

However slowly the crippling effects of the Depression re-
ceded from other well-known cities of the nation, hard times
hung on the heels of Hollywood with the stubborn devotion of
a lost pup. Barring a few indigenous fortunes (which had
somehow survived the bank failures) and a paper-thin crust of
new-rich stars, producers, technicians and land sharks (who
stayed afloat on precariously high incomes), the rest of us
gnawed on the hard bread of poverty, unemployment and low
wages. This situation continued right up to the eve of World
War II, when the unexpected flowering of the aircraft industry
in Hollywood's backyard brought to thousands of idle, un-
skilled extras their first taste of that stability that only a factory
payroll brings to a community.

Several things contributed to the length and severity of this
economic drought in a region that local boosters never ceased
hawking abroad as Everyman's Paradise. One major factor was
that Republican money remained tight throughout Roosevelt's
prewar terms. Hollywood's original settlers represented considerable retired and widowed money, and they preferred to
freeze their assets than give monetary comfort to the political
enemy.

Several natural catastrophes — unprecedented heavy rains,
floods, broken dams, mud slides and, lastly, the little-publicized
major earthquake — all dealt hard blows to both the morale
and the pocketbook of the embattled Hollywood citizen. Had
the quake, which rocked the greater Los Angeles area at six
P.M. on March 3, 1933, struck three hours earlier, the death
toll among children of all ages would have been appalling. In

three minutes flat most of the schools collapsed into rubble or became unusable shells.   However, the quake itself was nothing compared to the after-shocks of scandal when it came to light that political favorites who had been awarded quake-proof building contracts years earlier had adulterated their structures with so much sand that schools, bridges, dams and many other public works were about as earthquake-proof as if they had been built of glass bricks. For as long as four years after the quake, we children were still attending school in tents and makeshift shacks, while tough-minded taxpayers shot down every shady bond issue local politicians sent aloft.

Throughout this desperate decade, too, Southern California was inundated by ceaseless waves of destitute newcomers, refugees from all manner of troubles, near and far. Some were fleeing Al Capone's Chicago hatchet-men. Thousands of others were driven north from Mexico by President Calles' ruthless persecution of his country's large Catholic faction. Disreputable flivvers, top-heavy with wretched possessions and hungry kids, arrived by the score as farmers fled westward before the devastating Oklahoma dust storms. Uncounted German and Austrian refugees poured into Hollywood after 1933, pursued by the twin specters of Hitler's madness and the proliferation of concentration camps.

This invasion of Austrian and German theatrical talent alone — musicians, directors, actors, singers and technicians, many of whom were relatives of studio bigwigs, created a serious crisis of its own. As a direct result of defensive tactics to keep foreign newcomers from taking over what few jobs were open to Hollywood veterans, the Screen Actors Guild came into power far sooner than might otherwise have been the case. Special work "waivers" were issued to nonmembers of the Guild or Central Casting, supposedly valid for one specific job or picture only. The initial wave of sympathy for the persecuted newcomers was quickly supplanted by hostility, as picture people saw their hardscrabble day checks up for grabs to outsiders who could not speak a word of English.

But the continuing slump reflected most of all the vulnerability of a one-industry town that had suffered a near-fatal convulsion in converting to sound. The silent film may possibly have reached its artistic zenith by 1927, but as an organized business it had barely climbed out of its jerrybuilt cradle before becoming the first casualty of its own phenomenal popularity. At best the picture business had been what the cowboys described as a "baling-wire outfit" — a spread where everything is patched and tied with wire rather than being built properly from the beginning. When talkies forced the picture people to retool their plants they realized, almost too late, that the entire fabric would have to be razed before anything durable could go up in its place.

Not only were stars toppled by this industrywide shake-up; cameramen, directors and even producers were forced to start all over again at the bottom. Carl Laemmle, for one, never did regain the confidence of his backers, who gradually eased him out of his own Universal Studios. D. W. Griffith is the classic case of an outstanding talent who never managed to recoup the limitless influence and prestige he had once held in the world of silent films.

But then, it was not a time that called for greatness so much as for the mere genius of survival. Ironically, many mongrel companies landed on their feet and managed to keep alive on a near-solvency basis by turning out musical shorts and other types of canned vaudeville, most of which could hardly qualify as entertainment, but which somehow found a market with moviegoers who were themselves desperate to escape the rigors of reality. Some producers hit on a salable formula in low-budget comedies of the Thelma Todd–Patsy Kelly variety and the later Laurel and Hardy two-reelers, films that became masterpieces of the slapstick genre precisely because of the financial strictures under which they had to be produced.

But it was the shrewd independents of Poverty Row who identified the real staple of the industry and systematically set out to exploit the American moviegoers' hopeless addiction to

Westerns and Western serials. Nat Levine of Mascot was typical of the shoestring producer who worked out of a small, shabby office much as the saddlebag lawyer of old had worked off his cantle-board. Levine rented everything — stage, camera, equipment, crew, wardrobe, actors and horses — for the run of a production only. Monogram did the same.

These producers stalked well-known actors the way a puma stalks a weaner calf. As soon as his prey felt the pinch of being "between pictures," someone from Poverty Row would appear on the actor's doorstep, pen in hand, to make an offer. The offer was sure to be peanuts, compared to what Harry Carey, for one, had just received from MGM for playing the title role in *Trader Horn*. But the attraction of the independent was not unlike that of a frontier dentist — he relieved the immediate pain, and his work was over and done with quickly. There wasn't much money to be earned on Poverty Row, but what there was could be picked up in a few days or weeks. In fact, so many actors took this route to quick money a saying grew up in Hollywood whenever a large number of people began coming and going through a living room or an office: "My God, this place must be a short cut to Monogram!"

By making the eighteen-hour day his norm and by paying hungry name-actors near-starvation wages, the independent could grind out a feature in two weeks and a serial chapter in about four days. Another secret of Mascot's success was the use of three cameras and their crews. On a feature-length version of *The Girl of the Limberlost* in which I played a role, no actor was ever idle nor did a camera ever get cold. We were shooting at five-thirty in the morning, and while one scene was being filmed another crew was setting up for the next. Actors were rushed from one set-up to another without rest, and with barely time for rehearsal. (At Mascot you were letter-perfect *before* you got to work or you just didn't work!) Lunch was bolted down between takes. We sprinted through that feature-length juvenile masterpiece in five days flat, something of a record even in my book.

With a completely reshuffled deck of cowboy stars, Poverty Row perfected the art of making the small Western pay. In 1931 Fox gambled the shirt it didn't have on its ambitious *The Big Trail*. Luckily they more than broke even, but meantime the Poverty Row boys were daily gleaning the devastated fields of Hollywood talent and harvesting a highly profitable crop by slapping star labels on grade C Westerns. (John Wayne ricocheted back and forth between major studios and Poverty Row for years.)

Their success also depended on their use of as little sound equipment as possible, at a time when rental of a sound truck and technicians by the day represented quite an outlay of cash. They stuck close to the safe, silent film formula of taciturn hero in sight-action situations, and then they rented (at very low rates) miles of "stock shots" from film libraries and labs. These were fast action sequences, chases, stunts and falls, clipped from older movies and then spliced in with the new film in the cutting room.

I saw a classic example of the Spartanism of which these independents were capable on a location job that Father and I visited one afternoon in 1932, shortly after our return from Wyoming. Tim McCoy was making a serial in a lean-to stage somewhere out in San Fernando Valley when it was all still open, sun-drenched country. It was a barroom set, and one side of the building was left open so it could be cheaply lighted by playing silver-reflector boards against the sun.

But on the other side, just to the right of the camera, stood a relic of the early days that was already an antique when I toddled onto my first set at Century — a genuine kleig light. These were backed by heavy metal, and several tubes set upright, on the order of neon tubes, giving off the same gaseous, villainous light that caused the dreaded "kleig eyes" that had plagued actors in the early days. The actinic rays caused severe burns to the eyeball and many actors had to quit films entirely, because the kleigs made them weep ceaselessly on camera and left their eyes painfully inflamed for weeks after

160   THE HOLLYWOOD POSSE

exposure. But Tim McCoy's company was still wringing mile-
age out of this old dinosaur, which had been outlawed from
major studios years before.

It may come as something of a shock to outsiders to discover
that Hollywood was actually submerged in poverty during the
very years it was projecting its most glittering chrome and
platinum-blond image abroad. Millions of interviews and
studio portraits pumped out by studio propaganda mills
(whose mouthpieces were themselves earning only twelve to
twenty-five dollars a week and glad to get it!) convinced the
rest of the world that Hollywood was Camelot, and Beverly
Hills its only residential section, the neighborhood where
Garbo and Gable lived next door to anyone who lived in Hollywood.

Actually there were two Hollywoods, the packaged export
on which our very lives depended, and the real thing, on which
most of us practically starved to death. In the one, Hollywood
was the playground only of the rich — Colbert whipped up a
batch of scrambled eggs for a Photoplay home layout wearing
a gold lamé hostess gown. Stars went abroad only in gleaming
limousines, dining in such Olympian retreats as Ciro's and The
Trocadero, or lolled about their pools reading the Harvard
classics and listening to symphony records.

Barbarians from the outer marches of Monrovia or Minne-
apolis periodically poured into Camelot for the world premiere
of some "greatest motion picture ever made" and fought each
other among the green-lumber bleachers outside Grauman's
Chinese just to touch the guard hairs on Jean Harlow's white-
fox wrap. So much for the packaged export, which was
shipped all over the world, much like Mission-Pak baskets of
California glazed fruit, to satisfy the poor man's sweet tooth.
Now for the real thing.

Some extra people managed to pay their rent with fair regu-
larity, but among a dozen of our close friends not one family
could stay on top of the electric, gas, water and telephone bills

as well. One or the other was always being shut off or "temporarily disconnected." This brought into existence an unspoken
code of conduct that helped us cope with an abnormal situation which, for the time being at least, was our way of life.

If we were the ones whose telephone was working (but whose
water had been turned off), we let the next-door neighbor, who
was without phone service, call Central at our house and she in
turn gave us enough water to make supper. If our gas was off
it was no disgrace to put the makings of dinner in a roaster and
march upstairs to Mrs. Lundquist's kitchen. There we cooked
the meal while Mrs. Lundquist was downstairs using our
phone. The combinations and reciprocations were endless, and
fortunately everyone possessed a sense of the ridiculous, which
made it possible to laugh instead of cry over the way things
were.

Other friends who were not able to swap gas for water did
their part, too, and one Good Samaritan who helped us pay our
bills more often than I can count was Jack Padjan. He had
grown up in a small Montana cowtown with more saloons than
houses, but he said they supported the local undertaker by
fetching up at least one fresh corpse on his porch every Saturday night. Jack was about thirty-five when we returned to
Hollywood: he had finally settled there because the Carmel
Valley outfit broke up.

Padjan loved his friends, a fine horse, a pretty girl, a good
fight and a loyal dog in just about that order. He kept a
beautiful fifteen-year-old stallion in de luxe retirement at a
Hollywood barn all through the Depression, although the feed
bill alone took a week's wages. He also had a big Airedale
named Rusty, a wicked cow-dog that was death on coyotes and
wolves. Jack had worked stock with Rusty for years and had
almost killed a man who accused the Airedale of destroying his
sheep. "Rusty may have killed the goddammed wolf that got
your sheep," Jack told him, "but he won't touch stock."

Rusty was Padjan's shadow and usually ate better than his

master. One night, shortly after Prohibition had been re-
pealed, Padjan stepped into a cheap little restaurant on Santa
Monica and Western, one of those places with checked table-
cloths where they served the new 3.2 beer. Rusty's manners
were irreproachable, and he slipped under the table and lay
there quietly, while Padjan downed two or three welcome
before-dinner beers. When he was ready to order, Padjan signaled the waiter and asked for two T-Bone steaks, medium-rare
with French fries on the side.

When the waiter served the steaks he asked if Padjan was
expecting a friend.

"Nope. They're both for me," he replied with his most capti-
vating smile. Then, when the waiter left, he lowered one
platter quickly to the floor where Rusty set to work on the
steak in grateful silence. But a man dining at the next table
caught sight of this spectacle, turned white with rage and
charged over, grabbing Padjan by the shirtfront and pulling
him to his feet, the table between them.

"How come you're giving that goddammed dog a steak when
there's men in this town don't have enough to eat?"

Padjan never looked more like a Blackfoot than when he was
mad. His swarthy face turned a deep copper, and his usually
kind, hound-dog brown eyes became as icy-black as two
chunks of obsidian.

"Because he's a damned fine dog, he's mine and it's my
money — " With that he threw the table *and* the stranger halfway across the café, and then added, *"That's why!"*

Immediately several of the stranger's friends felt obliged to
finish the fight, while others took Jack's side in the dog-versus-
man dispute. When it was over the little café looked like a
Tom Mix barroom after the big fight, but as usual Jack quickly
recovered his dignified bearing. He gave the restaurant owner
twenty-five dollars toward repairs, and walked out with Rusty
at his heels.

"I didn't take no goddammed steak out of any bastard's
mouth to feed my dog," Padjan stormed at our house later.

"Hell, I didn't go out there to pick a fight. I got no wife, no kids — but no sonofabitchin' Okie can say I ever mistreated a good horse — or a good friend, for that matter."

And Padjan *was* a good friend. He brought steaks to our house when we hadn't bitten into anything gamier than creamed tuna or tamale pie for six months straight.

"Hell, Marian, you can't go out there and cook without no goddammed lights," he'd say to Mother when the electric company had pulled the switch on us. And he'd slip her a five. Or he would come home to dinner with Father after work and find the telephone dead when he wanted to make a call. "By God, Jack," he would say. "You can't untrack in this goddammed town without a phone!" And after he left there would be the sixteen dollars we needed for the two months' phone bill.

And then there was Ella — plain, good, work-worn Ella, who had run a boarding house in Padjan's home town until the Depression broke her. Padjan had brought her to Hollywood, put her up with her ten-year-old boy in a nice apartment just upstairs from ours. Lots of cowboys knew Ella from the old days, but only we knew that Jack was paying her rent. Young as I was, I realized this was a little out of line, according to the cowboy's code of ethics, but Mother, who was moral to her fingertips, took up for Jack and told us it was perfectly all right — if he did it.

Looking back, I realize that Ella was in love with Padjan and would have married him in a minute, but he knew himself too well. "Hell, I'm a ladies' man," he'd say if Father touched upon the subject. "Poor old Ella's had enough hell without marryin' a sonofabitchin' skirt-chaser like me."

Padjan had the kind of wild, savage charm that brought women to their knees. On one location job in Wyoming he met the twenty-one-year-old heiress to a famous female patent medicine fortune who was a guest at a nearby dude ranch. She fell madly in love with him, vowed that all she wanted in life was to be allowed to share his smile and his saddle blanket "forever."

"Hell, I told her the old lady didn't get rich makin' her *lady-forgit-your-pain* syrup just so's her granddaughter could run off with some no-good picture cowboy." Sure enough the matriarch got wind of the romance and threatened to disinherit the girl if she so much as laid eyes on "that Indian" again. Padjan made it easy on everyone by telling the unit director he was sick and getting an overnight transfer back to Hollywood.

About that same time Sally Rand introduced her notorious "fan dance" act at the Chicago's World Fair. "Hell," Padjan exploded when he saw a newspaper blowup of Sally and her plumes, "I worked with Sally on one of those damned Bible epics. I was playin' the centurion who gets converted to religion after spearing Jesus on the Cross. Now that's a hell of a time to throw Sally Rand at you — but there she was, playin' one of the three Marys on the other side of the Cross. Later we worked together on *The Iron Horse*, and I sure saw her on *that* location when she wished she had one of her peek-a-boo fans to hide behind!

"The whole company was on location and everybody including the director come down with a screaming case of dysentery. There was only a couple of old-fashioned outdoor two-holers at the country hotel where the company was puttin' up. Well, one afternoon the rush for them few seats was so great I raced out to one of them shacks and didn't even think to knock. Suddenly, there I sat with Sally Rand beside me. But she never lost her dignity, and God knows she was so bad off *she* sure as hell couldn't leave — nor could I. She just looked over at me serene-like, smiled and said, 'You look familiar. Didn't I meet you at the foot of the Cross?' "

✳

During the early years of the decade the moviegoers' tastes put the extra and the production assistant at each other's throats. The cheaply made bedroom farces with a minuscule cast were what budgetwise producers favored. Comedy seemed what the doctor ordered for a bankrupt nation. Poor people want to see the idle rich at play, said the producers. But if the rich took ship for London and the scriptwriter wrote in a crowd waving goodbye at the docks, studio budgetmen were advised to scissor the extras and show instead the star waving goodbye all alone in a big close-up.

Then suddenly a social phenomenon occurred that turned production policy upside down. The middle thirties witnessed an unprecedented American obsession with the historical novel. Women, whose last touch of glamor had been the jaunty plume of a cheap black Princess Eugénie hat, decided they wanted escape reading and plenty of it. After what they had been through they could only identify with literary heroes and heroines who had triumphed over wars, plagues, earthquakes and typhoons and managed to sandwich in a lot of sex and romance on the side. But being a generation that had teethed on motion pictures, these readers found the printed page only a teaser of what might better be made into a movie, capturing all the passionate, thundering spectacle on the screen. As a consequence, before the studios could even buy the screen rights to such best sellers as *Anthony Adverse* and *Gone With the Wind,* America's reading public had already deluged the front office with letters literally dictating which stars were to play Anthony, Don Luis, Scarlett, Rhett, Melanie, et al.

Overnight the reversal of policy sifted down from the top to the lowly casting directors. Production experts were told to shelve the low-budget drawing-room comedy with a cast of six people, and go heavy on crowds, mobs, hordes. What was needed now was *spectacle* — as De Mille had insisted all along. Second only to the all-star cast (usually topped with Gable and ending some ten credits later with such major luminaries as Lionel Barrymore and Dame May Whitty), the box office magic of the phrase "with a cast of thousands" was what studio copywriters were now told to capitalize on.

This meant of course that as many as three hundred extras

could be required on a single set, and not merely for one day, but for as long as it might take the lions to polish off the Christians, or General Sherman to take Atlanta. Whether an extra called Oklahoma or Oberammergau home he was equally grateful for this opportunity to lose his identity in order to save his life. No matter that callous directors often referred to extras as "rabble." No matter that working conditions were often brutal. The average extra was so grateful to be able to go home with seven-fifty in his pocket at the end of a day that he forgot the insults and discomforts. The cowboys alone, because of their background and the leverage which their particular skills often gave them, remained stubbornly independent. They might take up for the poor extra who had no champion, but they never lost that sense of their own dignity that made them as proud to be called picture cowboys as they once had been to be called top hands. They refused to be lumped together with the cast of thousands.

9

The Code of the West

THE COWBOYS carried with them into the world of movie-making a secret weapon, the very existence of which went unguessed by everyone in the industry outside the clan. A very real and indispensable piece of equipment it was, too, for it enabled them to function much as they had back on the open range. It was known simply as the Code of the West.

Counting no professional lawyers in their ranks, the pioneer cowmen of the 1880's roughed out their own unwritten laws based on the country, the nature of their work, the need to give each rancher a fair wedge of the range pie, and most of all their intuitive estimate of what was best in every man. They were realists and essentially honest men, for out West there was little time or patience for duplicity of any kind. The ideal was that a man either told the truth or kept his mouth shut.

The Code was not modeled after those laws that worked back East. Rather it was something fashioned out of their own unique experience. The number one necessity was to keep a group of fiercely individualistic patriarchs and their herds living peacefully together on the Promised Range. As a result it was a mobile, open, word-of-mouth rule. Like folklore, it was promulgated without benefit of the written word, and was perpetuated in a multitude of ways — in stories over campfires, indirectly through the instructive jest, and passed along by ballad or imitation whenever some unknown "Utah Carroll" went to his death because he chose to save the life of a friend. Virtues such as fair play, honor, loyalty and chivalry that have since been reduced to the hackneyed staples of the Western film were to them untarnished moral values to be prized above the price of a good horse.

This Code worked for the cowmen, far better in fact than the written laws that were later imported from back East, precisely because the latter failed to set the required value on character of the kind possessed by the men who had originally hammered out the Code.

The first rule of the Code was honesty. Not every man fulfilled it in its entirety, but those who didn't live up to it usually lived to regret it. In a vast, mercurial land where a neighbor's concern could (and still does) spell the difference between life and death by thirst, hunger, injury or cold, people did not flirt with promises. The fact that men lived by their word, and measured everything against it in a lawless region where there existed no other form of coercion, speaks volumes for the efficacy of the Code.

Courage was the second rule. Men who chose a life so laced with danger could not tolerate a coward in their midst. A co-worker whose "guts had turned to fiddle strings," as the cowboys put it, only served to increase the odds against them all. If a candidate for the chuck wagon trail lacked grit or had no sand in his craw, he had better try some other trade before he got himself or somebody else killed working at this one.

A grumbler was about as welcome as a Gila monster in a cow camp. The word "tired" was just never used. Until he was in agony no one else even guessed a cowhand was ailing. Death was as quick and common as cloud shadows on the gray sage plains, and doctors rare as rosebushes. A cowboy was expected to laugh his way to death's door and, if necessary, right on through it.

Loyalty to one's friends was the test of a true Westerner. In a country where no one let even a stranger go hungry, only a buzzard would feast on his friends. Another ironclad rule of the Code guaranteed that every quarrel was a private one, and no outsider had the right to interfere. The Art Acord "hoax" at Universal was originally believed by Bill Gillis to be just such a fight. Still more so was the long-standing feud between Blackjack Ward and Johnny Tyke. Outsiders wondered why the witnesses had stood around "helplessly" that day while a cold-blooded murder was committed. Actually, the cowboys were honor bound to do what they did.

Anyone who had the Code written on his heart, as the cowboys did, would have understood perfectly why Blackjack felt justified in killing Tyke for, as he phrased it, he had taken the fatal "six steps to hell," and each step was a flagrant violation of the Code: ". . . the first step — lying, two — horse-stealing, three — woman-stealing, four — cowardice, five — double-crossing a friend, and six — MURDER!" It was tribal, granted. But then the Code was not made for the settlements.

Generosity, without question, the Code demanded. A few saddle stiffs (the cowboys' term for mere hobos on horseback) may have taken advantage of it, but usually they were only riding through anyway, and not a part of the cattleman's culture. Ranch doors were traditionally left unlocked so that a hungry stranger seeking food or shelter from the weather could enter and eat what he needed. A note was left to inform the absent host, and thank him for the victuals; but to leave payment for his hospitality was an unspeakable breach of range etiquette. One was merely expected to repay in kind — or in services — when the opportunity arose.

In Hollywood this part of the Code operated in such a way that even outsiders were struck by the cowboys' touching concern for their own. Workmen's compensation wasn't even a term when most of the Chuck Wagon Trailers hit Hollywood. The studio was simply not responsible if a cowboy got hurt or even killed while performing before the camera.

On one Foreign Legion movie, where he was playing a villainous desert tribesman, Jack Padjan took a hard fall off a high parapet and broke his leg. The assistant director casually struck his name from the call-back list for the duration of the job. But the cowboys rallied instantly. The perplexed hospital attendants had scarcely finished washing off Jack's all-over coat of Bullamania before the "boys" began appearing at the hospital with personal loans of five and ten dollars. But Jack was luckier than most, for the director of the picture, Raoul Walsh, called the Cedars of Lebanon Hospital and arranged to have the entire bill for the injured extra charged to him. And that was as late as 1934.

Usually the studio bosses did not even get word of an injury or death, and if they did, it made no difference in the fate of the victim or his family. But whenever tragedy struck a Gower Gulch man, whether on the set or off, it was the cowboys who automatically went into action. Father was nearly always the self-appointed treasurer in these emergencies. Doffing his big, dark-brown Stetson with its rich cream satin lining, he "passed the hat" on the set, starting with the stars and the director, through the extra ranks and right on down to the lowliest carpenter on the job.

"Can you give something for old Pete's funeral?" he would ask in a tone that was more a command than a plea, and everyone dug down. Among the cowboys themselves there was a special psychology and significance behind passing a man's Stetson for the collection — the take had to at least amount to what the big hat cost its owner or it dishonored them. Desperate as they themselves were for money in those Depression times, I rarely saw a cowboy drop less than a five spot in Father's Stetson, and a "sawbuck" (a ten-dollar bill in cowboy lingo) was considered par. They went about their collections with great dignity, and many times it was just their fund that got the widow and the kids back home to her home town, or kept the rent paid until the sick cowboy was on the mend.

Looking back at the image of Father going boldly and without shame to beg contributions from stars and directors whose salaries at that time were astronomical, I marvel that those people did not burn with shame at their own lack of honor and responsibility. Still, with or without the help of outsiders, the Code stood by the cowboys just as they stood by it.

During the several years we spent ranching in Wyoming, and later in Montana and Colorado, riders were always passing through our place from nearby outfits, looking for strayed stock. Whether by accident or design, they usually showed up just at lunchtime, and Father never failed to invite them to stay. Whether it was the owner himself or some green kid wrangler, Father was instantly beside the rider. "Step down and eat with us. I'll take your horse to the barn while you go inside the lodge."

This was a duty which Father — and others of his mold — normally did not delegate to hirelings. He would lead the animals to the barn, unsaddle them, and tie them in a clean stall. Then he would go up into the loft to pitch down some sweet fresh hay, come back and pour a "shot of oats" (about a quart) into the feed box at the head of the stall by the hay manger — all carried out with genuine concern, and to the tune of lots of "horse talk," designed to calm the nervous animal made jittery by his strange surroundings. Father did not consider these tasks menial. To him it was all a single operation which fulfilled that part of the Code labeled "hospitality."

But one hot August day near Grand Lake, Colorado, Father and I were in search of some missing saddle horses when we rode into the yard of a neighbor's ranch. Our host (a newcomer to the region) was on his shaded veranda with his guests, sharing a cool drink. We walked our ponies right up to the hitching rack in front of the main lodge and Father called out to inquire if they had seen any strays with our brand.

"No, we haven't," the man said, "but why don't you have lunch with us? Just tie your horses up there at the hitching rail."

Without even glancing at Father, I knew the man was committing a mortal sin against the Code by (1) asking us to tie up our own mounts and (2) thinking we would permit them to stand, saddled, under a blazing noonday sun while we took our ease inside. On the other hand I was young and at just that moment felt myself near death from starvation. For one foolhardy instant I thought this rank breach of range etiquette might have been lost on Father, but of course it was not. I shot him a hopeful glance but saw his profile hard and black under the shade of his Stetson. He leaned his elbow on the flat pommel of his Herman Heiser saddle, while his horse played noisily with the cricket in his bit.

"Thanks anyway," he said after a significant pause. "We really have to push on until we find those horses. Besides," he lied, "we packed our own lunch." He touched the brim of his hat with his gloved fingertips, in itself a contemptuous gesture that put the man in the "gunsil" category where he belonged. As we rode out of the gate, hungry and dry, Father turned to me. "I'm sorry, dear, because I know you're hungry, but — "

"Don't worry," I smiled back. "I couldn't get *that* hungry!"

The original Code did not hold cattle stealing in itself a major crime, but weighed it against the circumstances surrounding it. Many small outfits, for example, fighting for their economic lives against foreign land and cattle syndicates, went so far as to make it a part of ranch policy to ask any hand who found a slick calf running with a branded cow to bring it in and brand it. The rider earned the price of a weaner calf in addition to his wages, in this modest poaching operation, but wholesale cattle stealing came under the heading of rustling, and that was a different case.

Slick-eared calves might be kidnapped, but no foreman was so tired of living that he would dare ask his cowboys to steal horses in the same fashion. To steal a man's horse in a country where his very life depended on it was not considered pilferage but premeditated murder. That is why cattle rustlers, by and large, were tolerated as an occupational hazard, while a horse thief brought out a posse on the double. One animal represented expendable merchandise, the other a man's sole means of survival.

The Code was particularly unyielding when it came to caring for horses and riding gear. The cowboy gave close attention to his horse's back — alert for the first sign of a saddle sore or a fistula. He checked his hooves regularly and noted the slightest lameness, translating it from experience into a spavine, a pulled tendon or a graveled hoof. He took pride in his equipment and kept it in good working order. A new saddle rope was soaked in water and stretched between two trees, to limber it up for use. He kept a sharp eye on his saddle, cinch, latigo and reins. He had to, for again, his life could depend on it.

What happened, then, when this idealistic band of men, to whom the Code of the West represented the real and ultimate human nobility, tried to live according to its dictums in a place as self-seeking as Hollywood? Nearly every point of the Code was completely at odds with the values — or rather, lack of them — which prevailed in this world of egocentric, cynical and crafty barbarians.

Here the most successful producers, directors and stars had usually fought their way to the top by destroying their enemies, betraying their friends, systematically forgetting favors, burying the competition in calumnies, and in every sense sacrificing their honor on the altar of their careers. Hypocrisy and character assassination were, one might say, the specialty of the house in Hollywood, where people with Messianic complexes built pyramids to their own immortality over the bones of whatever nobility they might have once possessed. Self-deceived, they lost their real identity and no longer knew who they were, only what they were — a great star, director, producer as the case might be.

But the cowboys felt no shame or disgrace at being mere riding extras. They knew who they were, and they were only concerned with doing their job well and making an honest living by it. It was inconceivable to them that anyone could look down on them or view their lot with pity. For their part, they could feel only contempt for the man or woman who forfeited his most precious possession — honor — in exchange for anything so trashy and perishable as fame.

If Hollywood baffled the cowboys, it also provided them, unwittingly, with what no other place on the face of the earth could have given them — a reasonably accurate facsimile of the very circumstances under which their abilities and virtues flowed. Dangerous situations, perilous speed and split-second decisions were, after all, their meat and drink, and making Westerns — both despite and because of the built-in hazards — created the conditions under which their courage, loyalty and self-sacrifice could be given full play. When a fellow-rider's life was at stake, they went into action with the speed of light, and as though the word "fear" had never been invented. In one of many perilous on-camera but not-in-the-script rescues, a young cowboy named Jimmy Van Horn saved a friend's life by his instant, unquestioning courage. Not even in an old-time cattle stampede could quick thinking have served a man better.

Leo McMahon, an expert young rider from Northern California, and Van Horn were riding in one of those ubiquitous cavalry charges, with about five hundred men involved. McMahon was riding the dangerous point of the flying V up front. They were on location in New Mexico, and as the charge rolled over the plain, Leo's horse hit a badger hole and went down. Van Horn, realizing that seventy percent of the horses would run over his fallen friend unless he was protected, set his own horse on its tail and then swung him broadside to the oncoming army.

"Leo had about as much chance as a wax cat in hell," Father, who was there, told us later. "But Van Horn stood off the first wave of riders until his own horse was knocked down

under him. After that the two boys sort of forted-up together — Indian battle style — behind their fallen horses,
while all two thousand hooves pounded over and around them.
We thought only a blotter would be able to pick those boys
up, but by God, they walked out, brown with dust and a little
bruised up, but all in one piece and miraculously alive!" Only
Van Horn's swift action and heroism had spelled the difference
between life and death for his friend.

On a location job in Arizona Leo had another one of his nine
lives saved, this time by Johnny Judd, who performed what
must be one of the most incredibly fast reactions to danger on
record. Judd was a cowboy who hailed from Indian Territory
in Oklahoma. He was a good, all-around hand, but his real
genius lay in the way he could handle a rope. "Johnny Judd
can do with a lariat what most men can't do with a pencil," Leo
said. He was not only an artist at executing rope tricks of the
usual rodeo type, but he could dab a loop on a horse or cow
under the most impossible conditions with as much ease as a
master angler fly-fishing a stream.

On this particular location job, the horses were being supplied by a local ranch and, anxious to get as much money out
of the company as possible, the rancher had pawned off several
bad horses on the studio wrangler as gentle-broke stock. This
kind of horse is far more dangerous than a mere green bronc
since he has either learned on the rodeo circuit or in the back
corral all manner of low tricks to keep men off his back. Leo,
without realizing it, had one of these spoiled broncs cut to him.
About lunchtime, when the company was between scenes, he
decided to try out his mount and see how he worked, before it
was time to ride him in the fast stuff scheduled for later that
afternoon.

The minute Leo stepped into the stirrup the horse cow-
kicked him (with his left hind foot) then reared in a usually
successful ruse to shake an unwanted rider. But Leo stayed
with him, still determined to get aboard, at which point the

horse laid his ears back and played his trump card — he stampeded. In that second the accident that every cowboy dreads most was happening to Leo — his foot was caught in the stirrup and he was being dragged by a runaway.

Johnny Judd just happened to be nearby, sitting on a nail keg enjoying his favorite pastime, playing with a rope. But this was no saddle rope, just a twenty-foot strand of ordinary limp white cotton clothesline he had picked up somewhere on the set and was experimenting with. When he heard the hooves of Leo's horse he knew by instinct it was a runaway. He jumped to his feet, looked in the direction of the hoofbeats and saw the horse heading toward him. In that split-second Johnny sized up the whole, deadly situation — the distance, the speed of the stampeding horse and the doomed rider, twisting along beside the animal in a cyclone of dust.

Father, who was sitting close by, said he could never understand where that great big open loop of white rope came from, "but it simply blossomed out of nowhere," and just as the runaway pounded past, Judd sent it sailing and forefooted the horse, neat and clean like part of a well-rehearsed rodeo act. There wasn't a tree or a post nearby to wrap the rope around and take his dallies on. Johnny simply planted himself in the earth and took root, his own body absorbing the shock of the horse who, with both front feet pulled out from under him, came crashing to earth. Before the downed horse could even struggle to his feet Johnny was beside him, tying him with a "piggin string" as an extra security measure, while he cut Leo free and helped the miraculously uninjured cowboy to his feet.

"I was just thankin' Johnny for savin' my life," Leo told me later, "when suddenly I noticed his eyes looked glazed. That's when I caught sight of his hands and realized the glaze was tears of pain. I've never seen such rope burns in my life. Each palm had a deep blue valley that cut almost to the bone, and all the way around to the back of his hands, too. Without gloves, without a tree or snubbin' post Judd had simply held on to that rope until his flesh was cooked, in order to stop that pony when he hit the other end, and save my life. How do you say 'Thanks' to a man like that?"

Quick as they were to do for each other in a pinch, the cowboys were notoriously slow to welcome would-be newcomers into their ranks. The initiation of an outsider was the acid test by which the cowboys took the full measure of a man, and the stranger in his turn could judge the degree of respect underlining his final acceptance into the clan. Over the years only a handful of outsiders were able to break through the invisible barricades that surrounded the cowboy's O.K. Corral at Sunset and Gower.

One of the finest of the younger breed was a rancher's son come to live with us, from Sonora, California. Spanish on his mother's side and Irish on his father's, "Sonora," as he was nicknamed, possessed all the good looks and hot temper of both parents. He got mixed up in movies by accident, when his father's ranch was used for location by a Hopalong Cassidy company. The producer insisted that, with his combined handsomeness and prowess in the saddle, he ought to be an actor, but Sonora wanted no part of movies. Finally, however, to shame him into coming to Hollywood the producer put him under contract in absentia and persuaded him to give Western films a try.

"Lord, I was green!" Sonora used to say when recalling his first months in Hollywood. "I honestly thought that what the picture people called a 'queer' was someone who had escaped from an asylum. I made the even worse mistake of believing every leading lady was what her name implied — a lady!"

On Sonora's first day's work as a leading man, the director called the female lead a whore and he sprang gallantly to her defense, literally chasing the director off the set. Then he stomped into the front office, demanded his contract, and tore it into bits. It not only turned out that the director had been quite accurate in his estimate of the leading lady, but Sonora earned the abiding displeasure of the studio boss who had first persuaded him to come to Hollywood. His impetuosity spelled the end of his career as a leading man, but only the beginning as a bit player and riding extra.

A superb rider who had literally grown up in the saddle, Sonora knew horses. Therefore, on his frst day of work with the Gower Gulch men he knew it was deliberate when the wrangler cut him a "lizard" as his mount. But he had a small part in the picture and a little speech to deliver from on horseback and Sonora had no intention of giving the cowboys on the job the satisfaction of thinking he was afraid of a mean horse. As soon as the cameras started to roll and Sonora's hip pocket hit the cantle-board, the horse came apart with him. He charged the lights, the camera, smashed $5,000 worth of camera and sound equipment, besides exposing every foot of film that had been shot that day.

As the bronc finally bucked himself off his feet and landed on top of Sonora, the man who was playing the part of the sheriff ran up to see if the young cowboy was still alive. Pinned under the horse, but still in the saddle, Sonora held out his hand and in stentorian tones delivered his one, well-rehearsed line of dialogue: "Sheriff, my outfit will take that job!"

"I'll forgive you the damages," the amused director told him later. "Any man who can deliver a line of dialogue with a horse on top of him has to be a born actor!"

But that didn't square away matters between Sonora and the Gower Gulch gang who had deliberately planted that bronc as a test. Four days passed, and as the company was on location in the little mountain town of Kernville, California, where Sonora did not know a soul, the silent treatment the cowboys were giving him began to rub his temper raw.

At last, on the night of the fourth day as Sonora sat alone in his hotel room brooding, he heard a loud pounding at the door.

When he opened up, seven cowboys, including the wrangler who had cut him the bronc, came charging in, brandishing two quarts of whiskey and yelling like Comanches hunting hair. Sonora didn't wait for explanations but piled into them one at a time as they came. He polished off Vinegar Roan first, then a wild-looking, black-haired half-breed named Cherokee. Henry Morse, the dignified-looking old gent with the white goatee, was the last man in and it was he who finally wrestled the furious Sonora to the floor, although he lost a good part of his prized beard in the struggle.

"Now, you listen to me, you slick-eared young calf!" Morse thundered. "Me and the boys come to make you welcome. We knew you didn't report to the director about that bronc, and that means you're on the square. Now help me revive the boys you just put on ice and we'll all have a drink to celebrate!"

The cowboys poured enough welcome juice down Sonora that night to float the hotel and Sonora knew that he had come through his initiation and been accepted. The following night after work, they were sitting around Sonora's room in their long underwear (the unseen part of the movie cowboy's costume, which protected the inside of his legs against saddle burns) when someone yelled up from below, "Give us a hand. The saloon's on fire!"

Since it was the only saloon in the tiny mountain town, its threatened destruction was seen as a dire calamity. Without stopping to pull on their pants, Sonora and his drinking companions stepped out the second-story window. "It seemed quicker than using the stairs, especially in our condition," Sonora explained innocently.

Vinegar Roan and Sonora joined the wild-maned Cherokee on the ground below. Inasmuch as Kernville had no firemen, and oblivious to the fact that they were still in their long-handled underwear, the tipsy cowboys commandeered the town's sole fire-fighting equipment, a little two-wheeled push-cart with a hose coiled at one end. They were running toward the saloon pushing the cart before them when they were suddenly confronted by the leading lady and the script girl, and it dawned on the cowboys that they were dressed only in their underclothes. With a yell Sonora let go of the cart and headed back to his hotel room, while the cart plunged wildly down the slope and vanished into the black icy waters of the Walker River.

"By God, I just can't stand here and watch them hundreds of gallons of good whiskey blow up!" Cherokee cried above the sound of popping bottles. He grabbed a short length of hose connected to the hotel's water supply, but the feeble stream was impotent to halt the flames. Finally, spotting a piece of galvanized tin lying on the ground, Cherokee held it as a shield before him and plunged bravely into the inferno, just as Sonora returned fully clothed to the scene.

As a newcomer to the clan Sonora could not be expected to know that Cherokee had one glass eye. Only Vinegar Roan, his closest friend, was aware of it at that time. And only he realized what was happening when, seconds after entering the burning saloon, Cherokee let out a spine-chilling scream of pain and raced out into the cold darkness, still yelling and clawly madly at his face. Pulling up directly in front of the leading lady and the script girl, Cherokee managed to pop the red-hot orb out of its empty socket, at which performance both women fainted soundlessly at his feet. The glass eye poised carefully between thumb and forefinger, the astonished Cherokee looked down at them and blinked. "Now what in the hell do you suppose is the matter with them?"

If the picture cowboys lived dangerously both on and off the screen, it is not surprising that their idea of fun and their practical jokes bordered on manslaughter. To plant a mean bronc was mere child's play compared to what they were capable of coming up with when really inspired. One cold winter night a group of cowboys were working on a studio back lot on a Western street. Seven of the men were cast as bank robbers, the rest as honest citizens. The business at hand called for the seven outlaws to boil out of the bank with their loot, three of them jumping into their saddles directly from the high wooden sidewalk above where their ponies were tied. The other four were to "pony express" their horses from below. It was about three in the morning (there being no such thing as overtime, of course) when the director was finally ready for the take. Although the "outlaws" had only downed a couple of straight shots to keep themselves warm, the drinks did make them just a hair less observing and careful than they might normally have been.

As the camera ground away, the robbers burst out of the bank, made their flying mounts at the hitching rail just below the sidewalk, and hung their spurs into their ponies' sides for the thrilling getaway. But at just that instant every one of the seven riders parted company from his horse and found himself in his saddle, either suspended in mid-air, or thrown violently to the ground. Some went as high as twenty feet before landing back in the Western street.

"Good God, what happened?" the director yelled as he watched the seven horses galloping bareback down the street and into outer darkness.

When the victims discovered the cause of their debacle they were on the verge of committing wholesale murder. Someone, between takes, had slipped onto the set and secured each of the seven saddles with stout tie-ropes to the strong underpinnings of the wooden sidewalk. When the horses took off and hit the end of those tie-ropes, every cinch and latigo snapped under the strain and the riderless mounts made the getaway alone.

It was a typical cowboy prank, one that would have surely injured seven less seasoned riders. But the victims of the joke were furious and they lined up every man on the job, including the terrified producer, demanding to know which of them had rigged the saddle trick. No one confessed, but the following night when the same seven outlaws entered the studio dining room for dinner, they found a case of Seagram's wrapped in black crêpe sitting squarely in the middle of their table. No one knew who had put it there, but a note was attached.

"I've dreamed of doing this for years," it read. "The look on your faces was just what I thought it would be — stupid! It really wasn't worth it. Guess I'll have to think of something else." The note was signed, "Sadly." To this day no one has ever discovered the true identity of "Sadly."

A classic example of a typically drawn-out and risky hoax occurred in the early 1940's when Father and Leo McMahon were on location in a little mountain town in Colorado. The same one-eyed Cherokee and Vinegar Roan of the celebrated Kernville saloon fire were the central figures who almost became the victims of their own practical joke.

At night after work, the saloon offered the only respite from boredom in the little one-horse town. As the location job wore on into weeks, Vinegar and Cherokee especially began casting about for some other kind of amusement than their endless games of gin and poker. One night when the place was crowded with local people, the picture crew and Gower Gulch men, Vinegar and Cherokee stood at the bar putting away more than their usual share of brandy. Observing them from a table in a far corner of the room sat a white-haired old man, obviously a native of the region. He sat there quietly, with only a plain tumbler and a bottle of bourbon set before him, drinking in regal solitude.

Suddenly the conversation at the bar between the two picture cowboys exploded into action: Cherokee knocked Vinegar's shot glass off the bar, and Vinegar reacted by drawing his .45. The ferocious-faced Cherokee replied in kind, and both men appeared to fire simultaneously. Apparently Cherokee's shot went wild, but judging from the scene that followed, Vinegar's bullet found its target. Cherokee let out a scream of pain that Leo said could be heard clear down in Denver, and literally emptied the saloon except for Leo, Father and the old cowman who was taking in the spectacle with his flinty eyes.

Clutching the bar with his right hand, Cherokee surrepti-
tiously scooped up a handful of catsup planted on the bar, and
then did a slow and ghastly turn until he was facing fully into
the room. Drawing away a crimsoned hand he revealed a
gaping gory wound where his left eye should have been. His
expression of unspeakable agony lasted several seconds before
he sank to the floor unconscious.

At this point the white-haired old gentleman rose to his feet
and strode with purposeful dignity to the bar where he confronted Vinegar Roan. Vinegar could see that the old man was
well over eighty; his hands hung loose at his sides like an
old-time town marshal. Recognizing the challenge in the old
man's eyes for what it was, Vinegar tried gamely to fight
through the glow of brandy and his own pent-up laughter to
explain what had happened, but he could only emit a choking
sound.

"The man you just killed was too drunk to know what he was
doing," the old cowman declared in a voice as smooth as silk.
And even as he spoke, the horrified Vinegar saw him brush
back his long black coat, revealing what Vinegar knew simply
had to be there — the worn, oak-handled butt of an enormous
.45 that had probably pacified the entire Colorado frontier.

"In my book that's murder," the old cowman was saying.
"Why not try me on for size?"

Realizing the hoax had gone too far, Cherokee resurrected
himself from the floor, leaping to his feet and laughing, at the
same time mopping away the catsup and reinserting his glass
eye in its proper socket.

"It was just a practical joke," he babbled. "It's only catsup
and my own fake eye!"

Without a word the cowman turned and walked back to his
table, picked up his bottle, and with a look that would have
kindled a prairie fire, walked stiffly out of the saloon. Never
again were Vinegar and Cherokee tempted to stage another
hoax around Cherokee's versatile glass eye.

10

Scissorbills, Streetwalkers and Barflies

IF the cowboys' philosophy and dress distinguished them from the rest of the cast of thousands, their language made them a race apart. Hollywood had always been a tossed salad of languages and accents: Jewish, Dutch, Swedish, German, Russian, British and Cockney, Mexican, Japanese, Theater Guild (an Eastern import much favored by drama coaches) and Deep South (which the same harried speech experts had just successfully beaten out of their Southern-born charges when the rash of ante-bellum movies swept on screen).

What placed the cowboys in a unique category was not an accent peculiar to their group or even a singular manner of bastardizing English. Rather it was because they spoke a *patois* composed of several tongues, each of them rich in imagery and idioms. The Anglo-Saxon Kentuckians turned mountain men, the French voyageurs, Mexican traders and Indian companions of the trail all bequeathed to Westerners a lingo spiced with so many cultures and allusions to frontier life that an outsider could eavesdrop for hours on a group of picture cowboys and never come within acres of grasping the actual topic of conversation.

These men carried with them to Hollywood favorite local phrases from whatever part of the West had been their particular stamping ground. Those from the Northwest — Washington, Oregon, Wyoming, Montana and Idaho — salted their talk with Indian words and terms. Many a devoted husband spoke of his wife as "my squaw" with no offense intended or taken. Feminine make-up was "war paint," and when a woman was angry she was either "on the warpath," or "on the prod." A tough horse was "skookum," while a wild Amazonian-type of female was often spoken of with mixed admiration and awe as being "a real Klutch." (The Klutches were a tribe whose womenfolk had also impressed members of the Lewis and Clark expedition a century earlier.) When a couple broke up or were divorced they were said to have "split the blanket." A horse among this group of cowboys was likely to be called a "cayuse," a pinto was a "paint horse," and a party was properly termed a "potlatch." They pronounced such Spanish words as *rodeo* and *coyote* with the hard Yankee accent so that they came out "*row*-deo" and "*ky*-oat."

Southwesterners and old-time California men, on the other hand, spoke a tongue generally softened by daily contact with Spanish. For them a wild horse was a *mustang*, a pet mount *mi cabello*, the horse herd the *remuda*, while *Quien sabe?*, *gringo*, *hombre* and *adios* fell naturally from their lips. For them a dance was not a "wing-ding" or a "stomp" but a *fandango*. They referred to a slicker as a *poncho*, and favored *reata* over the northern cowboys' twine (for saddle rope), *pinto* over paint. Southwesterners usually favored the Spanish hackamore over the gringo style bit and bridle, especially when breaking in a green colt. Some used the term *sombrero* instead of Stetson.

As the years of movie jobs piled up behind them the cowboys unconsciously evolved a third regional terminology, which developed in the course of perfecting their specialized work in the industry. They coined such originals as "Bullamania" for body make-up, "idiot bag" for the select gear carried by stunt men, and "chase horse" for seasoned movie mounts. By the end of the 1930's, "Running W," "tilt chute," "saddle fall," and "pony expressing" were already classics. Later came such other Hollywoodisms — strictly invented by the cowboys — as "gunsil," "scissorbill," "barfly," "streetwalker" and "calf money," each with a significance indigenous to the Western street.

Jack Padjan used cowboy lingo extensively, and managed to make it sound newly coined. A good-looking girl was "as pretty as a spotted pup," "pretty as a sunset," or she had "a smile like a field of sunflowers." An actress who was over-weight he described as being "beef to the heel," "built like a brick outhouse" or "six ax handles across the beam." One producer particularly despised by the cowboys for underpay-ing actors and extras was immortalized by Padjan as being "tighter than a bull's pizzle in fly time." When he was in a kindly mood he might describe a cheapskate as "a man who'd skin a gnat for its tallow." Once when disgusted by a would-be cowboy's show of cowardice in a dangerous chase, Bill Gillis described him as "shuddering like a dog passin' peach stones." The rear view of an obese woman wearing slacks drew forth his equally graphic comparison to "two fat hogs fightin' under a blanket."

To say that a man was "wiser than a tree full of owls" meant he had garnered decades of range experience. "Crazy as a peach-orchard boar" referred to the hogs that some farmers turned loose in their orchards to eat the overripe fruit. In the summer heat, however, the fallen apricots and peaches fer-mented on the ground and the razorbacks became so drunk from eating them that they would fearlessly charge a man on horseback or take on an entire regiment. "De Mille's as crazy as a peach-orchard boar," my father often said, "thinkin' he can put that many riders on a ramp and nobody get hurt."

Of course some of the old range terms underwent alterations in Hollywood that changed them radically from their original meaning. "Gunsil" in range parlance had referred strictly to a greenhorn or tenderfoot. At Gower Gulch, however, it came to specify anyone who attempted to do the riding extra's job but was unqualified and alien to the clan. In cow country, "scissor-bill" or "peckerneck" meant a cowboy who was lazy, a poor rider, or a careless hand, consequently a dangerous one to work with around stock. In Hollywood this label came to refer specifically to any nonriding extra who attempted to pass himself off to the director as a bona fide horseman on a riding job.

"That damned scissorbill almost killed a good cowboy!" Father would explode if an ordinary extra mixed into the carbolic brand of riding that he knew only a seasoned hand was experienced enough to survive. Such counterfeit cowboys were not disliked for tribal reasons only, but because they were indeed so often the cause of grave accidents and serious injuries. One freak accident that I recall vividly occurred in the making of a film immortalizing Custer's last stand.

"Sure, I can ride," Father overheard the extra telling the unit director. "I've been practicing every Sunday out at Griffith Park stables."

To the Gower Gulch men such "river sand" cowboys (who claimed to have taught themselves to ride by taking a rented horse at a lope down the dry, gritty bed of the Los Angeles River) were more dangerous than a man who had never seen a horse.

"That peckerneck is as deadly in a flyin' charge as a tarantula in a saddle blanket," Old Bill Gillis agreed, when he saw the young greenhorn struggling to hoist himself into the saddle. Bill finally protested to the unit director, telling him the extra didn't know how to ride and was a hazard to the whole company.

"Now, Bill," the unit man replied soothingly, "he'll be all right. You old-timers are always out to borrow trouble."

Father was not one to talk idly about the happenings of the day. That night when he came home from work, weary from riding in charge scenes since morning, he threw himself into his favorite chair, pulled out the little redwood bootjack from its place under the footstool and dragged off his boots.

"Anything happen today, dear?" Mother asked from the kitchen.

"No. Nothing unusual." But just after he had settled down

with the *Hollywood Citizen News,* the phone rang. It was Neal Hart.

"Hell, Neal, you should have been on the job with us today!" Father exclaimed. "There was the goddammedest accident you ever saw." With that hook opening he launched into a description of one of the goriest freak accidents in movie history.

"That scissorbill extra was riding the big bay, Dude, right up in the V point of the flyin' charge. Bill Gillis told everybody the punk couldn't ride, but nobody would listen to him or to me. Well, just as the charge had come to a rollin' boil and the ponies was all stretched out and flyin', that poor bastard's horse picked up a rock and stumbled. Dude always was a puddin'-footed runner, Neal — you know that — but that's another story — Well, anyhow, the gunsil didn't know how the hell to pull Dude up or even how to save himself, so when he felt the pony goin' down he panicked. Bill Gillis was ridin' in the spot just behind him and kept yellin' 'Fall forward — let the god-dammed horse go — hit on your shoulder!'

"But I guess the poor bastard was just too scared to hear, and figurin' he'd need both hands to light on when he landed, he threw away his cavalry sword a second before bailing off himself."

Father paused to light another cigarette, while Louise and I put aside our homework to listen and Mother stood open-mouthed in the kitchen door.

"What happened next couldn't happen again in a million tries. The sabre hit the ground, hilt down and blade upright, and when the extra fell he landed on top of his own sword, the blade borin' clean through him!

"Bill signaled to the men behind him that a lead horse was down, and then hightailed it over to the director to tell him to stop the scene. But by the time they got to him the poor sonofabitch was dead." Hardly pausing to listen to Neal's response to this recital of stark tragedy, Father rolled on. "And that wasn't the worst. All of us had tried to keep him out of the chase, but seems the kid needed the money. So afterwards some young friend come on the set to claim the body and the poor kid broke down and bawled like a baby. Then he told us the dead extra has just inherited a fortune from some relative back East. News came in today's mail, and he'd have been alive and worth a million right now — if he hadn't been buckin' so hard for that sixteen-dollar day check!"

Another "nothing unusual day" occurred when a Gower Gulch veteran was riding in a charge in a Civil War movie. The man's horse went down clean, and the cowboy landed free beside him. Then he picked himself up and sprinted for what — in the smoke and dust — he thought was the safety of the sidelines. Instead, he ran head-on into the oncoming charge. He was knocked down by the first horse to hit him and then run over by several others. Miraculously, he still wasn't badly hurt, and was crawling on hands and knees to safety when he was struck by a big team of blacks carrying a heavy caisson. The iron wheel of the gun carriage passed right over his forehead, scalping him as cleanly as though Geronimo himself had done the job.

"He'll never fork another horse, even if he lives," Father informed Neal that night over the phone. "He was barely breathing when they loaded him into the ambulance." But Father was wrong. Six weeks later the cowboy turned up on another set, an angry red scar knifing all the way from his crown to his left cheekbone, but with all his hair in place, and ready for work. The job? Riding in another cavalry charge!

"Tough as a boot and twice as hard to kill!" was a self-coined term by which the Gower Gulch men attempted to describe themselves. They were, in fact, as nearly indestructible as flesh and blood can be. Hardly a man of them walked without a limp, until the terms "gimpy" and "picture cowboy" came to be synonymous. All of them, including Father, had racked up all the routine injuries at least once — broken arm, wrist, leg, ribs, ankle and collarbone. Merely "pony expressing" a horse was forkéd or dangerous enough that Father once dislocated almost every vertebra in his spine executing such a mount. A studio doctor, with brutal candor, assured him he had cancer of the spine. When he recovered from the shock he got mad, went to a chiropractor and after two sessions was back at the studio "pony expressing" again. Not a few cowboys had survived a broken back, neck or pelvis, a fractured skull and concussion — not to mention such commonplace, but as yet medically uncatalogued, injuries as "bustin' a gut" and "having a horse put his foot through you."

Yakima Canutt, the incomparably great stunt man, was riding a series of broncs in a rodeo sequence on an MGM potboiler titled *Boom Town* when the last bronc of the day proved to be a sunfisher that turned up his belly and went over backward on top of his rider. He drove the saddle horn into Yakima's stomach, churning up his insides better than any eggbeater could have done.

"When I saw old Yak carried off the set with most of his stuffin' trailing after him," Jack Padjan said, "I knew he'd cashed in his chips for the last time." But doctors managed to put Yakima back together again "with whang leather and mare's milk," Jack claimed, and within a few months he was back doing his original and perilous wagon turnover and getaway for which, I was told, he received one thousand dollars a throw. It was worth every dime, especially when the wagon was loaded with explosives and set afire. Yakima went on to devise all of the remarkable stunts that distinguished the chariot race in MGM's 1959 version of *Ben Hur*. These stunts were executed by Yakima's two sons, trained by their father.

Rough as even "straight riding" jobs could be, there were unforeseen elements and accidents, which could turn a reasonably safe and routine location into situations where a man was lucky to get out with his hair still on. Such a location job occurred in the middle thirties in Montana when Jack Padjan

and a large contingent of cowboys were cast as horse soldiers
in still another version of the Custer massacre. Filmed on an
Indian reservation, the picture also employed a good-sized war
party of Indians to portray their own grandfathers' role in that
famous frontier fight.

"Them goddammed Indians just wouldn't untrack," as Jack
related it. "Not even after they was all painted up and
mounted, because they said they just couldn't savvy what the
unit man was tryin' to tell them he wanted. So then I went at
'em in sign language and in my bastard Blackfoot, best as I
could remember. I told 'em we were Custer's men and they
was Sioux and Cheyennes and whatever, hell-bent on driving
us and all other whites off their hunting grounds. When I
mentioned Custer's name some of the elders pricked up their
ears like a horse with a burr, and one old codger got all worked
up and said he had seen Yellow Hair firsthand. By the time I
got through jawin' them Indians it was time to call lunch, so
we took about an hour's break.

"Well, by God," Jack rolled on, "come time to shoot the
battle scene them Injuns all piled on their paint horses, but
half of them was so goddammed drunk they could hardly hold
on to the blanket. They'd been havin' themselves a powwow
during lunchtime over several gallons of whiskey they'd gotten
hold of somehow. They was breathin' smoke. When the director called 'action' you never seen so much goddammed
action all at once in your life. Them bucks hit the warpath for
real, all liquored up and painted and fightin' mad as a young
cow on the prod.

"We men of Custer's command was supposed to stand them
off for quite a while according to the script, but the Indians
was bent on wipin' us all out fast. Their arrows was the real
McCoy and they was firin' 'em at us so thick it looked as if
somebody had turned the wind machine into a mile-high stack
of cut willows. They would have raised our hair for sure if I
hadn't been able to talk enough Blackfoot to convince the old

chief who had seen the original Custer that we wasn't old Yellow Hair's ghost, and his men, come back from the dead."

If the men from Gower Gulch were hell on horses and hard on women, as they claimed, they were even harder on themselves and each other. On a typical rugged location job after riding fifteen hours a day and most of it stunt work, their idea of relaxing was to drink hard, straddle a straight-backed chair and play poker or gin rummy for high stakes until sun-up, when it was time to climb into the saddle for another man-killing day before the cameras.

The cowboys were all inveterate gamblers and wicked poker players. They came by this naturally, too, for card-playing formed the core of their recreation on the old-time cattle drives. "Poker winnings" constituted a vital part of every picture job, and they held many attractions: they were never listed on the income tax, they guaranteed enough of a nest-egg to enable a man to buy into the next pasteboard marathon, and best of all "the missus" need never know who won or lost how much on these far-from-home speculations. The average take for Father on a three- or four-week location job in Colorado, Utah, or Arizona was about $1500 worth of poker winnings. Pots in such games could truly be worth a man's betting his last blue chip on, especially when such prodigious spenders as one of the three Johns — Ford, Wayne or Houston — asked to be dealt in.

Sometimes Father, like the others, referred to such gambling gains as "calf money," meaning that he had earmarked it so he could retire from pictures, buy a small spread and raise fifty or so white-face calves every year for market. A lot of the men shared this undying dream of going back to the tall grass and timber, but the calf money virtually never found its way into the bank. Instead, it disappeared into the kitty of the next big game on a subsequent location job at Durango, Kanab or Sidona.

Once the bugs had been pretty well worked out of handling

sound on outdoor epics, Westerns became more sophisticated
and directors like John Ford and Henry Hathaway began striv-
ing for greater authenticity in an attempt to honestly document
the Old West as it really was and not as movies had so long
caricatured it. When such four-star Westerns began to be
made, the cowboys on the set became the acknowledged unofficial technical advisors to whom serious directors turned for
the last word regarding costume, customs and old-time terms.
When Ford was filming *My Darling Clementine,* he seated
Father and three or four other cowboys at a gaming table in a
saloon sequence where one of the stars was to deal them a
poker hand as part of the action.

Father, Neal Hart and Bill Gillis appointed themselves a
committee to call upon Ford and set him right about the
matter.

"John, in that part of the West at that particular date, gamblers wasn't playin' poker as the favorite pastime," Gillis explained respectfully. "Far more popular was a complicated
game we used to call *Jick, Jack, Ginny and the Bean Gun.*"
And then the cowboys proceeded to demonstrate the game
and how it was dealt. The director changed the script and
even parts of the stars' dialogue in order to portray history as
the cowboys themselves had known and helped to make it.

Similarly, if a horse came on the set saddled with a center-
fire rig — a single cinch — when the picture was supposed to
be laid in what the cowboys knew to be rim-fire country (steep
mountains and trails) where two cinches were employed,
they felt obliged "to raise Hell and put a chunk under it" until
the director changed the rigging to one that was proper to the
locale.

If an actor showed up wearing a Stetson with a Montana
pinch in the crown when he was supposed to hail from California or border country, where the crown was worn in either a
high, straight peak or flat Spanish *vaquero* style, the cowboys
gave the director no rest until he let them set the record right

by recreasing the actor's Stetson. With the passing of the old-timers, such authentic touches have slowly disappeared from the screen.

The term "streetwalker" in cowboy jargon bore no relation to a female hustler. (The older men still referred to them only as "sporting women.") It was a term applied to extra men who worked strictly on foot. The cowboy's scorn for those who worked on foot went deeper than his traditional disdain for the dude. It was rooted in his sense of honor, in his being a cavalier in its original meaning, a mounted gentleman as opposed to the yeoman.

When a job entailed the cowboys' working on foot they did so reluctantly, but never as mere "streetwalkers." They coined the deceptively humorous term "barfly" for any regular cowboy when he had to work on foot in a barroom, Western street or lynch mob sequence.

"I got six weeks on location at Tucson," Father wrote to me in 1953. "It's so damned hot out here that the buzzards run into the campfires at noon just to get in the shade of the skillet. But I'm ridin' old Cowboy and that's good luck for me. Then, after we get through here, I'll have another three weeks at the studio workin' as a barfly!"

The heart of the matter was the same deep-rooted sense of disgrace over being set afoot or grounded. At our ranches I used to watch Father spend twenty minutes making a skittery green colt sidle up to a gate so he could open it from the saddle, when the same task could have been accomplished in seconds if he had only dismounted briefly and done it on foot.

Even the boots they wore were designed to be comfortable only in the stirrup or propped up on a footstool. When the cowboys had to walk or stand a great deal in street scenes, they quickly developed painful blisters and corns. But pride forbade that they should ever swap their heel boots for the flat comfortable version worn without shame only by dry farmers and other such "plow jockeys."

Father illustrated the horseman's pride vividly when he told the story of two cowboys who had come in November of 1909 to the Felix McHugh spread in Calgary.

"It was fall, and there was no work punching cows, but the foreman told them if they were willing to cut poles for fence he had a job for them. So the two strangers rode out one morning, axes over their shoulders, with orders to cut down about three hundred jack pines in a stand of timber about ten miles from the ranch. They come back a few days later, collected their pay and rode on. Next morning we went up to the patch of pines with our wagons and teams to haul the poles down. When we got there we found the poles all right, but we also found a forest of topped jack pines about thirteen feet tall! And I remember how the foreman was cussing when a little cowpuncher from Wyoming looked at the felled trees and the tall stumps and then said squarely to the foreman, 'Hell, it was disgrace enough to have to cut poles — you didn't expect them to do it *on foot*, did you?'"

There was another job the Gower Gulch men were often called upon to do, but which detracted nothing from their cavalier status, and that was driving stage. Any man who could drive six horses up at a dead run had better know what he was doing, and he couldn't be found on every street corner, not even in Hollywood in the late 1930's. There were about three dozen cowboys whose experience qualified them, and they taught the younger and inexperienced men all they knew.

A dress extra might conceivably pass himself off as a rider and even manage to stay aboard a horse an entire day without disaster. But the scissorbill has never lived who could hire out as a driver and expect to survive his first hour on the job. The horsepower bottled up in six high-strung, speed-hungry stage horses has simply got to be felt to be appreciated. When an experienced driver climbs up on the box and takes the four

lines knowingly into his hands, threading them through his
fingers and letting them ripple over the backs of his ponies like
silk floss, he can feel that strength surging up through his
wrists and arms and across his powerful shoulders. He knows
right down to the horseshoe nails how much speed and power
each horse can turn on, and how much control those ponies
expect *him* to have over *them*.

The cowboys were paid sixteen dollars a day for driving a
team of two or six up, partly because of the special skills
required, but also on account of the risks that such driving
entailed. But the ordinary extra of that era working on the
same sets often faced many similar hazards, and received less
than half that wage.

When the mammoth production of *San Francisco* went before the camera in 1935, Mother was among hundreds of extras
who thanked God for the windfall of several weeks' work without interruption. But she soon learned that the earthquake of
1906 was a five-minute lark compared to the months-long disaster on the back lot at MGM. On the street scenes extras were
given no special instructions or chalk marks, but merely told to
"react naturally" to the unexpected and unrehearsed horrors of
this manmade facsimile of the real thing.

The special effects men turned in a performance worthy of
an Academy Award, constructing entire sets electrically rigged
to reproduce the wrenching jolts, the eerie undulation of the
earth and the giant chasms in the street which opened during
that historic April morning — all at the touch of a button.
When one such seam opened soundlessly and without warning
in the sidewalk beneath her feet, Mother barely saved herself
by leaping for a lamp post and hanging on for dear life.
While the cameras ground away, she watched in horrified
fascination as the great chasm slowly moved back together
again, at the unseen touch of an off-screen technician.

Mother thought the worst was over when they were finished
with the street scenes and moved to an inside ballroom set,

where revelers were supposed to be dancing 'til dawn. This sequence was rehearsed, but in the final take, when the dance floor began to tilt and pitch beneath the dancers' feet, the shocks were so great they accidentally tore loose the cables suspending one of several half-ton crystal chandeliers above the set. Extras registered enough genuine panic to satisfy a De Mille, and scattered in every direction as the giant fixture came crashing down into the midst of the scene, injuring one extra man seriously and spraying Mother and dozens of others with a fine mist of pulverized glass. From then on, no acting was required for the jittery extras to go through each scene in wide-eyed terror.

During the same period, Fox made *In Old Chicago*, another historical milestone whose high-point was the great fire that destroyed that city in the last century. Mother, Father and Louise all got work on that job, Father driving a buckboard and Louise and Mother as "streetwalkers." But here again, the ordinary extras found themselves engaged in what almost amounted to stunt work while being paid a straight seven-fifty day check. For several days they were required to work on fire sequences, running down streets while dodging flaming buildings that were collapsing on every side.

Later, as refugees who had escaped the catastrophe, Mother and Louise were assigned a cow and a goat, respectively, and told to work beside their tethered animals in the studio's back-lot version of Lake Michigan. Here they stood up to their armpits in icy water, fighting their animal charges who were just as unhappy over their plight as the two-legged extras. The blazing California sun beat down mercilessly and was reflected off the surface of the "lake." As a result of this, Mother and Louise both suffered second-degree sunburns even as their teeth chattered from exposure to the chill water.

After this grim experience Mother hesitated when Central Casting called her and told her there was a huge call in for extras to work on the back lot of Selznick's Culver City studio where he had rebuilt Atlanta for *Gone With the Wind*. By this time, under considerable pressure from the Guild, Central's operators had begun to announce in advance if an extra would be required to work under any unusual conditions. (No extra pay would be forthcoming, of course.)

"You will work in water," "This is a rain set," "This is a night job," was all that was required. The hungry extra merely gulped harder before he asked what time he was to report for work, but this way he could not claim a stunt check or adjustment from the assistant director on the set, for Central could produce proof he had accepted with full foreknowledge of what the working conditions would be.

For the *Gone With the Wind* job the girl announced in flat, professional tones, "You will work near fire and around explosives." Mother accepted, of course, for everyone knew the siege of Atlanta would last for weeks although the fire sequence was rumored to be limited to one big day.

Mother knew there were several cowboys working as drivers of ammunition wagons and army ambulances, but the minute she arrived on the set and the assistant signed her voucher, she was assigned to a male "streetwalker" as her partner, and given minute instructions for every action. This continued throughout the early days of the evacuation of Atlanta, but as the end drew near, and Sherman's shells began to blow up ammunition storehouses and the fire sequences were underway, it became increasingly difficult for the special assistants to map out each extra's actions. Once again it came down to what it had been on the *San Francisco* earthquake scenes: "reacting naturally."

On the last day, prop men went about soaking every door jamb and window sill with kerosene. Enormous wind machines, which looked like giant electric fans, ringed the set with smudge pots — the kind used then to protect California's ubiquitous orange orchards from killing frosts — placed before them. The smoke blown back into the burning set intensified the dramatic effect and made it even more difficult for the extra people and drivers to see where they were going.

To simulate Sherman's shells being lobbed into the Confederate stronghold, land mines made of dynamite had been planted everywhere, and the assistants warned extras on foot to watch where they were going as there was no way of clearly marking these mines without their showing up on the screen. Then came the prop men with their torches, working with frenzied speed. Suddenly the buildings burst into flame, the wind machines set up their frightening roar, and the incandescent nightmare of citizens escaping their doomed city began. Mother was still on foot, and for a time she had been assisted by her companion of the past weeks. But in this scene she was told to flee alone down a burning street. Dutifully she played her role until, completely winded and unable to go another step, she sank down exhausted on the curbstone. Ignoring the heat of the flames from the burning facade behind her, she was gratefully savoring this treasured minute of rest, when a prop man appeared from nowhere and called to her.

"Move on, lady! You've *got* to move on!"

"I don't care if I *am* in the way," she cried back angrily, not budging from her place on the curb. "I'm just too exhausted to go another step!"

"Please!" he pleaded from the shelter of the burning doorway. "You've *got* to move. One of those land mines is set to go off in a couple more seconds and *you're sitting on it!*"

Mother practically threw herself into the street and began to run again. Just then a team of four and a buckboard rolled up beside her.

"Hey, Marian. Get aboard," the driver called as he leaned down a powerful right arm to scoop her up into the driver's seat beside him. Instantly Mother recognized Handlebar Hank Bell.

"Oh, God, Hank. Am I ever glad to see you!" she cried gratefully.

"Hell, girlie," he said as he sent a stream of tobacco juice hissing into a wall of flame. "Don't make no sense me gallopin' out of town in an empty rig."

Mother clung to the seat as the team gathered renewed speed, too breathless from fear and exertion for further conversation, but numb with relief to be safe at last. Her sense of security proved to be premature, for just then an entire wall of flames collapsed on their right in front of the off leader, enveloping him in a shower of sparks. All four horses screamed in terror, reared and began to stampede.

"Hang on, girlie!" Hank warned Mother as the runaways' sudden leap forward lifted him to his feet. Despite his warning, Mother lost her grip and was thrown to the floor of the wagon, but managed to pull herself upright by grabbing the iron arm of the spring seat. As acres of flaming sets flashed by, Mother pinned her last hope for survival on Hank. His craggy profile, with the long sweeping mustache and his Stetson pulled down hard, were burned forever in her memory. She noticed, too, that he had taken two full wraps of leather around his powerful wrists and was hauling back on the reins with everything he had; at the same time he was jawing away at the leaders, scolding them as though they were children and could understand every word he was saying.

Suddenly the black smoke blinded her, and the loud roar of a wind machine told her they were virtually on top of the whirling blades. She screamed, and shut her eyes against what seemed the inevitable crash. Then she realized they must have passed through the worst of it, for she felt the wagon gradually slowing down. Looking up she saw Handlebar Hank, sweat standing out on his brow, his eyebrows knitted together in a scowl, but otherwise as unruffled as though he had just taken her for a Sunday outing.

Letting the frightened team settle down again and set their own slow pace, he turned to Mother.

"Well, I declare, it's a good thing I picked you up back there on the street. I swear it's worth a person's life to be a street-walker in this business — only safe place on a set like this is a-horseback or in a wagon!"

11

Western Union

UNTIL time and television finally did the old girl in, no eyelash-batting heroine in movie history had been rescued more often by cowboy errantry from the clutches of insolvency than had the motion picture industry herself. Virtually every producer in town, when confronted by a river of red ink, had at one time or another called out the Gower Gulch men to ford it. This crisis was, in fact, so commonplace that it gave rise to the bitter truism among the cowboys: "We've tailed more busted studios out of the red than longhorns out of quicksand, and with a helluva lot less thanks for stretchin' our rope."

From 1930 through the '60's, Universal was salvaged at least once in every decade by such disparate stars as Hoot Gibson and Audie Murphy, who had but one thing in common — the Western. Fox, which had been badly mauled in its struggle with Warners to be first with sound, healed its wounds with *The Big Trail*. Nor did Warner Brothers, whose knack for staying alive in the celluloid jungle traditionally consisted of converting yesterday's headlines into tomorrow's big film, disdain the lowly Western. When such contract wheel-horses as Errol Flynn, Alan Hale and Eugene Palette were not sprinting through Sherwood Forest or sailing the Spanish Main, they were kept riding hard on the sundown trail out at Warner's ranch. Even De Mille respected horse operas, for he shelved the Holy Land briefly while he shot two lowbrow but lucrative

sagebrush epics, *The Plainsman* and *Union Pacific*. Filmed in
the late 1930's, both went a long way toward bankrolling several less predictably popular ventures.

But the cowboys who had pioneered Hollywood's Western
street and were kept busy bailing studios out of bankruptcy
were no longer young men. Most were in their middle or late
forties, and some — Fred Burns, Neal Hart and Tex Cooper —
were well up into their fifties and sixties (although Neal dyed
his sideburns, wore a toupé, and pared fifteen years from his
official age lest the front office ground him as too old to ride).
Bill Gillis, the patriarch of Gower Gulch, also lied to the
casting men, but he was still in the saddle at eighty-three!

Although day checks in 1933 had sunk briefly to three-
twenty and five dollars, prices were comparably low and one
could still manage to buy carrots for a penny a bunch and a
loaf of day-old bread for a nickel. But by the end of the decade
with living costs up once more, Father found himself earning
the same seven-fifty a day he had taken home from Mixville
almost twenty years before.

As the terrible thirties shuffled toward their unlamented
grave, the temper of the average Hollywood riding extra and
streetwalker underwent a gradual but profound change. Gone
was the blind gratitude for any proferred picture job, however
poorly paid or menial. Gone, too, was the bounce, optimism
and innocence that the typical extra had brought with him to
Hollywood from his small-town or rustic origins. The industry
itself still held his unswerving loyalty as the likeliest place for
the lightning bolt of success to strike, but he was growing
disillusioned with his drivers. Yelled at by irate directors,
herded like cattle, and referred to as "the rabble," extras no
longer considered their livelihood the lark it had once been,
Ironically, as their bitterness increased, nourished by a growing awareness that they were being oppressed, the conditions
under which they were forced to work became even more
inhumane.

I myself worked on many street sets where there were no
chairs of any kind available for the hundreds of extras — men,
women and children of all ages. Instead, we were forced to
stand all day under a hot sun, even during the rest periods
between scenes. On one such outdoor set, where crowds of
exuberant Viennese were shown dancing in the streets to a
Strauss waltz, an older woman complained of feeling faint.
When I appealed in her behalf to an assistant, he replied, "Tell
her to just stretch out on the ground somewhere between
scenes, but she better be all right by the next take." Meal times
were at the whim of the director, travel pay from studio to
location was figured in the company's favor, while working
overtime was considered a mark of one's devotion to the studio
and/or one's career, as the case might be.

Under such tyranny even stars became rebellious, aware that
they, too, were being exploited. Newcomers who became box-
office stars overnight — Dick Powell is one example — were
tied to a seventy-five-dollar-a-week salary at their home lot and
were then loaned out to other studios for many times that fee.
The amounts charged in these intramural deals were among
Hollywood's best-kept secrets, but it was well known that the
lenders demanded all the traffic would bear and the borrower
cheerfully paid it, secure in the knowledge that the indentured
slave whose services he was leasing would recoup his investment a thousand times over. The star not only gained nothing
from these loan-outs, but in some cases his promising career
was killed by bad scripts over which he had no control.
Studios paying such high fees for a borrowed star could not
always afford a comparable amount for a top-flight scriptwriter.

But if a star rebelled or refused to work, the producer
slapped him or her under an interdict that was the Hollywood
equivalent of the Inquisition's power. The rebel's contract was
suspended until prolonged loss of exposure to the public, or
sheer hunger, brought him to his knees. If the renegade per-

sisted in his heresy the producer needed only to make a few
"family" phone calls around town and the actor was black-
balled throughout the industry. No studio would touch him,
not even Poverty Row. And this, not for being a card-carrying
Communist, but merely for daring to retaliate against the
studio whose "property" he was.

In March of 1933, the producers had forced contract actors
to take a fifty percent cut in salary. Free-lancers earning fifteen dollars a day had to accept a twenty percent cut in their
meager earnings. This was at a time when less than two cents
out of every dollar taken in at the box office found its way into
the pocket of the actor. Because they had no union to protect
them, actors were forced to submit to these cuts. But three
months later a group of six name players presided over the
birth of the Screen Actors Guild. Although it later became the
strong man of Hollywood, the Guild was born a weak and
sickly child who found it difficult to reach maturity in a climate traditionally hostile to any form of unionization.

It was the legal strength of the Humane Society that first
impressed the cowboys and won their cooperation in banding
together against the studios on behalf of horses. The Society
was a veteran scrapper and enjoyed a unique position of considerable power and nationwide prestige. It didn't count for
much in Hollywood, but it was still more than the cowboys
had going for them. In a nation distinguished for its sentimental kindness to animals, only matters of sex and religion
could provoke a stronger public response from moviegoers than
to be told helpless horses were being crippled and killed at
studios every day, merely for the sake of providing audience
thrills.

What handicapped both the Society and the cowboys in
their efforts to bring public pressure to bear on the studios was
their inability to get their message out to the people. Studio
brass and the heads of newspapers had the Los Angeles news
media pretty well sewed up. Not even a crusading journalist

would have dared lay his paper open to the wrath of a rampant
Louis B. Mayer, or a fire-eating Jack Warner, by printing a
shocking exposé of animal abuse on a Hollywood set. Even
assuming an individual cowboy had succeeded in getting his
story printed by some fearless reporter, he knew the price he
would have to pay. In retaliation, Central Casting would deliver him over to the torments of a silent telephone and a
jobless future; every studio gate in town would be automatically closed to him forever. Studios, like families, may have
quarreled among themselves, but here they could be counted
on to close ranks. The blacklist was Hollywood's supreme and
ultimate weapon.

A breakthrough came when the Society finally won a suit
against Warner Brothers over the carnage involved in making
The Charge of the Light Brigade. When it became apparent
that Running W's and tilt-chutes would eventually be outlawed by the courts, studios empowered their assistants to
negotiate "adjustments" on the set. What was euphemistically
termed "straight riding" paid seven-fifty, while a three or five
dollar "adjustment" was standard for a "simple" horse fall.
Now assistants began luring the cowboys with offers of as high
as twenty-five dollars each for Running W's. In most cases it
proved irresistible bait to a family man with only an occasional riding job coming his way. These adjustment checks,
which began to be offered with increasing frequency, did not
reflect any sudden outpouring of the milk of human kindness
on the part of the studios. Rather the "adjustment" represented
a positive reaction to a dread plague against which producers
had fought from the very inception of the industry.

To the average producer, unionization was a kind of tribal
nightmare that gave him bleeding ulcers by day and troubled
his dreams at night. As far back as 1923, when De Mille was
mounting *The Ten Commandments,* he had fired the outstanding cameraman, Alvin Wyckoff, who had been with him for ten
years and almost as many pictures, solely because Wyckoff was

involved in organizing a cameramen's union. "Get Franken-
stein's monster off the wall!" was a familiar command to increase the light when electricians were lighting a set. But the
producers knew in their hearts that the shadow of unionization
on their studio wall was a threat that only less light, not more,
could erase. Every demand for better working conditions,
hours or pay was met with increasing resistance. The front
office knew only too well the havoc that unions could wreak on
their captive kingdoms if they ever gained positions of control.

Carpenters, electricians, cameramen, hairdressers, make-up
men, the lowly property men, or "grips" as they were called, as
well as the cowboys and extras, had labored long and uncom-
plainingly in the boiler room of the industry, so that studios
might stay afloat and reap the profits earned by carrying the
"product" to distant ports. Now the sweating stokers who had
enriched their masters began to demand the same blessings of
union strength already being enjoyed by such humble souls as
coal miners, auto workers and Pullman porters.

Sandwiched between the top and bottom levels of the industry, which were both in their own ways undergoing token
unionization, were the extra people and the cowboys. Extras
looked to the stars for political leadership, fully aware that the
stars were prepared to pool their box office strength and had
even threatened to paralyze the industry with a general strike,
if it appeared the only way to gain their goals. The extras felt
confident that any privileges wrested from the monarchists at
the Bel Air Bastilles would eventually sift down to the Jaco-
bins manning the barricades at Sunset Boulevard.

The cowboys, however, could not identify with any of the
groups engaged in labor's fight with studio capitalists. Only a
handful of stars and directors did they consider friends, and
those were understandably Western in their background and
interests. Streetwalkers, who were traditionally avid fans of
the stars and the industry, baffled the cowboys with their
paradoxical sense of values. Carpenters and other crew mem-

bers were equally alien allies, for as a group they espoused all the constraining, blue-collar values against which the cowboys had been protesting when they rejected urban society and went West. Strangers to almost everyone in Hollywood except each other, loners by nature and welded together by a tribal code that set them apart from other men, the cowboys responded to the labor challenge of their day in their own distinctive manner.

"I wouldn't trust unions as far as I could throw a steer," Father said darkly. Neal Hart was equally cynical in his appraisal.

"It's just another way of getting control of a man's life and income," Neal argued one evening when he, Curley Fletcher and Jack Padjan dropped by our apartment. "Even this 'Social Security' thing Roosevelt has come up with is dangerous. I don't believe you can reduce a man's character to a number on a card. And the questionnaires they send around to fill out to make a man eligible! Why, it's un-American."

"The Guild could help us, though, Neal," Father said. "It's not like an ordinary union. It's people in the industry like ourselves. If the stars get in the saddle and can put a ring in the producers' noses, they'll get what they want."

"I don't see how that's goin' to give us any leverage," Jack contested.

"It could, if we'd organize on our own," Curley Fletcher put in. "We need an organization just for ourselves. We don't have any of the stars' problems and we don't need their help."

"You're right," Padjan agreed. "No star is ever gonna untrack for no goddammed picture cowboy. Their Code of the West is 'I've got mine!' "

"But we've reduced our Code to that, too, Padjan, when we accept adjustment checks for less than what everyone agrees is a fair price."

The controversy pro and con the union movement raged for several weeks that spring. It was carried on over the telephone, on the set, over dinner tables like ours and, of course, in front of the Columbia Drugstore. Gradually the ferment among the cowboys evolved into a meeting with the purpose of forming their own distinctive labor union. This first session was scheduled to be held in a small rented hall on lower Sunset Boulevard, near Olive Hill, but at the last minute it was moved by common vote to Gower Gulch.

It was a pleasant April evening and passers-by paid little attention to the cowboys as they drifted down Sunset and strolled in from neighboring avenues. In the pool of yellow light shed by the street lamp in front of the Columbia, nearly two hundred and fifty men crowded the sidewalk. The speakers took turns addressing the assembly from atop an apple box that served as platform and podium.

"What we need is an organization of cowboys, existing for the good of the cowboys and for which riding extras will be willing to make some sacrifices of their own," the first speaker told them.

"For example," he went on, "when an assistant offers any of you men two-fifty or three dollars for a saddle fall, it's your duty to your union to refuse it."

"What do you think a saddle fall should be worth?" Curley Fletcher asked from the crowd.

"I don't think anybody should do one for less than five dollars," the speaker insisted. "If we all hold out for five, we'll set a standard and force the studio to pay it, or they don't get no fall — not from nobody, and not for a dollar less!"

That, of course, is where the boot pinched. With times still as hard as they were, who could afford to hold out for five dollars and then run the risk that the next man to whom the assistant made his offer would do it for only three?

Then Artie Ortega spoke up. "Did you hear what we Indians managed to get with our organization?" Artie was a short, stocky California Indian who hailed from Weed, and had been a co-star in very early silents with his wife, Mona Darkfeather, who was much-publicized as an Indian princess. He had since become a riding extra as well as one of Father's closest friends. He was very popular among all the cowboys.

"I heard the Indians was tryin' to organize, too. What were you able to get out of it?" asked half-Indian Jack Padjan.

"Well, on *The Man of Conquest* set some of our people were told to use sign language in a scene, and when we did, we asked for a full speaking part adjustment. After all, talk's talk, however you say it. Well, the studio refused, so we went in a body up to the Screen Actors Guild and they ruled in our favor and our people got paid what they deserved. Now we're pushin' for sixteen-fifty a day, if we wear our own native costumes, and we're going to get it, too, because we've already wrung that rate out of De Mille on *Union Pacific*."

"God knows, that's gettin' blood out of a turnip!" someone laughed.

Still, the first meeting closed in an uproar of dissenting voices. The only thing the two hundred and fifty men agreed upon that night was the name of their outfit — The Riding Actors Association.

Subsequent meetings were equally uproarious. Such touchy matters were raised as could a cowboy be suspended for playing cards on the set. Who in his right mind could vote "yes" on a rule like that? Should one member of the Association report another if he knows he is sneaking a couple of drinks on the set? One Chuck Wagon Trailer quoted the old range law, "No whiskey with the wagon," to support his point, but it was generally agreed that sooner or later every member would be up for a fine on that count. As for reporting such infractions, it was against their Code to engage in tale-bearing of that sort, even if it was supposedly for the good of the Association.

The leaders of the group tried circulating a questionnaire so as to categorize their potential membership, but this led to mutiny. The cowboys still adhered to the old adage that no one asks my name or where I came from unless he intends to back up his curiosity with his .45. They considered their average income (minuscule though it was for most of them) strictly their own affair. Also requested were such unpublic facts as whether a member was married or living in a common-law arrangement. Men who could ask such questions weren't to be trusted with the answers! To no one's surprise, the whole Riding Actor's Association fell apart like a rotten saddle in a rain storm after only a few tumultuous weeks of meetings and membership drives.

A simultaneous battle the cowboys had to fight was that with the barns who, in the long period from the mid-1930's through the 1960's, supplied studios with horses, saddles, wagons, stagecoaches and all the other special gear needed to put horsemen and drivers on a picture job. They also provided wranglers and special animal handlers. The friction between the cowboys and the barn men had increased over the years, as had the number of serious accidents linked to worn-out equipment.

The days when a Universal studio or a Mixville kept their own horse herds and tack rooms were already a fond memory by the time Harry Sherman was making his Hopalong series. The many livery barns and stables that had started out supplying mounts and equipment had been narrowed down to about three major outfits by 1940. "Fat" Jones's place at Griffith Park was perhaps the most successful.

The barns had a thoroughly unenviable job. They had to feed, house and keep in working condition a vast number of tough, experienced picture horses, veteran animals, yet still young enough to do the job. Feed was never cheap, blacksmiths' fees climbed steadily, land values around the Griffith Park area, after a severe slump, rose to the point where it was no longer an economical location for the barns. Still, Jones and his counterparts had to stay close to Hollywood and San Fernando Valley where the majority of the action took place. Some studios shooting program Westerns went regularly to Lone Pine, about two hundred miles north of Hollywood.

There, local ranchers took care of location companies' stock and equipment needs, and usually charged lower rental fees.

For a long while Father and his friends believed the barns and their personnel were just plain careless; later, when they had occasion to make a study of the situation, they realized that they, too, were generally overworked and underpaid. Horses, equipment and wranglers worked on the same tenuous day-to-day basis as riders, which made it almost impossible for the barns to have anything left over to invest in new equipment or proper repair.

On a busy day in Hollywood when De Mille, John Huston, John Ford, Raoul Walsh and Henry Hathaway were all in the saddle at once, the barn people had their hands full. Wranglers had to see the horses were at the studio before dawn. On location a rope picket line was set up and the horses tied to it. Cowboys arriving on the job picked out their mounts, usually old favorites they had ridden many times, occasionally a new addition to the standard *remuda* that they wanted to try out. Wagons or carriages were frequently taken to the studio a few days ahead of shooting schedule and kept in a prop department or warehouse for the duration of the job.

When several such companies were rolling at once on their big-budget spectacles, there was hardly time for a returning wagon or carriage to be checked out for breakage or faults before it was due to be hauled off to another job. The same thing was true of saddles, cinches and other crucial gear. Even horses were kept working relentlessly, the barn trying to make as much hay as possible while the sun of studio prosperity shone. But due to the inevitable neglect of animals and equipment, many needless injuries occurred. Father was involved in two such barn-related accidents, one of them, an unscheduled horse fall, almost costing him his life.

The first occurred on a big location job out at Chatsworth. The movie was *High, Wide and Handsome,* a musical about a turn-of-the-century circus troupe, and this colorful sequence was to show them traveling between shows across a green rolling countryside. Father was one of seven cowboys hired to drive the circus tallyhos, and Louise among the seventy-five extras.

Most of the extras were put inside the coaches, but several girls were ordered to ride on top of the tallyhos to lend more color and spirit to the scene with their flowing skirts and bright bonnet-ribbons. Father objected to outside riders, on the grounds that it would make the coaches top-heavy and danger-ous, especially as they were to drive their teams of six horses at a dead run. His warning went unheeded.

When all was ready for the final take, seven ornately carved and painted tallyhos took off across the meadow, their passen-gers singing merrily, parasols a-tilt and ribbons flying in the wind. No one remembered exactly what happened next, but the driver of the lead tallyho said he heard something snap, like a main axle, and the coach simply keeled over under its load, throwing the occupants against the trees that lined the road.

Hard on the heels of the first wreck came the second, when the driver tried to veer away from the smash-up dead ahead and was unable to safely maneuver the top-heavy load. In rapid succession five out of the seven tallyhos were overturned, only the last two drivers having enough warning to slow their teams down and maneuver them around the others. Father was driving one of these, and as soon as he stopped his team he hit the ground running. The meadow looked like a battle-ground — crippled ponies caught in a tangle of harness and wreckage, frightened and injured extras, women and girls in their bright skirts scattered all over the landscape, in little pools of pink, blue and yellow satin.

While a grip man raced a stand-by car to the nearest ranch to call for a fleet of ambulances, Father, crew members, cow-boys and extras laid out quilts under the shade of the trees and placed the injured there. An assistant director gave Louise some brandy and told her to offer some to anyone who needed it. Among the injured Louise recognized Harry, a middle-aged extra with whom she had worked many times. His face was covered with grime and blood, his clothes torn and he was moaning softly, "What happened? What happened?"

"Your tallyho tipped over," Louise explained soothingly. "Here, take a sip of this and you'll feel better." She wasn't surprised when he helped himself to a long drink. Harry was well known as one of the laziest extras in the business, wily at hiding out on a set, but also the first on deck any cold night when warming drinks were being passed around.

When the stand-by chauffeur offered to drive back to the studio clinic any of the less seriously injured people, Harry volunteered, "Save the ambulances for the others. I — I don't think I've broken anything."

Touched by Harry's generosity, the assistant armed him with a pint of Southern Comfort to anesthetize the pain, and Harry managed to turn the journey into something of a lark. But once inside the studio clinic he began to murmur ominously about "internal injuries" and possible "complications." Harry was well aware, as were all the extras, that, while studios provided no compensation, settlements were not unheard of when gross negligence could be legally proved.

"It was pure and simple negligence," Harry told the first studio lawyer who questioned him, "and I intend to sue Paramount for everything it's got!"

The worried official whipped out a checkbook and pen and explained the studio would be happy to settle out of court for "let's say five hundred dollars?" Harry continued to haggle, but after a bit more footdragging, he finally let himself be persuaded.

On the steps of the clinic a hale and hearty Harry strolled over to Father and Louise and astonished them both by flashing a studio check for one thousand dollars.

"But Harry, what if you really do have internal injuries?" Lousie asked earnestly.

Harry laughed. "I might have a hangover from the brandy,

but hell, I wasn't even on a tallyho. I was hiding out behind a tree when I saw the smash-ups. Figured I could look as hurt as anybody else with a little borrowed blood and dirt and there might be money in it."

The ten or fifteen extras who had really been injured did not come out so well, but Harry walked away that day the highest paid streetwalker in the business.

Not long after the faulty tallyho had led to mass injuries out at Chatsworth, Father got a call to report to location over at Vasquez Rocks. This rocky defile had been the real-life robber's roost of Tiburcio Vasquez, a native Californio, who turned bandit and became the scourge of the invading *gringos* during the early years of U.S. occupation of the former Mexican territory.

Arriving at the location, Father discovered that he was the last man to reach the picket line; all the best horses were gone and only a blue roan was left standing there still unclaimed. One glance told Father why the horse had been so judiciously passed over. The condition of his hooves was outrageous, for they had overgrown by two inches his last pair of horseshoes, which the barn blacksmith had tacked on at least three months earlier. Now with long, almost pointed hooves, he was what the cowboys called "rocker-footed."

It was sheer carelessness for the barn men to have allowed a horse in that condition on any set, let alone a chase sequence in the treacherous malpais and shale rock of Vasquez Canyon. As he automatically checked the cinch band and latigo, Father briefly considered leading the sorry-looking animal over to the director and telling him he refused to ride. But to do so would cast aspersions on his own riding skills. "Better just ride the rocker-footed bastard," he muttered to himself as he swung into the saddle, and then, leaning over, he combed the roan's tangled gray mane with his fingers and said, "Okay, Blue, you keep your feet under you, do you hear?"

"All right, Monty," the unit director called to Father, "fall in with the posse. This is the follow-up of the Western street stuff we shot yesterday. You men have ridden several miles out of town and spotted Casey and his bunch headin' for the hideout up the canyon. Now, I want you to get bunched close together in this take, tight as a fist, and when the camera gets you comin' out through the narrowest rock draw here, I want your ponies so wide open you'll look like you were shot out of a cannon. Got the idea?"

The men nodded silently, settled into their saddles, reset their Stetsons one last time on their brows, and threaded their horses slowly back up the defile to an open sandy wash several hundred yards up-canyon from where the camera car would pick up on their chase. This gave the horses the space and distance needed to build up the speed required by the time they hit the pass.

In the first take, Father felt Blue turn pudding-footed under him, but managed to pull him out of it by the time-honored trick of yanking up on his bit, which brought the roan's head up sharply and automatically lifted his front quarters out of the stumble. But the first take did not satisfy the director. He wanted the posse to come on faster and in a tighter bunch. The men went back up the canyon still farther and started the chase again, so that this time when they hit the defile all fifteen horses were flying and the posse seemed to fairly explode on camera. But when Blue hit the loose shale rock he stumbled over his own front feet, and this time Father could tell by the feel of the fall and the terrible forward thrust there was just no way to pull him out of it.

Father hit the rocks first, dead ahead of Blue, who went down on top of him, rolled over on him twice in his struggle to get to his feet, and then walked away leaving the downed rider to be run over by three other horses before the men in the posse could even see that Blue was down.

Finally Neal Hart planted his horse's rump on a dime in the center of the trail, squaring him off as a shield against the last few oncoming horses. A second later, he was kneeling beside his friend's unconscious form.

The only way to transport the injured man the twenty miles from Vasquez Rocks to the nearest Hollywood hospital was to lay him on a pile of quilts on the bed of a wooden station wagon stand-by car. The jolting ride over unpaved roads was guaranteed to finish up any work that Blue and three other horses had left undone.

"Marian, I've got some bad news for you," Neal told Mother from a phone booth at Cedars of Lebanon. "Jack's been pretty badly busted up in a fall out at Vasquez. They think his back's broken. You better get over here as fast as you can."

A neighbor raced us across town in her car, and we found Father lying unconscious in a darkened room, his clothes gray with dust, his boots and spurs still on his feet. His face was the color of chalk. Standing at his bedside, I was afraid to hold out any encouragement to Mother. Then a nurse came in and briskly set about taking off his boots. As if by some primordial instinct he opened his eyes and said in a rasping voice, "Get your hands off my boots!"

The startled nurse jumped back and went for a doctor, while Father turned a glazed eye toward Mother, Neal and me.

"Where the hell am I?"

"In Cedars of Lebanon Hospital," Mother told him reassuringly.

"Well, goddammit, I'm gettin' out of here before they give me a blood transfusion!" Propping himself up on his elbow, he tried to rise, but as he did so, his face contorted in pain.

"Jumped-up-Jesus, I must have busted a gut!"

"Not this time, Jack," Neal laughed. "But the doctors think you broke an arm, a leg and a wrist. All things considered, for a man who had four horses go over him, you're in good shape."

"Feels like the saddle horn went plumb through me."

"I'm not surprised," Neal chuckled. "You and old rocker-footed Blue sure gave that unit director one hell of a free fall!"

Father's own insurance covered him this time, and the studio was forced by State Workmen's Compensation to make a small settlement in his favor. He utilized the two months of his convalescence to put together a project he had long been mulling over in his head. It was a prospectus to be submitted to the production heads of studios, outlining a system by which all horses and equipment used in action films would be subject to continuous inspection by a committee of experienced cowboys or otherwise qualified specialists.

These examiners would visit the barns, check on the animals, saddles, wagons, coaches and all other rigs used in pictures. The salaries paid for their services by the producers would be saved many times over, Father argued, considering the costly accidents they would prevent. These caused expensive delays in shooting schedules, loss of valuable horses, and sometimes the death or injury of innocent studio employees. A careful and regular check would be the best accident insurance the studios could carry.

"When the Guild gets enough power," Father told the executives he interviewed, "studios will be forced to pay out far more in compensation than the cowboy barn checkers would earn."

Predictably, the producers, to a man, rejected his proposition. They smilingly assured him that he was overestimating the hazards of riding extras' work, and grossly exaggerating the incidents of negligence on the part of barn men and wranglers. With great bitterness, Father was forced to shelve a plan that he had spent ten years developing and two months working out on paper.

What Neal had jokingly referred to as a "free fall" was still another sore point between the working cowboys and the studios. A free fall was what the front office most often described as "an unavoidable accident." It resulted almost automatically whenever a director set up a situation in which the cowboys' more experienced judgment told them there was a ninety-five percent chance of multiple accident and injury if the plan were put into action. They would far rather set up specific stunts and falls, however individually dangerous, because there was at least a modicum of control over the outcome. But letting nature take its course in a badly planned melee was a cheap way for a director to pick up some really exciting spills on camera, without having to put out adjustment checks to get them.

On small-time outfits, where the budget couldn't cover the additional expense of stunt checks, directors gambled on the overall action to provide a sprinkling of such good "accidental" spills. Although it amounted to a policy of getting something for nothing, the cowboys considered it one of the dangers one ran into occasionally on one of "Pop" Sherman's Hopalongs, or working for Poverty Row. But the worst offender, according to the cowboys, and the man for whom there was no budgetary excuse, was Cecil B. De Mille.

The cowboys not only disliked him, for reasons already explained, but they distrusted him as well, for sooner or later on every job where the Gower Gulch men worked with De Mille, he seemed to find a subtle way of squeezing free falls out of them. It was over one such episode that the long and bitter feud between the cowboys and De Mille finally exploded into open hostilities. Father and Neal Hart were leading participants.

12

"Kill De Mille!"

FORTY mounted Crusaders, encased in helmets and armor, forced their nervous horses four abreast across a narrow drawbridge toward the gates of a medieval stronghold. Defending the fortress, an equal number of Saracen zealots charged the attackers, their horses balancing precariously as they sprang forward in short, catlike jumps along the runway.

As the two bands battled on the narrow, crowded ramp, one Crusader's horse lost his footing and, with a shrill cry of fright, slipped over the side, carrying his helpless rider with him into the dry moat some thirty feet below. Moments later a second, third and fourth animal were similarly forced off and shouts of alarm went up from soldiers on both sides as they saw their men plunge downward. At last, above the clangor of arms and the cries of the injured, a single voice rang out like a trumpet from the battlements. At his command alone, the slaughter ceased as suddenly as it had begun.

The year was 1189 A.D., the place an Arab redoubt somewhere in the Holy Land. But beyond the papier-mâché turrets it was actually 1935 on an indoor set at Paramount, where a battery of lights, as hot as boiling oil, poured down on the heads of the medieval armies. Beneath burnooses and breastplates, Saracen and Crusader alike were Gower Gulch men, transformed into twelfth-century warriors by Western Costumers and that exacting god of battles, Cecil B. De Mille.

De Mille's epic *The Crusades* was in the making, and the great director sat enthroned on the boom just to the right of the cameraman. He was dressed, as always, in his ceremonial short-sleeved shirt, riding breeches and army-style puttees and boots. His profile belonged on a Roman coin, with its bland, unwrinkled features and high-domed brow. His bald pate was tanned the same deep bronze as his muscular arms, from twenty-five years of uninterrupted exposure to the California sun. De Mille had become a living legend in Hollywood, as convinced of his own immortality as any Roman hero returning from the wars, and as dedicated to erecting monuments to commemorate that fact as any pyramid-building pharaoh.

Over the years, De Mille had become that rarest of Hollywood celebrities, a devoted husband who lived to celebrate his golden wedding day with his first and only wife. His children found their father amusing, generous, sometimes eccentric, but always the most indulgent of papas.

He inspired in a steadfast corps of women that kind of lifelong selfless dedication rarely found outside the pages of the Old and New Testaments. At this point in his career, seven of these loyal female followers formed the heart of his working staff. Among them was faithful Jeanie MacPherson, who worked until her death as trusted editor of all his films. Most of his workers died in harness, grateful that they had never worked anywhere else but in "The Bungalow" as De Mille's Paramount headquarters were reverently referred to by employees of "the Chief."

As a group, De Mille's assistant directors — who were under the withering fire of his sarcasm and temper all of their working hours — displayed an incredible capacity for swallowing invective in the course of their frenetic years spent as drivers for De Mille. But even more striking to anyone who watched them survive even a single day on a De Mille set was their staying power. Some, like Hezzy Tate, worked decades under his banner, when it was common knowledge that one day in the job could take ten years off any man's life expectancy.

Whatever sweet, magnetic charm bound these loyal workers to De Mille, he managed to keep it successfully concealed from most of the actors and virtually all of the extras who ever worked for him. When the tenderhearted husband and father, and the appreciative, witty Chief left home and Bungalow, respectively, he underwent a Jekyll-Hyde transformation. The De Mille of the mob scene set was an arrogant, sarcastic, dictatorial tyrant who brooked no resistance or opposition to his absolute authority on a set. When a De Mille assistant director called for "Quiet on the set," he meant total silence. But when De Mille himself took the mike and demanded "Quiet!," extras knew that meant they should simply stop breathing.

Famous though he had become, his artistic progress had not been particularly spectacular. Except for filming increasingly gargantuan epics, not infrequently overblown re-makes and improvements on his own earlier masterpieces, De Mille had made little creative headway over the years. To the cowboys he seemed to have become only a more flamboyant and self-assured version of the petty tyrant who had taken up his megaphone on the Red Sea sands and denounced them publicly as a frightened and cowardly crew.

As was ever the case on a De Mille epic, months of historical research had preceded actual filming of *The Crusades*. He had employed a crew of research experts to mine whatever was to be dug up about the period. He personally studied thousands of pictures showing the costumes, castles, armor and weaponry of the time. During this stage of gestation of a De Mille spectacle, anyone on the Paramount lot who had even a cringing acquaintance with the Great Man knew better than to refer to some former triumph in his glittering career as being his all-time best. When about to give birth, all the De Mille genius was focused on that creation soon to see the light. "This is my greatest work!" was the manner in which he referred to every current production; and "Yes, Mr. De Mille!" was the only way any sane man dared respond.

After combing all the libraries and other sources for every fact and figure bearing on his theme, De Mille just as methodically set about throwing out that data that did not match up to his own conception of good history as being good theater. This was a De Mille hallmark and one in which he took considerable pride. Not every historian had such resources at his command nor, indeed, was so high-handed in his disregard for history.

In *The King of Kings*, for example, he had improved upon the Bible itself by whipping up a torrid love affair between Judas and Magdalene — a sexy episode that, of course, took place back in her salad days, when she was still plying the oldest profession. According to De Mille, her subsequent conversion to the teachings of Jesus caused her to renounce her life of sin and spurn her former lover. This made more sense to De Mille, as it gave a logical reason for Judas to betray his Master. It seemed incredible to De Mille that Judas or any man would turn in his best friend for a lousy thirty pieces of silver. "There simply *had* to be a dame behind it!" was the rather un-Biblical phrase he used when justifying his gilding of Scripture's scarlet lily. (This sex-angle motive behind the Crucifixion was mercifully left on the cutting room floor, lest it offend orthodox moviegoers.)

Similarly, when preparing the script for *Unconquered*, his epic treatment of the French and Indian War, a researcher turned up a fact of passing interest — that there had been a small contingent of Scots among the troops who lifted the siege of Fort Pitt. Inspired by this kernel of truth, De Mille went history one better and had none other than the heroic Black Watch of World War I fame march into the frontier post dressed in kilts and with skirling bagpipes.

So, too, on *The Crusades* he found ways to go history one better. He ordered armor and chain-mail "copied to the last rivet from originals in the Metropolitan Museum," but came up with a special armor for horses and men which, although tending to be a bit clangier than the original, he judged would allow the horses more freedom of action and greater speed in the battle scenes. He felt his point would be well taken when it came time for the biggest scene in the picture, the Battle of Acre, where Richard the Lion-Hearted wins his great victory over the Saracens.

Perhaps, then, it was only fitting that he who had brought the Crusades to life after centuries in history's cold storage should be the one whose cry of "Cut!" would draw back the colorful tapestry of Crusaders attacking a Saracen fortress, revealing the harsh realities of life in Hollywood at the height of his own glorious reign.

As soon as the cameras stopped turning, Father and Neal Hart spurred their horses off the ramp and onto the sidelines where they threw off the weight of helmets, armor and weaponry, and ran to the edge of the moat to the aid of their fallen comrades.

Jumping into the wooden-floored moat they found it slippery with the mingled blood of men and horses. It was painful work easing the Crusaders out of their battered armor, but they did what they could to relieve their immediate sufferings. Carefully they handed them up to the ambulance attendants who had raced directly to the set in response to a frantic assistant's call.

It was obvious from the first that all four men had suffered serious injuries in the fall, the extent and gravity of which would not be fully known until after X-rays and complete examination by the hospital staff at Cedars of Lebanon. After the fall they had been further hurt by the thrashing of their horses, who were trapped in the deep moat with them.

While others carried the men into the waiting ambulances, Father and Neal remained behind in the moat to try to quiet down the panicky horses. They were sickened by what they found. Every one of the four fallen animals was so badly smashed up it would have to be destroyed. Taking the pistols which a prop man handed down to them, they carried out the picture cowboy's most detested chore — shooting a valuable and well-loved picture horse that had been crippled needlessly. This dirty business behind them, the two men climbed out of the moat and strolled over to a quiet corner of the set to light up a much-needed cigarette.

"I told De Mille he couldn't put four mounted men abreast on that small a drawbridge without forcing somebody off," Father said, trembling with suppressed rage. "Now four good picture horses are headed for the slaughterhouse — and maybe four good cowboys, too."

Father's indignation was heightened by the fact that, just before the take, he had headed a delegation of experienced riders who called on De Mille to explain that only falls could follow the kind of crowded action he was demanding. But the director, stubborn as always, and passionately determined to wring every drop of dramatic action out of his battle scenes, refused to alter a word of his instructions. "You will do the scene exactly as I mapped it," De Mille had told them.

Drawing silently on his cigarette and looking deceptively youthful under his dark auburn hairpiece, Neal Hart frowned. "Jack, you know damned well it was no accident. It's not the first time the Old Man's squeezed 'free falls' out of us. I can't even count the times over the past twenty years that he's put the cowboys in spots so tight any sane man would know you couldn't ride out without somebody gettin' hurt or killed. Believe me, if I didn't need the long run on this job, I'd walk off this goddammed set and tell the old sonofabitch to shoot his Crusades in Hell."

Father glanced toward the boom where De Mille was looking down on the rescue work with the aloof bemusement of Yaweh paying a surprise visit to earth.

"I'll tell you one thing, Neal," Father said stubbornly, "I'm going to see that those boys or at least their families get something out of this mess. Come on, let's go over and talk to God and see what we can work out."

Neal shrugged pessimistically, ditched his cigarette, and walked across the set with Father. Two or three other cowboys who had been in the original delegation joined them. When they reached the boom, it had been lowered to a point just above eye level. Once more Father stepped forward as spokesman for the group.

"Mr. De Mille, the boys and I would like to talk to you about the four men who just got hurt."

"What is there to talk about? I'm sorry they're hurt, if that's what you want to know." De Mille thrust his head forward, concentrating the powerful beam of his gaze upon the cowboys.

"Well, we feel those falls were — well, unavoidable under the circumstances. The boys are going to be laid up some time — if they pull through at all — and the hospital bills are going to be pretty hard on their families — "

De Mille's face was a study of disinterest.

"Anyway, there's one way you could help, and the front office wouldn't turn down a request if *you* made it. That would be to put in for adjustment checks for those four — say, fifty dollars each for stunt falls into the moat. That would help."

De Mille delivered himself of a short, contemptuous laugh. "I hardly see why those men should be rewarded with stunt checks for falls that were clearly due to their own incompetence. All I asked of them was simple, straight riding. If they had known how to do so, obviously they wouldn't have gotten hurt."

As if on cue, the boom pulled away from earth and De Mille was once again lifted high into the sky above the Holy Land.

This speech, to which De Mille did not give a second thought, was tantamount to calling Wyatt Earp a sonofabitch to his face. With it he brought his twelve-year-old feud with the cowboys full circle, and past the point of no return. Although he was unaware of it, at that moment De Mille began to live on borrowed time.

At first the cowboy-Crusaders retaliated by simply making life as miserable as possible for De Mille by means of a silent protest which no one could pinpoint as revenge. The morning after the accident they were working on a village set with hundreds of extras as townspeople. De Mille was in a particularly bad humor. One woman was sent back to wardrobe because she was wearing tennis shoes under her gown. Another was dismissed for appearing with red nail polish. An extra man was severely reprimanded for smoking. It was past one P.M. The extras were wilting under the hot sun, and nearly faint from hunger. They had been on their feet in that same square since seven-thirty. Suddenly De Mille's attention was drawn to a not-so-young blond stunt woman who often doubled for the ingenues in Westerns. De Mille leaped from his chair and strode across the platform to the loudspeaker.

"You over there by the well," he said in a voice that made the ground tremble. "You were talking!"

A deathly hush fell on the already quiet set as De Mille continued. "All right, then. Since it was so important you had to tell your girl friend, come up here on the platform and tell everybody on the set what you just said!"

The stunt girl flicked a forbidden cigarette to the ground, switched her twelfth-century gown as though it were a madam's kimono, and made her way across the painfully silent set and up to the platform.

"Go ahead," De Mille said, his voice dripping sarcasm as he handed her the mike.

"Well, if you really want to know," she proclaimed in a husky voice, "I asked my friend when that bald-headed old sonofabitch was going to call lunch!"

After a second of stunned disbelief, De Mille's command rolled like a thunderclap across the set: "LUNCH!"

Later that day, when King Richard's longbowmen were assaulting a castle, the director took his place beside the camera behind a high protective wooden barricade. This was designed to shield both De Mille and the camera's lens from the shower of arrows, which were specially made with rubber tips to avoid injuring crewmen and performers. De Mille directed the action through a small opening in the screen, a hole just large enough for his mouth.

As this tumultuous scene began, Father found himself fighting side by side with his long-time friend, Jack Lorenz, an expert archer who had instructed such skillful Robin Hoods as Douglas Fairbanks, Sr., and Errol Flynn in the fine art of using the bow and arrow.

"Just watch me end this take fast!" Lorenz shouted in Father's ear as they moved forward with the besiegers. He released an arrow and sent it winging toward the castle. A second later Father heard someone yell, "Cut!" From behind the barricade De Mille emerged, purple with rage and tugging at a rubber-tipped arrow which appeared to be halfway down his throat. Lorenz had scored a double bull's eye through the hole in the screen and into the director's open mouth!

Shooting was suspended as De Mille, furious beyond anything the cowboys could recall, demanded over the loudspeaker, "Which one of you cowboys tried to kill me?" The silence that followed was eloquent proof of the solidarity that could exist between the cowboys when the chips were down. But the director's question had planted a seed that Father, Neal Hart, Hank Bell, and four other Gower Gulch veterans discussed seriously over lunch.

"Well, how *would* you kill the old bastard if you had the chance?" Neal asked no one in particular.

"Shootin's too quick and clean, and hangin's too good for him," Hank muttered. "Especially since four good cowboys are holed up in Cedars of Lebanon Hospital, thanks to that drawbridge fall."

"I'd like to stick De Mille inside the goddammed tin can I've been wearing all week and push *him* into the moat," Neal ventured.

"We could try the old Apache trick of stuffing him down a red anthill and bastin' him with honey," another man suggested jokingly.

"There's only one way to do the job," Father said earnestly and with characteristic impulsiveness. "It would take all seven of us to do it, but by God we could kill him clean or scare hell out of him tryin'!"

"Go on," Hank urged, leaning forward.

"It can be rigged so that everyone will call it one of those 'unavoidable accidents' the front office is always so fond of reporting to the papers."

"I'm with you, Monty," Hank volunteered. "But what's your plan?"

Father replied with a single, chilling word.

"Stampede!"

"When?"

"Where?"

"Why not tomorrow out at Muroc Dry Lake? We're shootin' the big battle scene there."

"If it's the kind of stampede I think you mean," the soft-spoken Neal put in, "you know as well as I do you can't always control a runaway — especially seven of them at once — " His voice trailed.

Father finished his coffee in silence, rolled a cigarette carefully, and said in a cold voice, "That's a chance a man just has to take. After all, there's more ways to skin a cat than stickin' his head in a bootjack. I figure runnin' him down is as good a way as any."

They nodded, and then rose as one man and walked out of the studio commissary.

The self-chosen seven reached location early the following morning in order to have first choice of the several hundred horses tied up at the wrangler's rope picket line. They knew exactly the mounts they were looking for: each one had to be a notorious cold-jawed picture horse known to stampede the minute the director called, "Action!"

"If each one of us is mounted on a chase-spoiled runaway," Father had told his fellow conspirators, "every crewman, cowboy and wrangler on the set will have to testify honestly that the 'tragedy' was one of those freak accidents when seven runaways all just happened to light out in the same direction and at the same time."

For himself, Father picked out a big, Roman-nosed palomino named King who invariably bolted the minute a picture charge began, and never stopped running until he was completely winded. The other cowboys selected their mounts with equal care, but not a single man on the job outside the conspirators was given an inkling of the murder plot.

The white, hard-packed sands of Muroc Lake, a favorite De Mille location and familiar to the cowboys from that fateful day on *The Ten Commandments* when the Red Sea had parted between them forever, was dazzling under an April sun. Ironically, the one-time Red Sea was serving as the site of the Battle of Acre, which was fought in the Holy Land in the twelfth century and had ended for the Crusaders in crushing victory over the Saracens.

Three hundred and fifty mounted knights, encased in heavy armor and further encumbered with cross-emblazoned shields, lances and broadswords, sat their restless horses after forming the battle line. Arrayed against them was an equal number of Saracen cowboys, dazzling in their gem-bedizened burnooses and floating white robes, their jeweled scimitars and scabbards catching fire in the burning sunlight.

De Mille, impeccably dressed as always, stood regally surveying the panoply spread out beneath him. Everything was exactly as he had envisioned it during the long, tedious months of preparation, the uncounted hours he had pored over sketches of the authentic costumes and the light-weight metal armor he himself had developed. This master of spectacle had spared nothing, least of all himself, to make the Battle of Acre the high point of the film which he felt sure would be the crowning achievement of an already illustrious career. Now he was about to savor the full and sweet reward of these labors. In a few minutes all this grandeur he had carried about in his head for so many months would be captured on film and safe in the studio vaults, ready for the plaudits of posterity.

Two of the cameras had been planted just below ground level not far from where De Mille stood, so placed as to get unusual angles and shots of the horses' hooves during the battle scenes. These cameras were protected by a low, winged, wooden barricade in the shape of a V, from behind which De Mille would direct the spectacle. But until the charge was underway, he stood apart from that protection, checking out every horse and rider with his eye. Father, Neal and the others had not spent years working with De Mille for nothing. Each man of the seven was as familiar with the director's habits and idiosyncrasies as he was with the fatal flaw in the headstrong horse under him.

Battle flags fluttered, nervous horses caracoled all along the length of the tightly drawn battle line, and time and again an animal had to be whirled and reined back into position. Long ranks of gleaming knights, completely sealed inside the helmets that the cowboys hated so, leveled their lances as the assistant director gave the warning call. Father leaned close to Neal's ear and muttered through his lowered visor, "He won't climb down into the camera pit until he sees the charge is rolling. If we hang our spurs into these cold-jawed babies right now, we can do the job before the Old Man even sees us coming." Neal nodded and lifted his free hand upward in the pre-arranged signal, then dropped it just as quickly. The seven runaways felt the spurs of their riders at exactly the same moment, and all of them bolted as though someone had just set fire to their tails.

De Mille was distracted by a call from one of his camera crew and was momentarily looking away from the battlefield as the seven knights virtually exploded from the front ranks of the Crusaders, visors lowered, lances couched, with their runaway horses streaking across the hard-packed sand as tight as they could run. Suddenly, someone in the pit caught sight of the band of seven horsemen and yelled, "My God, Mr. De Mille! Look out! Those horses are runaways — out of control!" But it was already too late for De Mille to save himself.

Unaware of the band of stampeding horsemen until they were almost upon him, the fatal and "unavoidable accident" had almost come to pass when the totally unexpected occurred.

Streaking over the hard white sand the palomino King was just a few yards from where the unprotected director stood, when he suddenly broke stride and turned into the wickedest rodeo bronc Father had ever found himself aboard. At the very first crowfoot, Father's helmet was turned completely around, the eye holes in the front of the visor switched to somewhere behind his ears. Riding completely blind, he was forced to throw away his shield and sword in order to stay aboard the most reliable runaway horse in the business, who had suddenly turned himself into a tornado.

Every one of the other six conspirators was having exactly the same incredible experience. Their horses had panicked, just as old King had done, terrified by the frightful racket made by the armor, and determined to unload what sounded to them like all the empty tin cans in the world inside a metal drum.

Normally nothing could have stopped these stampeders, but now, almost on top of their human target, they turned into wildly plunging broncs. And behind them thundered the entire main army of Crusaders and Saracens, whose jittery, chase-trained horses had bolted as soon as they saw King and the others leave their ranks. The earth shuddered as close to twenty-eight hundred iron-shod hooves drummed on the hard-packed sand of the lake bed. But the faster the horses ran, the more deafening became the thunderous clangor set up by the armor. Soon all the Crusaders found themselves riding twisting, sun-fishing broncs.

The Saracen horses, infected by the general hysteria and

noise, and further terrified by their own riders' billowing, cloud-like robes, also decided it was time to unload their frightening riders. Soon they had succeeded in decimating the proud ranks of the Prophet even as King Richard's host had gone down in ignominy.

As for De Mille, he stood rooted to the spot where — except for this inexplicable turn of events — his dead and mangled body would now have lain. White-faced and incredulous, he watched as the magnificence of his two great armies melted before his eyes. As far as he could see, the flower of Christendom and the cream of Saladin's proud host were jolting across the sands, the mile-wide battle site littered with jettisoned shields, splintered lances, smashed saddles and bent and battered helmets. All his meticulous planning to make this the Crusaders' and his own finest hour had been turned into the biggest wild-horse race and rodeo ever staged, with no less than seven hundred bronc riders in the vast dry lake arena at once!

De Mille went to his grave totally innocent of the fact that he had been all but murdered twenty-five years earlier on the set of *The Crusades*.

As it was, his life was saved, quite ironically, by the special armor he had created. Production was considerably delayed while a quieter armor was devised and the sequence re-created. The cowboys at the hospital recovered, and De Mille lived on to fight with the Gower Gulch men for another quarter of a century.*

* I myself did not learn of the episode until fifteen years later, in 1949, when Neal and Father came to dinner at my home. They began to open up about their long feud with De Mille, and since they were the last two of the seven conspirators still alive, said they did not feel they were betraying a trust in telling me.

13

Last Stand at Disneyland

WITH the release in 1939 of John Ford's starkly beautiful *Stagecoach*, Hollywood's least-esteemed entertainment staple was suddenly lifted to a new plateau of respect and prestige. Directors who had formerly scorned even outstanding Western scripts were now in open competition for the biggest stories available with the magic frontier theme. Film critics began referring to the Western as an "art form," and praising those directors whose deployment of actors and extras against overpowering scenic backgrounds struck an aesthetic balance. Some critics were even known to single out the work of stunt men and solemnly evaluate the effectiveness of a certain chase or fall.

Of more immediate practical value to the cowboys than this long overdue recognition of their "picture riding" was the industry's stampede toward high-budget outdoor epics. There were several contributing factors making this a long-range renaissance rather than just one more minor revival of the *genre*, and of first importance was the simultaneous maturation of Technicolor.

After years of trial and error with various processes, Hollywood had about concluded that color was too unstable and disappointing to warrant the additional production costs involved. We had all been through recurring periods of enthusiastic experimentation with the medium, when stars and extras arrived on the set for a color sequence wearing the required "Panchromatic" make-up. This new grease paint was said to be "revolutionary." All we could observe was that it went on a luminous orange-pink, and had to be accompanied by a bizarre wine-dark rouge that was quickly dubbed "black lipstick." Experts assured us that what we looked like to each other (positively ghoulish!) was not at all what the processed film would record. However, what usually came across on screen in these pioneering efforts was an entire cast that seemed to be suffering from an advanced case of jaundice.

The release of *Gone With the Wind* in the same year as *Stagecoach* not only cost Ford an Oscar (*Gone With the Wind* carried off most of the major ones) but it forced Hollywood to reassess its judgment of color. Although Ford had achieved his finest camera work in black and white, Selznick's epic proved beyond a doubt that Technicolor had indeed come of age. And what better way to celebrate the Western's newly acquired status than to dip the drab, two-tone frontier in the same dye pot that had just brought Tara and Twelve Oaks so brilliantly alive?

Scenery, formerly considered too distant and costly, now lured location scouts and cameramen high into the American Rockies and far out onto the brooding deserts of Chihuahua and Sonora. A far cry, both spatially and photogenically from such visual clichés as Lone Pine and Vasquez Rocks, these distant sites possessed the added merit of assuring riders from four to six weeks' work on a single location job.

Another contributing factor fostering the big Western was the movie fans' addiction (carefully cultivated by producers for almost a decade) to the historical biography. These abridged and highly glamorized film lives ran the gamut of European and American immortals from Cellini, Marco Polo, Disraeli, the Rothschilds, Dr. Pasteur, Lloyds of London, Thomas Edison and Alexander Graham Bell all the way down to George M. Cohan and the Dolly Sisters. Now the biographers had caught up with the frontier, placing new emphasis on the psychological and documentary approach.

But probably the prime reason for the longevity of the post-*Stagecoach* obsession with the West was the increasing number of aging male stars in need of work. As the West had been populated by a predominantly male, bachelor society, studio writers capitalized on this happy coincidence by producing stories featuring several craggily handsome matinée idols not previously identified with cowboy roles. This made it possible for as many as four or five ranking contract stars (approaching or past fifty) to stay professionally alive by sharing screen credits in a single major Western. While their female counterparts retained their youth by means of face lifts, false eyelashes, and being shot through silk, the men grew seamier, with nothing to hide the ravages of time except a heavier tan and more grease paint. The harsh extremes of the great outdoors explained away their "premature" age. By boarding this bandwagon, such older lovers as Clark Gable, Gary Cooper, Alan Ladd, Glenn Ford, Robert Taylor, Henry Fonda, Tyrone Power and Walter Pidgeon extended their careers as romantic leads by another fifteen to twenty years.

At a considerably lower stratum, *Stagecoach* gave a badly needed transfusion to an all but expiring Poverty Row. Monogram, Republic, Mascot and even Universal imitated the all-star trend with their own "trio" series, which also resurrected the mordant careers of early cowboy stars. *The Rough Riders* starred venerable Buck Jones and Tim McCoy; *Trail Blazers* did the same with Hoot Gibson and Ken Maynard. And still there was room on the back lots and Western streets for four or five more "trio" series, culminating in *Border-G-Men* which starred Russell Hayden, James Ellison and a very adult Jackie Coogan.

What this activity meant to the Gower Gulch men in terms of morale, steady work and hard cash was nothing less than a windfall. Reliable riders were now put under weekly contract

by directors well aware that such virtuosity and expertise
could not be found among location natives. The Hollywood
veterans were entrained or even flown to Durango, Colorado,
or Sidona, Arizona, and put up at the best hotels with the stars,
all expenses paid. On the set their judgment and knowledge
were respectfully solicited, their suggestions or objections
cheerfully deferred to, by directors who recognized them as
technical experts in their own field. In turn they had their
favorites among the great films produced in that period, rating
Wagonmaster, Red River and *Cowboy* as the genuine classics.

A Gower Gulch man could return from a six-week contract
location on a big production and take his pick of jobs on any
one of a dozen major studio or Poverty Row potboilers. Fat
Jones's barn teemed with activity. For the first time in twenty
years the cowboys were assured of total employment. Father
not only earned an excellent living doubling and doing stunts,
but there was plenty of "calf money" around. He was also
assigned speaking parts and small roles: a dust-bowl sheriff in
Harry Sherman's *Five Faces West*, a kindly deputy in *Four
Godfathers* at Republic, a mountain man in *Northwest Passage*, and an early frontiersman in De Mille's *Unconquered.*
Perhaps the finest riding he ever did on camera was on Raoul
Walsh's *Dark Command* in 1940, when he worked throughout
the film as double for Walter Pidgeon.

But while the cowboys were at the peak of their powers and
constantly in the saddle, there began an imperceptible thinning
of the ranks. One evening in 1940 when I was visiting at home,
Ed Hendershot dropped by unexpectedly to tell us Tom Mix
had just been killed.

"Poor Tom's had his share of hell the last few years," he said
sadly. "Tried a comeback at Universal and Tony fell with him.
Then he hired on with the old Sam Dill circus. It was a
motorized outfit, you know, and after my Flo died I heard Tom
had bought out Dill and was touring the show under his own
name, so I joined up for a while." (I had read how Mix had

rather pathetically told newsmen that the sawdust trail had been his first love and the circus was something that got into a man's blood. There were also publicity stories proclaiming he was earning $20,000 a week once more as star of his own traveling circus.)

"I finally quit Tom for the last time in 1937," Ed went on, "and there was scarcely fifty people left in the company. After that I heard he had another bad fall in the arena, and was hurt again trying to save his animals and tents when a prairie rainstorm blew the whole damn show apart." Mix finally gave up on circus life and moved his remaining livestock to a little place outside of Hollywood. He planned to go on a personal appearance tour, although he was then sixty years of age.

"Tom didn't live to see sixty-one," Hendershot said, tapping the ashes of his cigarette carefully into the narrow cuff of his faded Levis. "He was drivin' his big cream-colored Cord convertible across Arizona on his way to Florence. Knowin' Tom, I'll bet he was goin' like a bat out of hell, and probably drinkin', too — he was seldom off the stuff these past ten years. He come onto a road crew and swerved onto the loose shoulder gravel but his car just shot off the embankment and turned over on him. They say his neck was broke on impact and he never knew what hit him." Newsmen noted later that the great Tom Mix had died in character — wearing his fanciest boots, his big white Stetson, and carrying $7,000 in cash and travelers' checks tucked under his diamond-studded belt buckle.

Shortly after Mix's death, another well-known cowboy star died of burns received when he rushed back into a fire he had just escaped, in a heroic effort to rescue others. More than five hundred people perished in that post-Thanksgiving Day conflagration in Boston's Cocoanut Grove Club, but the only name that made nationwide headlines was Buck Jones.

Despite his new prosperity, Father had never given up on the idea of ranching. In 1941 he took the settlement money from his fall at Vasquez Rocks and leased a dude outfit in

Montana for the summer. Had its situation proved practical he would have bought it. As it was, there were many operational drawbacks to the location that made its purchase unwise. But that summer proved to me that he and Mother were an ideal pair to serve as host and hostess on a successful dude operation. Father's gift for storytelling, his concern for greenhorn riders, and especially his care for children's safety around livestock were outstanding. He won the lifelong friendship of his guests, who assured him they would come to any ranch he operated, no matter where.

We returned to Hollywood in the fall, Father with a sizable nest-egg and ready to negotiate on several ranch properties he had in mind. But now, as circumstances at last permitted his long-deferred dream, another national tragedy clouded his plans, just as the Depression had overtaken him earlier in Wyoming. The Japanese attacked Pearl Harbor, and all recreational travel was virtually frozen.

Over the years Father, Neal Hart and one or two other cowboys had served as deputies under Los Angeles Sheriff Gene Bizcaluz. It was largely an honorary title, but on the other hand, they had not been chosen simply because their horsemanship could decorate the Rose Parade. On several occasions when mud slides, heavy floods and the 1933 earthquake brought wholesale disaster to the area, the cowboys were called to serve full time as long as the emergency lasted. I recall particularly the devastating flood of 1937, which ripped through the Tujunga Canyon, stripping the stream bed of trees, boulders and homes, and hurling a wall of water and debris down into the San Fernando Valley. Father and Neal Hart worked side by side around the clock at the Colfax Bridge, where some of the heaviest damage occurred. They risked their lives to rescue survivors who were carried downstream clinging to rooftops or bits of flotsam, and saved horses and other livestock from the roiling brown torrent.

With the outbreak of the war, the Gower Gulch men at once volunteered their services to the sheriff in whatever capacity he could use them. Hank Bell patroled out in the Malibu area, which he knew well from his days as line rider for Mrs. Ringe. Neal worked with air raid warnings, and Father was made a block warden in his neighborhood. Every evening after a long day of riding at the studio, he would come home, eat dinner and then set out on his rounds to make certain the blackout on his block was being properly observed. The cowboys, it seemed, were a perfect choice for positions of responsibility in times of crisis.

But despite the prosperous job outlook in Hollywood and the constraints of wartime rationing, Father continued shopping by mail for the ranch of his dreams. One morning in the early spring of 1943, while I was living nearby their apartment, I dropped in on Father and picked up the mail from their box downstairs. Mother was out working at MGM and, when I handed the bundle to Father, he threw aside all but a single letter which he tore open with avid interest.

"Good news?" I asked.

"The best!"

"You've bought a ranch." It was not a question, but a statement of fact, for I could read him so well.

"It's a beautiful spread." He grinned. "Just outside of Grand Lake, Colorado, at the western entrance to Rocky Mountain National Park. Snow-capped mountains all around, miles of trails, nine solid log guest cabins and a good main lodge . . ."

"Lights — plumbing . . . ?" I queried as though standing in for Mother.

"Lights are from carbide gas in a buried tank, and the bathrooms are just Chic Sales outside . . ."

"Have you talked to Mother about it?"

He sighed and sank into his chair. "No, not yet. You know,

I've got a cache of calf money, enough to settle the deal right now. I thought we could leave for Colorado in a couple of weeks when the weather breaks. I figure it's better to spring these things on your mother all of a sudden, rather than let her build up a storm by knowing too long in advance."

Mother's aversion to ranching was hardly a family secret. What made it so difficult to deal with was that she adapted to the life so wholeheartedly once she got there. In Wyoming she had been the incarnation of the pioneer woman, and in Montana every guest became her personal friend. But she resisted being pulled up from Hollywood, losing her apartment, her Guild card, their newfound prosperity.

"Once Sharkey sees this place she'll love it," Father assured me. "It's just that she's got her friends here in the picture business."

"So do you," I reminded him.

"Well, that's true, but maybe not for long. None of the boys wants to stay on here forever. If my plans work out in Colorado — and hell, there's no reason they shouldn't — I figure our place can become a real home ranch for good men like Hank and Ed Hendershot, and even Sonora . . ." His voice trailed sadly as he spoke of the young cowboy who had become like a son to him. Sonora was now fighting somewhere in Europe.

"Anyway, I want to get my family away from civilization. God knows how long this war will drag on, and I'd feel more secure if we're all on our own piece of land."

Having by then completely severed all my connections with the motion-picture industry, and working at research and writing as a career, I was highly portable. Besides, I loved ranch life, and I realized Father would need all the man and woman power he could get. The West had been literally stripped of cowboys and other hands. But I was determined Father would make a success of this ranch, and I was willing to do anything in my power to help him realize his dream. He was past fifty, and there would not be many more such opportunities.

Mother put up stiff resistance to the move.

"I'm just too old to go on pioneering like this!" she insisted stubbornly.

"But it's a magnificent location, Sharkey!" Father argued.

"I can't eat scenery, and besides I just won't go through that cooking thing again."

"I'll hire a full-time cook."

In a spirited show of pre-women's lib, Mother observed drily, "You're talking about at least two hundred dollars a month in salary — which I was never paid in Wyoming all those years!"

Three weeks later Louise, Mother and I once again set out for another "sight-unseen" ranch, asking the usual questions as each new vista opened up on the highway ahead. "Is this the spot?" "No, not here. It's just a little farther, now."

✳

Our three years in Colorado made the stay in Wyoming seem like one long vacation. Mother, characteristically, fell in love with the place. She also decided it was ridiculous to "throw away" two hundred dollars a month on a cook who couldn't feed twenty-five guests (and good friends) as well or as economically as she. Besides, there was our own garden, chickens, eggs, milk and hogs. Father's marksmanship kept the table supplied with fresh venison to help stretch the guests' meat stamps. With the help of a crew of Mexican *braceros* we got through haying season. I served as cabin girl, dishwasher, laundress, dude wrangler and guide, with Louise pitching in between the births of two of her three children. Once a week, with the sole aid of an ancient gasoline-driven washing machine and wringer, we laundered eighty sheets and forty pillowcases between breakfast and high noon, when it was time to have a hearty lunch on the table for two dozen starving dudes fresh from the trail.

But if the summers were rugged, the winters were man-killers. And since there were no caretakers left to take on the job for them, and I had to spend at least half of the year with my husband who was then stationed at Fort Ord, California, Father and Mother were forced to put in two long winters there alone. Two feet of snow on the level is not uncommon for the Grand Lake area, and still cows had to be milked, chickens fed, eggs gathered, coal and wood hauled. When illness and the heavy round of chores put Father in bed, Mother took over, hitched up the team of dappled grays to the hay sled, hauled and scattered feed in the upper pasture where the livestock was foraging.

A wealthy young sportsman paid a visit to the ranch late in the second spring. A maddeningly unseasonal blizzard was peppering the windows, and Father's animals were still being fed last summer's hay. The war looked as if it would go on forever, and Father was in the right mood to sell. When I learned the news that he would operate through the summer of 1945 and then turn the place over to its new owner in the fall, I was stunned. It seemed even more ironic when both the European and Pacific wars were over by late summer of that same year. But there was one aspect of the Colorado venture that had escaped me, and which alone explained why Hollywood now attracted Father more than ever before.

"This whole country is fillin' up with gunsils," Father remarked on one of our last rides together along the river that ran through the property. "They just don't do things the way they should be done — they're not the same kind of people I used to know." Indeed, they were strangers to the Code. The incident of the neighbor inviting us to lunch while leaving our horses at the hitching rail in the hot sun flashed into my mind. The dream ranch could not be made to exist if the old range customs were gone. Among the new generation of ranchers, everything was becoming mechanized. The young men who had remained at home and those returning from war were both truck and tractor crazy, always relentlessly haranguing their

dads: "Get rid of the horses — we don't need them anymore!"
No matter how superb the cutting horse or how spectacular a
man's horsemanship (and Father was still a fantastic rider,
even then) there was no one left now to appreciate them.

Father was in his mid-fifties when he hit the Hollywood trail
for the last time. The men who still lived by the Code could be
found there, and he realized they were among the last of their
breed. He bought a small house far enough out in San Fernando Valley (or so he thought) to put him safely ahead of the
urban blight that was devouring the country out there at an
appalling rate. Although he had made more money on the
Colorado venture than at any other time in his life, Father had
no intention of retiring. Riding jobs had never been so numer-
ous, and riding was the one thing he could not live without.

Old friendships were renewed, and younger wayfarers welcomed home. The dashing, romantic Sonora, who had served
three years as bombardier and tail gunner in Flying Fortresses
over Europe, returned to Hollywood. He had suffered a
serious leg wound, and leaned heavily on a cane; his once
devilish Irish eyes had gone melancholy. But as soon as he was
able, he returned to picture work, and it seemed only fitting
that this youngest of the Gower Gulch men should have been
among the last of them to talk to the oldest — Bill Gillis.

"Old Bill was a beautiful man," Sonora told me, when describing that last meeting. "He had the face of an eagle, but
the soul of a gentleman, and was one in every sense of that
word. God had been good to me. I had been in the army five
years and I had survived. When I went to work on my first set
after returning from war, Bill was on that job. I saw him walk
across the sound stage, coming my way. He walked the way
old cowboys do — stiff from the hips down, arms swingin' free,
shoulders pointed a bit forward. He was so thin you could see
his heartbeat through his pale blue shirt.

" 'Howdy, boy. No see-um tracks for many moons!' were the
words he greeted me with. Then he went on, 'Did you initial

one for me?' He meant, did I score an enemy plane during the war, with his brand in mind. We talked the whole afternoon. He asked a million questions about the war, and although I wasn't in a mood to talk about that part of my life, he listened avidly. When the company called it a day, he thanked me. 'I reckon I feel like I was there now, boy. Thanky!' "

Three days later Hank Bell called Sonora to tell him that Old Bill Gillis had crossed his last desert. For a Gower Gulch cowboy he had gone the very best way a man could go — in his sleep, peacefully, still riding, and with a call-back for to-morrow. Although the front office had never guessed it, he was *ninety-three years old!*

✳

When I returned to Hollywood briefly in 1948, I had been away five years. Perhaps because of that absence I was better able to see and feel the changes than those who had never left home. The war had completely altered the character of the city we natives had always called an overgrown tank town. The aircraft industry had brought in a tremendous wave of newcomers, and the postwar years saw an even greater inundation of ex-GI's who, during wartime service, had tasted the sweetness of Southern California's climate and returned by the hundreds of thousands to raise their families there.

Hollywood Boulevard had grown seedy, partly from neglect, partly from having catered almost exclusively to transient soldiers and sailors for the past few years. The shops that lined the famous street were run down, the signs above them cheap. The better stores had moved out to Wilshire and Beverly Hills. A Greyhound bus station occupied the place where Joe Posada's Boot Shop had been. Joe had vanished. Across the street where the Waterhole once stood, a red neon hammer silently rose and fell, pounding nails into the upturned sole of a giant neon boot atop Zinke's Shoe Repair.

The Sunset Strip, not long before the fanciest address an agent, nightclub or interior decorator could have, had sunk to being a slum with a view. The bridle path where Father and I used to ride White Man and Tim was paved over, and the streets were lined with sleazy strip joints and clubs.

"Movies are better than ever!" proclaimed the banners decorating countless crumbling neighborhood moviehouses, and many of the old-timers believed the slogan. But there were ominous portents of decline on every hand. Entire wardrobe departments, which had employed dozens of skilled seamstresses, were being closed down and these long-time, faithful employees turned out to look for other jobs . . . doing what? "Gable's back and Garson's got him!" was a hollow attempt to revive the prewar attitude toward Hollywood's frivolities.

At the time of my return, television had just torn through the industry with all the savage suddenness of a tornado in the Texas panhandle. But Hollywood was picking through the devastation with the air of a determined survivor. It would be twenty-five years before the auctioneers began putting the grand old ruins of Hal Roach, Paramount, Selznick and MGM under the hammer, but the die had been cast the day William Boyd convinced Harry Sherman that the Poverty Row producer could have no earthly use for all those prints of his old Westerns, and bought them for something like seventy-five dollars apiece.

What appeared to be nothing more than an actor's sentimental interest in his old films proved a turning point in Hollywood history. With the marketing to television of his "Hopalong Cassidy" series (some thirty-six in all), Boyd reaped millions from the residuals of repeated showings, and became the first White Hat to gather to himself what had formerly enriched the studios. After that, it was only a matter of months before producers realized that every worthless can of old program film might now earn a fortune in reruns. What matter that they were destroying the studios, the star system, the very market that had built Hollywood in the first place? There was money to be made, and if one waited too long, the gravy train would have passed, perhaps never to return.

Once again, it was the Western that blazed the entertainment trail in the new medium, and held its lead to the point of saturation. By 1960 television was not only rerunning just about every Poverty Row Western made since sound came in, but at least fifty of the made-for-TV shows fighting for prime time were Westerns, too.

Father, who had never gone to a move theater willingly in his life, thoroughly enjoyed watching television. In the early days when "Hopalong Cassidy" and other program Westerns provided most of the movement on the small screen, he sat glued to his set, but for a different reason than a stranger might suppose. They weren't movies to him. Each one was a location he knew, a job he had been on, with horses he himself had ridden, and horsemen he had known a lifetime.

"Hey, Sharkey. Come in here and look at this!" he would call to Mother while she was preparing dinner in the kitchen. "I'll be damned if that isn't Hank Bell and Fred Burns in that chase. See, Fred's ridin' that chalk-eyed pinto. Remember? He's the pony that used to blow himself up and fall down every time I tried to cinch him tight."

Later, when the major networks began producing their own Westerns, I asked Father what he and the other men considered the most authentic of the lot.

" 'Wagon Train' has it over all the others," he said with a ring of authority. "Ward Bond's the real article, and it comes across in the show."

Once I ventured a rare question, and received a typical cowboy answer.

"What do you think of the Western as an art form?"

Father pondered for a moment before answering solemnly, "Well, it's as classic as Italian opera — " and then, as a logical afterthought, "and it's a helluva lot more American!"

Along with a sudden diminution of outdoor action, the TV Western introduced a new kind of hero, every bit as wooden as Gene Autrey's singing cowboy. This White Hat was part lawyer, part psychiatrist, sometime Shakespearean scholar and, of course, a dyed-in-the-wool pacifist. The old carbolic chases, with dozens of horses spilling over the brink of a cliff and making it to the bottom in three or four incredibly dangerous jumps, were becoming as rare as the men who could make them.

"She ain't very big," Fred Burns said of the nascent TV industry, "But then, neither is a Gila monster. He gets a hold, his jaws lock, and he pumps his poison into you. That's what's happened to pictures. The industry's as good as dead."

"Television spells for the industry what the Conestoga spelled for the Indian," was the way Jack Padjan put it. "The Blackfoot thought them wagons was just a passin' bother. The truth was they'd come to stay."

A concurrent problem was the increasing expense of turning out a major Western.

"Hell, it costs a studio fifty dollars a day just to put an empty horse on a set with his wrangler," Father told me when we discussed the situation one afternoon. "The Guild started out with a good idea, maybe, but thanks to them we've been priced out of business. For straight riding or driving six up a man can get thirty-three dollars and fifty-four cents a day now. But, at the same time, for just leading a camel a gunsil can draw down sixty-one dollars!"

As the Guild drove wages up, it also drove studios to the expediency of "runaway" productions. England, Spain, Egypt and Israel became the new Griffith Park and Lone Pine for Hollywood's "cast of thousands" spectacles. While cowboys with Guild cards went without work in Hollywood, De Mille would film his re-make of *The Ten Commandments* in Israel itself, employing the most tractable Egyptians and Israelites of his career. These people were the real article, who cheerfully fought each other and drove their chariots into the Red Sea for a paltry fifty cents a day. Well might De Mille rejoice that at last he had triumphed over his two most implacable enemies — the cowboys and the unions.

During this period of transition when television was threatening to blow the cowboys' Hollywood apart, I decided the time had come to seek out the old-timers and try to record the high points of their lives, both in and out of the industry. They were, of course, lifelong friends, but getting such information from these men was not as easy as it at first appeared. I invited them to dinner at my house, I capitalized on every occasion when they dined at Mother's table, but although they are a storytelling tribe, the cowboys could also be infuriatingly reticent if they suspected one was trying to pry special information out of them. The old range code of "Nobody ever asks my name or where I came from" was never obsolete among them. They might gossip all of a Sunday afternoon, but just let someone outside the tribe ask them to illustrate with a specific example their own or another cowboy's display of heroism or chivalry, and the river of unself-conscious recollection suddenly ran dry. And it remained dry for the rest of the day.

Perhaps the Gower Gulch men had been infected by Hollywood's refusal to see its own collective experience as history. The industry demanded sacrifice, fierce loyalties, hard work. Never were so many strong egos met in one small arena. But whenever I spoke to former silent stars and extras about their role in history, the universal reaction bordered on self-contempt. "Making pictures, history? You're out of your mind!" It was much like asking a now-successful call girl to identify the madam of the low brothel where she had gotten her start.

In a sense, Hollywood may have been the precursor of our throwaway society. When talkies took over, virtually no one valued silents any longer. Studios burned the films to recover the silver nitrate, or let them turn to dust or jelly in the cans. Stars and directors were utterly rejected, tossed like salt over

the shoulder of a very superstitious industry that loathed fail-
ure and sought to ward off its spell by pretending it had ceased
to exist.

The cowboys, of course, had put out heroic servings of
courage, selflessness and performance over the years. But they,
too, were unable to see their accumulated efforts as a unique
body of experience. Salvaging their stories and collective history was slow work and had to be carried out on their own
terms and almost without their awareness. And even as my
collection of notes grew, the older men began slipping away.

Neal Hart was the first of Father's closest friends to go. He
lingered for several months out at the Motion Picture Hospital
in Woodland Hills. There in the shadow of hills where the two
had ridden stirrup to stirrup in movie chases over thirty years,
Father kept his daily vigil at Neal's side. When he learned, to
his astonishment, that Neal had been raised a Catholic and
wished to die in that faith, Father made all the necessary
arrangements to assure that, even if he himself could not be
there with him, he would have a priest at the end.

Father was working on a big Western at Paramount and he
took up a very special collection for Neal. Times were good,
and the old brown Stetson bulged with almost three hundred
dollars. Father was determined that Neal's would be the finest
tombstone any picture cowboy ever had. He designed it himself — a large marble marker with a cowhorse in bas relief, his
saddle empty, his head down and trailing his reins. Under his
feet was inscribed the simple epitaph: "Neal Hart. Another
good cowboy gone West."

The Gower Gulch men went in a body to the Catholic ceme-
tery, all dressed in their best dark "funeral and wedding" suits.
Proud and eager to present this last tribute to their old friend,
they were stunned when the church officials refused permission
to install such a "profane" monument on "consecrated ground."

Jack Padjan was perhaps the only Gower Gulch man to quit
pictures completely, although he never left town. He had

always had a magic touch with horses, and a millionaire Beverly Hills hotelman selected him to manage his racing stables and stud farm in Northridge. Just before the war Jack had met Mary, a loving, dark-eyed country girl from Northern California who, he declared, "had a smile like a field of sunflowers" and was "as pretty as a spotted pup." On the property and cottage assigned to him he settled down at last, with the aging stallion Buttered Toast, some "bummer lambs" for Mary to fuss over, and several generations of Rusty's pups.

"By God, Nugget Nell," he told me the last time I saw him, "you can't untrack out at my spread without steppin' on some goddammed stray cat or lamb or chicken Mary's taken it into her head to gentle." I smiled when I saw them together, Jack with his bronzed, beaked profile and his wiry black hair frosted with gray. Mary had a good touch, for she had gentled Padjan the only way it could have been done — not with a hackamore but with a soft rope halter.

There were still other leaves left on the tree: Hank Bell, Sonora, Slim Whittaker, Artie Ortega, Leo MacMahon, George Huggins and Bob Burns; the latter two were tall, slender white-haired old gentlemen, Southern by birth, but Westerners by choice. Together they had formed a closely knit social group out in San Fernando Valley, comprised of friends and their own grown sons, daughters and grandchildren. They held a square dance every Wednesday night in a hired hall, and invited me to join. For several months I attended these dances faithfully. George played the fiddle and Bob Burns called, both men possessing an impressive repertoire of melodies and calls.

Watching these happy, unsophisticated people, I felt that I could be attending an old-fashioned barn-raising of a hundred years ago, the crowd was so much the same. And yet there was a difference. I felt a twinge in my heart as I looked at the cowboys' straight, lean bodies, their eyes bright with merriment, but their hair now gray or white. There was no frontier

ahead for them, no new pioneering to be done. It was a long
time since we had put together those ridiculous two-reel
comedies at Sunset and Gower, since they had stubbornly sat
their horses at Muroc Lake, defying De Mille. And yet, something of the old spirit was still in the air. I could catch it
between the "squares," in stray wisps of conversations. "I told
the assistant, 'Who says I'm too old to do that stunt?'" "Yes,
we're called back for tomorrow . . ." ". . . believe it or not, I
got a double whammy!" (a ninety dollar adjustment for speaking a single line of dialogue).

On July 18, 1955, an unprecedented event rocked the industry. On a formerly desolate plain outside of Hollywood, thirty
thousand guests watched the assembling of a remarkable
parade, while millions more witnessed it on television. One of
Hollywood's best-known producers stepped proudly before the
cameras and assured a waiting world: "Disneyland will never
be completed as long as there is imagination left in the world."
Only those of us long accustomed to searching the faces of
movie crowds and finding old friends there would have noticed
two men in that pageant who had played key roles in getting
the parade — and, indeed, Disneyland itself — ready for this
grand opening in mid-July. One was a short, stocky man, with
swarthy complexion and black hair, who cut a proud figure on
the driver's seat of a stagecoach made exactly five-eighths the
size of a standard model. His team was comprised of six dun-
colored ponies, which nature had also made just about five-
eighths the size of a normal carriage horse. It was the California Indian from Weed — Artie Ortega. Nearby, mounted
on a high-stepping bay with four white socks, and followed by
a docile string of thirty well-trained pack mules, rode another
familiar Gower Gulch man — Jack Montgomery.
I never learned all the details of how Father and Mr. Disney

got together. I did know, of course, that Father's Aunt Alice had been assigned the youthful Walt as her driver in Europe after World War One. Serving as a Gray Lady for the Red Cross, she was quite taken aback when her taciturn young driver proceeded to draw and paint strange-looking animal caricatures all over her black touring car! Aunt Alice forgave him, however, and in the late 1930's Mr. Disney had invited her to come to Hollywood as his guest. She dined at the Disney mansion and was given a personally guided tour of the studio by Walt himself. All of this impressed Aunt Alice, who had been head of the Drama Department at the University of Nebraska for nearly twenty-five years. But those of us who were natives considered working at Disney Studio tantamount to being condemned to the galleys. Everyone agreed his people were the poorest paid and his artists almost never given screen credit for the original artwork they created.

Like almost everyone else in Hollywood at the time, Father believed that Disney's star had set. The demise of the big feature-length cartoon had been hastened by the harsh realities of war, and no one thought Disney's animal documentaries would accomplish much more than to keep the studio going at a Poverty Row level. But of course they all underestimated Disney's remarkable resourcefulness, and his positive genius for persuading big corporations to take all the financial risk required to bring the biggest fantasy of his career into being.

Early in the spring of 1955, Father learned that there was a unique job open over at the proposed Disney amusement park, for a man wise in the quirky ways of the mule. It was not an easy position to fill, as few men in the area possessed the specialized knowledge and background. It was Disney's dream to make available in his park all of those things he himself had wanted to do as a child. One such cherished activity was a trail ride on a real, live mule. A trader named Pope provided the raw material in the form of thirty or so stubborn, temperamental and completely unbroken bronc mules gathered from some godforsaken corner of the Texas range.

When Pope's spokesman approached Father about the possibility of his taking on the job of breaking the broncs, training them and laying out the ride, the time was ripe for Father to make a decision. He was looking for something permanent. His home on a once-quiet side street had been completely surrounded by encroaching business and a freeway was scheduled to be put through the living room. Television was eating at the vitals of the movie industry and he felt it was only a matter of time before the old town was terminal.

"The job will pay one hundred dollars a week," the spokesman assured him, "and Walt wants people who will be steady, and happy with him."

While Father was trying to make a decision, Artie Ortega called and told him he had taken a job driving miniature stagecoaches out at Disney's new park. Father was extremely fond of his old friend, and if Artie was going to be "on the lot" with him, it would be like having a long contract job, with a perpetual call-back for tomorrow. Meantime, Mother learned there was another Disneyland job available, as wardrobe mistress to the six dance-hall girls who performed regularly at the Golden Horseshoe Saloon.

Although Mother's total needlecraft skills consisted of sewing on buttons and snaps, she rightly assumed that these would be exactly the repetitive emergencies one might encounter backstage in a Saloon-theater. The job paid seventy-five dollars a week, and when they added up their pooled potential income it looked too good to refuse. And, unbelievably for Hollywood, *it was permanent.* Disneyland promised the brightest of all possible futures.

Father sold the Valley home and bought a new house far out in Anaheim. "There's nothin' out there at all," he told me, "and it seems the right direction to go to get away from the tide of humanity filling up the Valley."

From early March until the eve of the opening parade, Father struggled to gentle his long-eared charges. At the same time he designed a narrow but safe trail to be built for the mule train rides. Bulldozers scooped out tons of earth, but heavy spring rains caused them to ooze back down onto the sandy plain. Bulldozers again forced up more earth, buttressed by concrete embankments, to create mountain passes and curves where all had been flat before. Meantime, Artie was breaking out his ponies, teaching them to handle the coaches, and laying out the route his rides would take. Everything was fever-pitch haste, but Mother and Father took a Sunday out to celebrate their fortieth wedding anniversary.

I was living in Santa Barbara, but after two months of their constant urging, I agreed to come and see the wonders of Disney's park. At the Golden Horseshoe Saloon I found Mother happily engaged in keeping her six blond chorus girls in good repair between numbers. Mother was a great booster for Disneyland, as enthusiastic as a child over the River Boat, the Jungle Ride and Main Street. She also felt that the park gave people a wonderful place to escape from the pressures of the outside world. The way Anaheim was booming as a result of Disney's enterprise, it appeared the outside pressures would only increase.

Going into Frontierland I located the mule corral, but as I started to enter through the gate I overheard an argument and sensed trouble was brewing. I saw Father leaning against a hitching rack in front of the barn where he kept his mules. Two young men in blue jeans, flat-heeled boots, and wearing country boy "straw Stetsons" with the side brims curled as tight as paper cones, stood beside the water trough facing him.

"This is our kind of job, that's clear on the face of it," one of the men was saying in a stubborn, angry tone. I stopped short of making my presence known, for I could tell by Father's expression he was furious — rolling a Bull Durham cigarette very slowly, a sure sign he was trying to give his temper time to cool down.

"The mule rides are strictly for the children," Father said at last, as though spelling out the facts with infinite patience to retarded minds. "It has nothing to do with labor unions, loading and unloading produce or merchandise or anything of the kind."

"Not in our book!" the other man shot back. "Any time you load a kid on a mule and take him off it again, that's Teamsters' work and we aim to see that Teamster members get it!"

This stand-off between three grown men in the center of a miniature corral was absurd, and yet it was as cunningly real as everything else I had observed at Disneyland, except that the men were not scale-models like the river boat, the saloon and the crocodiles.

"And just don't you forget that, old-timer. We mean to take over all the loading in this park, and the sooner you get that straight the better." The two young men swung their legs over the low corral fence and strolled away.

"Well, what was all that about?" I asked, entering the corral with studied nonchalance.

Father glanced at me, then at the backs of the disappearing Teamsters, took one last drag on his cigarette and threw it to the ground. "Just a bunch of goddammed union toughs determined to get a slice of the cake," he growled. "Come on, let me take you around."

He showed me the barns where his mules were kept carefully sheltered from the sun in summer and rain in winter. It did not surprise me that he knew each one by name. There was a quart can sitting in an open bag of oats, which he filled automatically as he led me to the stalls, dribbling a shot into the feed box of every animal we visited.

Father had gentled each mule himself and then taught them to work as a string. They were sure-footed, patient and remarkably obedient to his commands. When some twenty children had been carefully mounted on as many mules, he took the lead on his saddle horse, setting the pace and keeping a watchful eye on his charges as they made the circle around the simulated mountain trail and back again. It certainly wasn't a trip down the old Mormon Trail to the canyon floor, but it must have seemed as exciting to the kids. At the end of a certain number of ten-minute trips, Father returned the first string to the cool barn, and replaced them with fresh mounts.

I gathered from his conversation that the Teamsters were not opposed to his continuing to lead the mule trains; they just wanted control of the loading and unloading at union wages. To Father that meant losing control of the safety factors, the same conflict that had created so much bad blood between the cowboys and the barn men. "All you need is a rotten cinch, or a busted latigo and you've got all the elements for a bad fall — or a series of falls."

Later, Father and I strolled over to the stagecoaches, where we found Artie between rides, talking to Hank Bell who was on his first visit to the park.

"Hank, why don't you take a job driving coach, too?" I asked.

"Why, girlie, I'd break up one of these toy coaches just climbin' onto the driver's seat," he laughed.

"I weigh every bit as much as you do, Hank," Artie replied.

"Yes, but mine's stretched out over a lot more territory."

As we looked at the charmingly small coaches, each made five-eighths to size, in accordance with the overall scale of the park attractions, Hank made a shrewd observation. "They may look cute, but they're top-heavy as hell."

A few months later I had reason to remember Hank's remark, when Father called to tell me Artie was in the hospital with a broken pelvis. I never did learn from Father whether the Teamsters had achieved their goal of getting on as "loaders," but whoever was serving in that capacity for Artie had failed to keep idle spectators safely away from the docks when the highstrung ponies were brought in to be loaded. On this particular afternoon as he was coming in to pick up passengers, the noisy onlookers terrified his team, and they bolted. In an effort to keep the runaways from charging through the crowd and injuring hundreds of bystanders, Artie risked trying to turn them sharply out onto the track. The unwieldy little coach, as Hank had predicted, would not maneuver properly and heeled over on top of its driver.

"At Artie's age I don't expect he'll be climbin' back up on the box behind six up again," was Father's bitter commentary. As it turned out, Artie was on crutches for months and remained crippled for the rest of his life.

I was not surprised when, a few weeks later, Father and Mother both quit their "permanent" jobs with Disney, sold their place in Anaheim, and returned to Hollywood. Out at Disneyland, the highly popular stagecoach rides were soon discontinued, a sign perhaps that men and animals are animated by a more complex set of values than those which so effectively control the mechanical crocodiles in their manmade slime.

When I visited my parents in their new home in the Valley, Father talked seriously of buying a little spread up around Sonora, California, where he could run a few head of saddle horses and teach his grandchildren how to ride. But in the same breath he hastened to assure me he had no intention of quitting pictures — just yet.

"At least not until I finish this big location job coming up with Bob Mitchum on *Pursued.* Sonora, Slim Whittaker and Hank are on it with me. We're all established as members of the posse pursuing Mitchum. We've got special business and speaking parts all through the picture. Besides that, we're sure to pick up extra chink doubling the principals. They're most of them just actors, who can't ride for sour apples."

It hurt me to have to admit to myself that good men like Father, Hank and Slim had been trapped, long ago and unwittingly, in a prefabricated fantasy called Hollywood. It may have been unfenced, and with no fixed admission charge, but in its own way it was every bit as much a set piece as Disneyland itself.

Denied those authentic situations where their horsemanship

had once counted for something to other men, they had settled for the only place offering an opportunity to live out a shadow-play version of the real thing. But they paid a high price to go on playing cowboy for the rest of their lives, in an alien society that underestimated their values and derided their Code. It pleased me, then, to hear from Leo McMahon that for at least one of the old Gower Gulch men there had been a moment of truth as genuinely heroic as anything the cowboys had ever known before they took that first fateful drink at the Waterhole and were seduced by the deceptively sweet taste of Hollywood's counterfeit West.

14

"We'll Judge by the Riding . . ."

IT WAS in the early summer of 1954 that two veteran Hollywood cowboys went on a fishing trip to Durango, Colorado.
Bob Burns — eyes as blue and honest as a Western sky, and
with the courtly manners of a Southern colonel — was one.
His companion, a tall, dark-eyed cowboy, lean as a lodge-pole
pine, and still wiry despite his sixty-odd years, was known as
"Pancho" to many of his friends. Both men were past what
other people in Hollywood considered retirement age, but Bob
and Pancho refused to quit. Their fishing trip was only a blind
for the real reason they were in Durango.

Leo McMahon was stunt co-ordinator on a modest little
Western entitled *Denver and Rio Grande* that was due to be
shot on location there. The two old Gower Gulch men decided
if they worked through Leo and the assistant right on the job
they would have a far better chance of being hired than if they
tried to go through the front office back in Hollywood where
there were so many young "river-bottom" riders to choose
from.

"I'll do my best to get you boys riding jobs," Leo promised
when they visited him in his hotel in town. "Meantime, why
not come on out to the location site with me tomorrow afternoon? I've got to line out the route of a buckboard chase
across a big meadow with a helluva deep washout runnin' right
down the middle. I need your knowledge and experience in
goin' over the lay of the land."

They met Leo the following afternoon, but before they started walking across the meadow he confessed, "I'm sorry, Pancho, but I spoke to the assistant last night about putting you on, and he — well, he just thinks you and Bob are a little old for the carbolic kind of riding this job calls for."

"Hell, Lee," Pancho countered. "Didn't I do all the stunts for the lead in *Johnny Guitar* a couple of years back? I swam that little buckskin through the river ten times in one day. I can still ride the tail off of those damned river-bottom cowboys they're hiring now, and so can Bob."

"*I* know that," Leo agreed, "but *they* don't. Besides, this isn't like the old days when a man got busted up all on his own. Today if a cowboy gets hurt, the studio has to pay. They're a helluva lot more careful about accidents than they used to be, back before the war."

"We understand, Lee," Pancho replied. "But me and Bob will stick around the set anyway, just in case. Maybe I can talk to the assistant myself. He knows me, I think. Now, let's give a look-see at this chase route."

The three men stood near the center of the meadow and took in the whole panorama carefully with their eyes — eyes that were wise with decades of reading prairies, plains and mountains.

From the highway just behind and above them, the land fell away gradually. A deep wash cut across the section from left to right. To their right the arroyo was almost level, but it deepened until at one point it was five hundred feet to the bottom. Another wash lay to their left, easily twenty feet deep. The cowboys reckoned it was about eighteen feet across at its narrowest point.

"I figure if the team and buckboard stay over there to our right, where the wash levels out, we can get the effect of a dangerous crossing without the risks of really doing it," Leo told them.

"Well, it would sure as hell smash up a team and wagon to

head over the deep part in the center," Pancho said, squinting at the terrain. "And looks to me like there's plenty of dog-holes out there. It's deceptive, this kind of place. It looks like smooth and rolling meadowland, but it's rough, dangerous country when you start puttin' a horse over it."

As the three cowboys paced off the land, a local wrangler drove in on a buckboard pulled by what the experienced Hollywood riders immediately sized up as a team of half-broken broncs. Leo signaled to the wrangler, and then shouted at him. "Okay, Mac. Just tie the team up to that fence there, and I'll be along directly." Soon after that, a few cars began to park along the highway. Their curious occupants looked, got out, and finally strolled down toward the meadow to watch.

"Looks like word's gotten around already that we're goin' to shoot a picture out here," Leo grumbled. "Bunch of tourists are startin' to gather."

Pancho's dark eyes glanced up at the gathering crowd. Even though there were only two horses on this location site, it always made the old man nervous to see greenhorns — and especially children — turned loose around livestock. "You never know what it takes to set off a bronc," he said to himself.

As the three men strolled close to the timber that encircled the meadow, a rider emerged from the trees to their left on a big, long-legged sorrel horse.

"God damn, but that's a good-lookin' horse!" Pancho exclaimed.

"That sure is a gunsil ridin' him," Bob Burns added, and Pancho agreed.

As Leo and Bob chatted, Pancho kept staring at the horse that the dude was sitting at the edge of the timber. Finally, his interest got the better of him. "I'll be back in a minute," he told them. "I'm goin' over and take a closer look at that sorrel."

As he started toward the dude and his handsome horse, the old cowboy instinctively shot another searching glance up toward the huddle of spectators. This time he noticed that the wrangler had walked off and left the team of broncs alone. At the same instant his whole body stiffened, for he saw a little girl in a bright pink dress playing practically underneath the hooves of the jittery team.

"She's beggin' to get her head kicked off," he muttered to himself, and automatically changed his course. He started uphill at a fast walk toward the group of tourists to find her parents and warn them to keep their child away from the horses. He was still two hundred yards from where the little girl was playing around the team when he heard the all-too-familiar scream of a frightened horse. In a single motion, the broncs reared, snapped their tie-rope and blindly started barreling in his direction at a dead run.

Knowing the deepest part of the arroyo lay directly behind him, Pancho tried to flag down the runaways by fanning his Stetson at their heads. He only managed to make them veer slightly toward the level section of the wash. Then, as the buckboard hurtled past him, he froze. His trained eye had caught one last, heart-stopping detail — the flash of a pink dress! The little six-year-old girl, who had been playing around the team only seconds before, had somehow gotten aboard the wagon. There she was, hanging onto the spring seat for all she was worth, screaming in terror as she saw herself being carried beyond all hope of rescue.

All three cowboys were caught flat-footed. The only horse around was the big sorrel, and his dude rider just sat there, hunched over in the saddle like a human question mark, not knowing what to do. Before anyone else could untrack, Pancho bolted for the sorrel. Grabbing the reins in his left hand, he jerked the startled dude out of the saddle with his right, and threw him to the ground. Slapping the sorrel on his rump at the same instant as he vaulted into the saddle, he hoped the strange animal knew what pony expressing meant.

Bob and Leo stood helplessly grounded in the center of the meadow and watched as Pancho and the sorrel lit out in the wake of the buckboard. The team was a good two hundred yards in the lead, running absolutely blind. They were stretched out and flying, the buckboard in the air behind them all the way, bounding, tearing up mesquite, sage and anything else that lay in its path. The child, her long blond hair flying and her dress snapping like a pink flag in the wind, clung to the seat. Her screams came faintly back to them.

The cowboys understood better than anyone that the country was mined with prairie dog and badger holes, slashed with unseen washouts and other traps. Only they could appreciate what was happening out there on the prairie between a peerless horseman, sixty-five years old, and a horse he had never laid a hand on until seconds before. Not only was the horse a total stranger to him, but he had never set foot over an inch of the land he was now putting the sorrel over at breakneck speed.

"The old man sure ain't standing still," Leo said proudly to Bob. Pancho had his spurs buried in the pony's sides, and the two men watched in fascination as, sitting straight as a giant spike driven into the saddle, he sent the sorrel streaking over ground so broken it would have slowed a bobcat to a trot. There he was, the cowboy whom the assistant had said was too old for "straight riding," making the ride of his life.

The broncs were now churning across the level part of the wash and had begun making a big arc until they were gradually turning around and heading back directly toward the deepest part of the cut which, a few minutes earlier, Pancho himself had estimated was close to five hundred feet deep.

As he saw the team begin to double back toward him, Pancho realized he could never hope to overtake them by tracking directly in their wake. His only chance to save the child was to jump the arroyo himself at the deepest point — which he figured was also the narrowest, although still eighteen feet across — and head the runaways off before they themselves reached the brink. Between one stride and the next he made the decision that Bob and Leo realized was loaded with danger. They sucked in their breath as they saw him bend the sorrel in a fast, ground-eating swing to the left. They knew the old man was stacking all his chips on the slim chance that he might have a jumper under him.

Like Indians, the cowboys had a sign language all their own, and only experts such as Leo and Bob could possibly read meaning into what happened next. Pancho now began to feel out the horse, trying every old trick at a dead run. First, he put the pony over a big clump of sage. The sorrel cleared it neat and clean. On the next test, however, the horse turned pudding-footed and plowed right through the bush. His friends knew exactly what was on the old man's mind and what he was trying to prove. "This pony may be counterfeit, and if it is, I'm due to ford the Jordan before next payday!"

"How does he figure, comin' on a situation as fast as this, knowing he's ridin' a stranger?" Leo asked Bob in amazement. Bob shook his head.

Each of them at some time in their lives had picked up the mangled body of some unlucky cowpuncher who — trying to head off the lead steers in a stampede or on some other kind of ride — had taken the same desperate gamble and lost. They knew that trying that kind of jump with an untried horse was inviting a walk-down with almost certain death. But Pancho had outridden and out-drawn that villain too many times in his long life to back down now.

The big trick was to make the sorrel turn on every ounce of horsepower he had locked up in his ginger-colored hide. As the split opened up before him, Pancho's eye was measuring down to the last whisker the width and depth of the wash, while his body weighed the degree of willingness and spring, reluctance and fear surging through the horse beneath him. When they hit the wash the horse was wide open, and to those who witnessed it, the man and saddle looked as if they were sitting on a door knob, the horse was running in such a tight bundle.

Pointing the pony like a jackrabbit at the very narrowest part of the ditch, the old man hung his spurs into his sides and brought his quirt down under his flank with everything he had. Then the cowboys heard a wild caterwauling that sounded as though a dozen Comanches had just taken to the warpath. In that instant the two old friends realized that they were witnessing one of the greatest rides either of them had ever seen, on screen or off, before or after Hollywood. With that blood-chilling war cry, and by the way he turned his own body into a carefully balanced spear, a master horseman was literally lifting the undecided sorrel off his feet and thrusting him across the abyss.

Horse and rider hung above the arroyo for what seemed to Leo and Bob an eternity. Finally, they hit the other side, with only crumbling inches to spare, and the sorrel gamely clawed his way up the opposite bank. Pancho let out a triumphant cowboy squall. The cowboys sent an echoing yell of encouragement back to him.

The way from there along the chasm's edge to where the team was heading was short and clear, but the old man knew he would have to wring one more miracle out of his winded mount if he was to beat the runaways to the rim. Rising in his stirrups until he was standing on tip-toe, he took a twist of Indian-red mane in the fingers of his left hand and tipped his body forward as lightly as an arrow about to leave the bow. He was using horse-talk now, the cowboys realized, telling the pony exactly what he wanted him to do and convincing him that he was the only horse alive who could do it. The sorrel pricked up his ears, put on one last, incredible burst of speed and drew alongside the team only twenty feet from the chasm's edge. It was an old, old range trick. And it had worked!

Leaning out of his saddle, Pancho grabbed the near-horse's head-stall. Running alongside the leg-weary broncs, he turned them from the brink of the bluff and eased them to a stop.

Immediately, Pancho scooped up the terrified child and placed her in the saddle in front of him. She was badly bruised and still crying hysterically, but at least she wasn't dead on the bottom of the wash. The old cowboy took his time jogging back to the highway, sweet-talking the little girl to quiet her, letting the lathered sorrel cool down slowly, and leading the tired team behind him as though they were two well-broken plow horses coming in from a hard day's work.

When he drew near the highway, the child's frantic parents came running toward him and literally tore the girl from his arms. Without a single word of thanks to her rescuer, they grabbed their daughter, ran to their car, and drove away. Apparently they had had enough Western chases to last them a lifetime.

As Pancho swung out of the saddle, Leo and Bob said simultaneously, "Well, you old sonofabitch. You sure made him jump over the moon!"

Just then the dude came striding angrily up to where the three cowboys stood. "I think you had a lot of nerve taking my horse from me like that and then trying to kill him by making him jump that arroyo!"

The old cowboy took two steps toward the lank youth. He stopped, hip shot, directly in front of him, his hands on his belt, his dark eyes going over every inch of the stranger with the thoroughness of a currycomb.

"Why, you lousy dude gunsil, you! You don't deserve to stand in the shade of a horse as good as that. I'll give you five hundred dollars for him any day you care to sell."

"I won't sell him!" the young man shouted angrily. "And I still think you had your nerve — "

Pancho started to walk away in sheer disgust, and then, succumbing to an irresistible impulse, he spun around and drove the toe of his Joe Posada boot into the seat of the dude's pants. "You take good care of that horse, you goddammed scissorbill," he warned. "And if I ever hear that you've mistreated him, I'll come back from hell's rim rock and take him away from you!"

Sometime later when Leo tried to describe that day's events in front of Pancho, the old man cut him off sharply: "What happened outside of Durango is nobody's concern," he cautioned him. "And if I ever hear you or Bob mention it, you've lost me for a friend."

Ironically, Leo was thus forbidden to tell the assistant director about Pancho's fantastic ride and rescue, and it lost the old man any chance of landing his cherished riding job.

True to his character and his Code, Pancho went to his grave without ever telling a single friend or even the members of his own family about the day he made his greatest ride. The little girl, who is alive today because of his courage and horsemanship, does not even know his name. Her parents never bothered to ask.

It was several years later, in response to a letter of mine asking Leo to relate some of his most unforgettable experiences with the Gower Gulch men, that he told me this story.

"Watching old Pancho make that ride," he wrote, "I realized that here was a cowboy truly wise in the ways of the old West. He was as tall in the saddle as any man who ever lived, a friend you'd be proud to ride the river with, all the way. When he died I wished to God I could cement his spurs to his tombstone, just above his name." And then, at the end of his letter, Leo added:

"His name was Jack Montgomery."

Reading that, I remembered a song Father taught me years ago when I was a little girl. It was one of his favorites. Looking back, I think he liked it because it had a special meaning for him and the men with whom he rode —

> *I dreamt that they held a great Round-Up*
> *Where cowboys like dogies did stand,*
> *To be marked by the Riders of Judgment,*
> *Who are posted and know every brand.*
>
> *Then Saint Peter stood up in the grandstand,*
> *A six-gun held up in each hand,*
> *And he said, "Boys, we'll judge by the riding*
> *Who goes to that sweet Promised Land."*

Hollywood did not, of course, judge by the riding. But, fortunately, Hollywood did not win every pot, either. Father's last ride proved that the Gower Gulch men had never really needed a director or a script to tell them how to save the heroine. They just came by it naturally.